ECONOMICS FROM THE CONSUMER'S PERSPECTIVE

Lewis Mandell

SCIENCE RESEARCH ASSOCIATES, INC.
Chicago, Palo Alto, Toronto, Henley-on-Thames, Sydney, Paris, Stuttgart

A Subsidiary of IBM

ACKNOWLEDGMENTS

The following material is reproduced by permission.

p. 29   Excerpted from HISTORY OF THE AMERICAN ECONOMY, by Ross M. Robertson. Reprinted by permission of Harcourt Brace Jovanovich, Inc.

p. 41   Mincer Chart. Reprinted by permission of the National Bureau of Economic Research, Inc., from *Schooling, Experience, and Earning,* by Jacob Mincer, New York, 1974.

The following material is copyright ⓒ by the University of Michigan and used with the permission of the Survey Research Center of the Institute for Social Research, University of Michigan. P. 35, table 4-2; p. 94 table 7-1; p. 120, table 9-1; p. 121, table 9-2; p. 151 table 10-3; p. 164, table 11-1.

Library of Congress Cataloging in Publication Data

Mandell, Lewis.
    Economics from the consumer's perspective.

    Includes bibliographies and index.
    1. Finance, Personal. 2. United States—Economic conditions—1961-   I. Title.
HG179.M26   330   74-34343
ISBN 0-574-19205-0

CONTENTS

TO MY CORE FAMILY
Nancy and Eyli

PREFACE

This book represents the author's best efforts to distill from the widely accepted principles of economics that which is most *useful* to the student in the ordering of his or her own life. In reviewing economics from the perspective of the consumer, I have been forced to deviate from the approaches of the traditional introductory economics textbooks, which are government and business policy oriented. I have brought in instead materials typically taught only in graduate and upper division economics courses, such as human capital and time constraints, as well as materials typically not taught in economics, such as principles of insurance and actual use of present discounted value. In the same vein, I have deemphasized many of the theoretical approaches that are least relevant to the consumer and, wherever possible, tried to substitute logic and examples for the mathematics and graphs usually employed to illustrate important economic principles.

This book is intended for use in a variety of courses, including a one-semester introductory economics course emphasizing personal economic decision making, an economics course for nonmajors, a course in consumer economics or personal economics, or, with appropriate supplementation, personal finance, home economics, or a more traditional, two-semester introductory economics course.

Reflected in my approach is my career as a behavioral economist which, aside from giving me a lot of interesting data for illustration, has forced me to go deeper into many economic concepts to explain the basis of theory in terms of human behavior. A second advantage of my career, which is often evident, is my continued association with social scientists of other disciplines, particularly sociologists and psychologists, who offer much to my own profession particularly when we focus on the economic behavior of the consumer.

Many individuals have helped shape the ideas that have gone into this presentation. Most important have been my former colleagues in the Economic Behavior Program of the Survey Research Center of the University of Michigan's Institute for Social Research. The program's founder and long-time director, the great economist-psychologist George Katona, convinced me, along with many others who worked with him, to accept the fact that economic theory is constantly changing, and relevant theory can best be learned by continual observation. My association with James Morgan and the late John Lansing are also evident in the book, as are the ideas supplied by many other friends and colleagues in the Economic Behavior Program, including Robert Marans, Jacob Benus, Jay Schmiedeskamp, Martin David, Burkhard Strumpel and many others cited throughout this book.

Thanks must be given to the many people who aided in the physical production of this book. My editor at SRA, Paul Kelly, with the assistance of a number of reviewers helped shape the presentation. Dick Carter, also at SRA, served as project editor. The manuscript was typed numerous times by several indulgent persons including Margaret Hinz, Eileen Silvestri, and my wife Nancy, who also helped this book by continually demanding more examples. Geeta Balakrishnan helped me with the bibliographical references and the chapter summaries, and my colleague at the University of Maine, Donald Savage, suggested many changes which were incorporated.

L.M.

1

A CONSUMER'S INTRODUCTION TO ECONOMICS

The Declaration of Independence of the United States proclaims that "All men are created equal," yet from the time that a baby is removed from his mother's womb, certain economic forces are at work to insure that some people will be more equal than others. The smart baby that chooses rich parents begins life a step ahead of his contemporaries who must work a good deal harder to achieve at least their share of the good things in life. This is not to acknowledge that money is everything, but as one American humorist has observed, "I've been rich and I've been poor . . . and believe me, rich is better."

THE DISTRIBUTION OF INCOME, WEALTH, and WELL-BEING

There is unquestionably a great disparity in the United States between the rich and the poor. According to the Survey Research Center at the University of Michigan, in 1970 the 10 percent of families with the highest incomes earned more total income than did the entire 50 percent of families with the lowest incomes. And even more amazing, the wealthiest 5 percent of families have more than

40 percent of all wealth, while the poorest half of the nation's families together have only 3 percent of it (see table 1-1 and figure 1-1).

While many people are aware of this great disparity between rich and poor, few realize that this is only part of the story. In terms of well-being and enjoyment of the material things in life, the richer are even further ahead. Those families who have higher incomes also tend to get more for their money than families with lower incomes, largely because they are more sophisticated and better consumers.[1]

In shopping for an automobile loan, as an example, the more aware consumer knows the meaning of the annual percentage interest rate and tends to shop for the loan with the lowest rate. The less aware consumer, on the other hand, will often ignore the interest rate even though the Truth-in-Lending Law requires that he be told this rate, and take the loan with the lowest monthly payment and a much higher interest rate. By the time the loan has been repaid, the less aware consumer may have paid several hundred dollars more in interest than the smart consumer.

Similarly, the more aware consumer is alert to the causes and symptoms of inflation and will take actions to protect himself from its harmful effects. If he has savings, he will put them in a form that increases in value with increases in the price level. The less well-informed consumer, on the other hand, may see (if he is alert enough) any savings that he may have eaten away by inflation.

As a result of these and many other occurrences in our economy, we can see why some people (usually those with high incomes or more education) are even better off than their income or wealth would indicate, while those who don't understand the system tend to see their often meager incomes eaten away as the result of their ignorance.

Are Things Improving?

Many people have the naive notion that the difference between rich and poor is disappearing in this country. They feel that everyone is melting together into a vast middle class partly because of aid given to the poorer families, and partly because progressive income taxes take more from the rich. This is really not so. According to data collected by the Survey Research Center over the past 25 years, the distribution of income was more nearly equal from the end of the Second World War until about 1960. Since then, however, there has been little change—if anything, the

---

[1] A recent study lends support to this observation. In Lewis Mandell's article entitled "Knowledge and Understanding of Consumer Credit," in the *Journal of Consumer Affairs,* Vol. 7, Number 1, Summer 1973, he reported results of a national study showing higher income individuals to be more knowledgeable about consumer credit.

TABLE 1-1

The Distribution of Income and Wealth in the United States

(1) Decile	(2) Share of Total Income in Decile	(3) Cumulative Share if Total Income	(4) Share of Total Wealth in Decile	(5) Cumulative Share of Total Wealth
Lowest	1%	1%	0%	0%
Second	3%	4%	0%	0%
Third	5%	9%	0%	0%
Fourth	6%	15%	0%	0%
Fifth	8%	23%	3%	3%
Sixth	9%	32%	5%	8%
Seventh	11%	43%	7%	15%
Eighth	12%	55%	11%	26%
Ninth	16%	71%	18%	44%
Highest	29%	100%	56%	100%

The lowest decile in income consists of the 10 percent of the population with the lowest incomes. They have only 1 percent of all the income in the United States (column 2). The second lowest decile has 3 percent of total income and together, the lowest two deciles (the poorest 20 percent of the population in income) have only 4 percent of all the income (column 3). The half of the population (from the lowest through the fifth deciles) with the lowest incomes have only 23 percent of total income.

The lowest four deciles in wealth have less than half of one percent of total wealth (rounded to zero in column 4). The poorest half of the population in wealth (wealth deciles through the fifth) have only 3 percent of total wealth. The wealthiest 10 percent have 56 percent of total wealth.

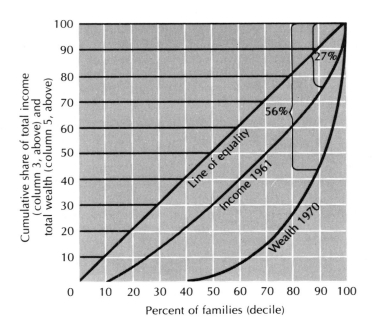

Fig. 1-1
Lorenz curve showing
the inequality in the
distribution of
income and wealth in
the United States

very richest seem to be gaining on everyone else again. And in spite of supposedly high income and inheritance taxes, the small percent of very wealthy families still control a great proportion of the wealth.

Much of the explanation for this lies in the disparity in economic knowledge that often is associated with wealth. Taxes are just one example. While high-income families are supposed to pay an extremely high percentage of their incomes in taxes, their knowledge of the law, or loopholes as they are called by those who don't use them, helps many of them to pay a lower proportion of their income in taxes than most of the rest of us.

If the law in the United States discriminates, it is more on the basis of knowledge than anything else—smart people know enough either to benefit themselves or to hire an expert—a lawyer or an accountant—to give them help. As an eminent jurist once said, everyone has an obligation to pay the smallest legal amount of tax. The smarter you are about taxes, the less you usually have to pay.

The Internal Revenue Service does not go out of its way to help the great number who overpay in taxes each year. While the middle-income person may not be able to use the big loopholes, such as oil depletion allowances, he often out of sheer ignorance overlooks many tax breaks for which he is eligible.

We have also seen our economic system get more complex over the past decade—a situation that favors the more aware even more strongly. As an example, the huge programs of assistance to the needy which have arisen since the Kennedy administration are so complicated and administered by so many different agencies at the federal, state, and local levels, and have changed so often that the needy person must have great sophistication to get what society has legally granted him. For example, in state after state, desirable public housing fills up immediately with the sophisticated needy (and often less needy) while the unsophisticated tend to be ignored.

Furthermore, the past decade has seen an increase in the complexity of the goods that all of us—the poor, the rich, and the rest of us—consume. For example, there are so many gadgets, options, and variations in features on today's automobile that it is hard to find two recent cars that are exactly alike. On what basis can we make an intelligent decision, unless we happen to be automobile mechanics?

And even if we know cars, how can we evaluate washing machines, television sets, or houses? Even the all-around Mr. Fixit can not be expected to know everything about life insurance, social security, and installment debt—all of which have gotten far more complex in the past ten or fifteen years.

Here again we see that the knowledgeable can cope better with the increasing complexity of our economic system; indeed, they thrive on it. While new options in life insurance throw most people into a panic or cause them to accept the often poor advice of an insurance salesman, the sophisticated consumer sees in the new options potential benefits to himself which he can then evaluate in terms of cost and benefit.

The more aware consumer also knows when he needs expert advice. Persons who do not feel qualified to evaluate automobiles, toasters, or washing machines can turn to such unbiased evaluations as *Consumer Reports,* but here again, those who are sophisticated enough to avail themselves of such services are rarely the ones who need it most.

Similarly, the more aware consumer will seldom buy a house without the advice of an attorney. Yet the less aware consumer, who is even less well qualified to deal with such a large and complex matter himself, will often forego the attorney to save fifty or a hundred dollars—a foolishly small sum of money relative to the purchase price.

Within the past few years, a growing sentiment has arisen for greater government protection for the consumer. While this is very useful, the government simply cannot act fast enough to provide full protection for the consumer against unsafe products or unfair and deceptive practices. Each year a staggering number of new products and services are offered and the government is hardly in a position to render a complete examination to each one before it reaches the market.

Unfortunately, much of the highly touted consumer protection legislation falls short of its intended goals. The Truth-in-Lending Law is valuable primarily to those who understand the meaning and value of an annual percent rate of interest. The Fair Credit Reporting Act, which gives consumers access to their credit files, is almost unknown to the general public and particularly to those who most need its protection.

So long as this country offers free entry of new products and competition in the marketplace—a great benefit to consumers—the ultimate protection of the consumer's welfare will lie with his own knowledge and behavior.

To summarize what we have said in conceptual terms, each family has certain *financial resources* that may be measured in terms of income or wealth. The overriding economic objective of the family is to use these resources as efficiently as possible to maximize its well-being or standard of living, which may be seen as the *product of resources times consumer efficiency.*

ECONOMIC WELL-BEING = RESOURCES x CONSUMER EFFICIENCY

Consumer efficiency relates to all of the things we have mentioned in this chapter and may be called "getting the most for your money." We can now see that if (as we have stated) families with more economic resources also are efficient consumers, their economic well-being is that much greater than their poorer counterparts.

STUDYING ECONOMICS

Many people, especially the young, who are smart but not sophisticated feel very unsure of their abilities to cope with the economic system—to buy a house, to take out a loan, to get insurance, to withstand inflations and recessions. As a result, they sign up for a course in economics hoping to learn a few rules of survival that they know they will need.

They end up by learning a little economic history, something about life in the Soviet Union, and a lot about business and government policies. Since only a small percentage of students end up running businesses and few indeed emerge in a major economic policy-making position for the government, most of what they learn is never used and rapidly forgotten.

This book attempts to take the vast body of knowledge that economists have assembled about our system and use it to help people make the right decisions in their role as consumer. We know that whatever else we are in life—football players, lawyers, homemakers—we are all consumers and will be until the day we die (and even afterwards, since our mortal remains must be dealt with).

For well over a century and a half, some of the greatest minds in Western civilization have been applied to the study of economics. The system has been dissected, analyzed, and explained, and some writers and philosophers (most notably Karl Marx) have suggested alternative systems. It is now common for nearly all branches of government as well as most large businesses to employ economists to help make decisions.

Consumers have also been studied in order to help make policy for business and government. Unfortunately, the well-developed and sophisticated body of economic knowledge needs to be utilized to give guidance to consumers in making their critical decisions. Yet many of the principles of economics that guide businesses and governments are directly applicable to the household, which may be viewed as a kind of small business.

There are several ways in which the study of economics can contribute to the consumer's ability to make wise decisions:

1. *Evaluation of the true costs and benefits of making a decision*
Every decision made by a consumer has costs and benefits associated with it. Some of these are obvious; others are very subtle but very important to the consumer. In the scores of years that economists have been studying businesses, they have uncovered many ramifications of decision-making which are not at all obvious to noneconomists. In deciding

whether to buy a washing machine, for example, most people look at the operation cost as well as the price. How many people anticipate the machine's *depreciation* over the years or even provide for mounting repair as it gets older? How many people look at the annual cost of having, say, $200 sunk in a washing machine when that $200 could be in a bank earning money? These are real costs that no businessman would overlook in making an acquisition, but are often overlooked by the consumer in making his own decisions.

2. *Understanding consumer motivation*

Consumers have certain patterns and habits that are well known to business and marketing experts and the advertising men on Madison Avenue, but are less well known to the consumers themselves. The developing field of psychological economics has been studying consumer motivation, and quite a number of things are now understood. It goes almost without saying that the consumer should know and understand himself in order to govern his economic life in the most beneficial way.

3. *Understanding business*

An understanding of business has two important uses for the consumer. First, he must deal with business in the course of most of his economic actions and try to get the best deal for himself. Similarly, business, in dealing with the consumer, is out to do the best it can for *itself*. Consequently, while they are not exactly enemies, they are antagonists and should study each other well in order to do best in their dealings. Business already spends a good deal of time studying the consumer; the consumer should also understand how business operates and why.

A second reason for studying business is that many *economic rules that govern business decision-making are equally applicable to the household.* Investment decisions, acquisition of plant and facilities, and debt or financing decisions, among others, have their reflection in the household.

4. *Understanding government economic policies*

For many reasons which will be dealt with in later chapters, the role of the government in the economy has steadily increased and will undoubtedly continue to do so. The direct effects of government economic policies on the consumer may be seen in areas such as taxation, social security and unemployment compensation. Indirect effects result from government fiscal and monetary policies which attempt to guide the economy on an even keel and keep unemployment and inflation low and economic growth high.

5. *Understanding terminology*

Economics, like most other scientific disciplines, has developed its own jargon or terminology. Yet while the consumer can go through life without understanding the conversation of chemists or sociologists, economic talk has great meaning in his life. The newspapers are full of terms such as *inflation, recession, GNP, balance of payments deficit,* and *balanced budget.*

Equipped with an understanding of the meaning and implication of these terms, the consumer is in a far better position to make correct decisions to better his economic welfare.

SUMMARY

1. Income and wealth are not evenly distributed in the United States. On the contrary, a relatively small proportion of families receives a large proportion of total income and has a much larger proportion of total wealth.

2. Compounding the uneven distribution of income and wealth among consumers is the distribution of ability to utilize their resources to get the most for their money. For various reasons, those with the most income and wealth often use their money more rationally than others. Since total consumer well-being is the product of resources and the efficient utilization of these resources, those consumers who are financially better off often enjoy even higher levels of relative well-being.

3. The focus of this course is to use well-established principles of economics to help the student in his lifetime role as a consumer. The study of economics can help him better understand
   a) business
   b) the economy
   c) government economic policies
   d) economic terminology
   e) his own motivation
   f) the problem of evaluating costs and benefits in decision-making

QUESTIONS FOR DISCUSSION

1. Why do people with more money also tend to know more about spending it wisely? Is this always true? Give examples of cases where this may not be true.
2. Draw a Lorenz curve showing the distribution of rights to vote in elections. Are these rights more equally distributed than income

and wealth or less? What does this mean about distribution of political power in America?

3. In what ways can the study of economics help the consumer? If everyone studied economics, what would happen to the distribution of economic well-being in the population?

distribution of income and wealth
Lorenz curve
deciles
cumulative share
economic well-being
economic resources of the family
consumer efficiency
costs and benefits
consumer motivation

NOTE: You, dear student, are the consumer advisor with a column in the local newspaper. Readers have written in with problems requiring your help; they appear at the end of several chapters. Please help them by replying to their questions, using what you have learned in the chapter to give the best answers.

Dear consumer advisor:

There's an old saying that the rich are always getting richer and the poor are just getting poorer. Do you agree or disagree?

A. Cynic

Dear consumer advisor:

My husband and I work very hard to earn money so we know the value of each dollar. However, my husband has certain habits of spending money that I consider wasteful. For example, when we bought a house my husband insisted upon having a lawyer look over the papers and this set us back nearly $100. And on top of that, he hired an appraiser for $50 to look it over when anyone could see that it was in good shape. How can I get him to stop wasting our money?

Thrifty

SELECTED REFERENCES AND SOURCES OF DATA

Katona, George, Lewis Mandell, and Jay Schmeideskamp. *1970 Survey of Consumer Finances*. Ann Arbor: Institute for Social Research, 1970. (See chapter 1 on distribution of income.)

Lampman, Robert. *The Share of Top Wealth-Holders in National Wealth, 1922–56*. Princeton: Princeton University Press, 1962. (Distribution of wealth and its components.)

Mandell, Lewis. "The Changing Role of the American Consumer," *Michigan Business Review,* Vol. XXIV, No. 1, January 1972, pp. 22–26. (Discussion of need for further consumer education.)

Projector, Dorothy and G. S. Weiss. *Survey of Financial Characteristics of Consumers*. Washington, D.C.: Federal Reserve Board, 1966. (Results of a very large and detailed study of consumer wealth.)

U.S. Bureau of the Census, *Current Population Reports,* Series P-60. (Regular reports on distribution of income in the United States by various classifications.)

2

AN INTRODUCTION TO THE STRUCTURE OF THE AMERICAN ECONOMY

In the preceding chapter, we learned that the consumer does not live alone in a vacuum. The decisions that he makes affect others, and their decisions may ultimately have an effect upon him.

To begin with, the consuming unit, or the family, is only one of more than 65 million in the United States. As we will discover, decisions made by any of them can have an impact upon the possibilities open to any of the others. As an example, consider the family that would very much like to buy a certain model of a new car which has been widely advertised and which it feels that it can afford. Obviously this family will not be alone in making a similar decision; but depending upon the total number of families who want such a car, that is, the total *demand* for this car, the possibilities that this family can march out to the showroom and drive the car away may be affected. Our family may find that the availability of such cars is not currently equal to the quantity demanded. In other words, more families want that car at the advertised price than were produced by the company. In this case, they may have to wait several months for delivery.

A more relevant example occurred in some areas of the country during the recent fuel crisis. Fearing that stations would soon run out of gasoline, thousands of persons

flocked to service stations to fill up their cars—and wherever possible, cans, jars, and other receptacles as well. The net result was that the stations did, in fact, run out of gasoline where they would not have under normal non-panic circumstances. This is an example of a *self-fulfilling prophecy* in economics—where if enough people believe something will happen and act accordingly, they make it happen.

Yet the entire American economy is broader than just the 65 or so million consumer units. There are the *business sector* and the *government sector* as well. The business sector consists of several million businesses ranging in size from the giant General Motors down to the plumber who operates out of his home and by himself. The government sector consists of not one but many thousands of governments ranging from Washington, which employs over two and a half million persons, through the state, county, and local governments.

There is a fourth sector, the *foreign sector,* which consists of all of the other countries of the world with whom our nation trades. While the impact of import-export on our lives has increased greatly since the onset of the oil shortage in 1973, it is still relatively minor when compared to the domestic sectors with whom we must deal on a daily basis. The foreign sector will be covered in chapter 18.

Each sector has certain objectives, and conflicts between as well as within them have a great impact upon the consumer (consider the problem of too many people wanting the same car).

Conflicts between sectors may be more pronounced. A former cabinet official who had been president of General Motors once made the observation that what was good for General Motors was good for America. Now, in some senses this statement may be true since when GM does well, more people are employed, incomes go up, and there are many more shiny new cars on the road. In another sense, however, there is a real conflict between the business and the consumer sectors—consider the ecology, the preservation of our environment. As we will see later in this chapter, the objective of a business is to make profits, and one way a business may keep expenses down is to dump its waste products into the rivers and streams, as many businesses have done. This assuredly is a good deal cheaper than treating the waste products and removing the impurities. However, the consumer who lives downstream, whose enjoyment of life comes from boating or fishing or perhaps even from sitting on the banks and watching the river flow serenely by, is definitely going to be hindered by this "economical" business practice.

The government sector may also be in occasional conflict with the consumer. The government is financed largely through taxes, and when a decision is made to increase the availability of government services, it must be partly at the expense of the take-home pay of the consumer.

The above examples are perhaps simplified illustrations of how the consumer lives within a structure of the American economy and is affected by decisions made by other consumers as well as by business and government.

THE ECONOMIC SYSTEM

It is now time to look at what an economic system is and what its goals and objectives are. Very basically, an economic system is an organization for *producing* goods and services that people want or need and *distributing* them to the consumer.

Take a simple example. A man sailing his boat from California to Australia runs into a storm and ends up shipwrecked on a deserted island. He must sustain himself until help comes his way, so he fashions some crude weapons and goes around killing animals and devouring them. Here the economic system is very simple. This man is both a producer and a consumer. He has no problems of distribution. If, however, he is joined on that island by a downed airman, the economic system becomes more complex. Production may become somewhat easier—one man may be able to chase the game into a trap set by the second, but then the problem of distribution looms: do they share equally, are there some choice parts of the game that one would prefer over the other? These things must be worked out.

If our two men are left on their island for some time, they may decide to engage in agriculture, plant some edible foods, and this requires even more planning and more thought for production and distribution. With larger numbers of people, the production possibilities become greater. They can do more, yet the problems of who produces and who gets the results of the production also become more complex.

The very large economic system, such as that of the United States, is really a more complex enlargement of our basic example of the two men on the desert island. Almost every consuming unit in our society contributes to the production of the goods or services, and every unit helps consume them.

A question may be asked at this point: Why have an economic system that encompasses more than one consuming unit? For example, with the two men trapped on the desert island, why doesn't each do his own thing and live on his own part of the island?

Aside from perhaps a basic human need for companionship which most of us have, there are two major reasons why economic cooperation is preferable. The first reason is the *avoidance of conflict*. In any physical region, whether it is a small island, a large country, or the entire planet Earth, there are limited resources available. If more than one party wants these resources, the resolution can be made in only two ways: either they can fight for them (violently in the case of war, or nonviolently in the case of a court "fight" or competition in the marketplace), or they can agree to share them.

Throughout the history of humanity both fighting and sharing have been tried many times. Individuals and nations have gone to war thousands of times over the past centuries in order to lay their claim to scarce economic resources—possession of the iron and coal producing regions of Europe has instigated more than one war.

Conflict is a very wasteful way to settle the ownership of scarce resources, particularly if your side is not guaranteed to be a quick and easy winner. So our two men on the desert island may decide that rather than fighting for possession of a fertile area, a garden, or a wild boar, they should join forces—thus a larger economic system helps avoid conflict. A second reason is somewhat less obvious but critical to an understanding of economics. This is often called *economies of scale* or *additional returns due to specialization.*

At a very basic level, there are some things that one person cannot do alone but which two may be able to. Assume that the shipwrecked sailor has some important implements in a box in his cabin, but that since the boat is underwater he alone does not have the strength to pry open the door and get out the implements to make their lives a little bit easier on the island. A second example could be in ploughing the land. One man working alone may not have the strength to pull the plough, but two may be able to.

There are more complex examples. The men may have different skills, and each pursuing his own skill may be able to maximize the total product. For example, one may be a hunter and the other a gardener. If each had to hunt and also grow a garden in order to provide sufficient food for survival, neither could live very well since the hunter may be very inefficient at growing a garden, and the gardener a lousy hunter. If each did what he was best at and shared the result, they could both enjoy more meat and produce than they could have done on their own. Similarly, in a large economic system with people working in unison, the total product available for consumption becomes larger than if each individual worked on his own. In addition, specialization in the large economic system makes possible goods that could not be available if each man had to produce them on his own. One man could not possibly produce an automobile all by himself. He would first have to start out in the iron fields of Minnesota mining the ore, smelting it, rolling it, fabricating the metal, getting the rubber for the tires and so on. But numerous people, each performing tasks at which they are trained and relatively efficient, make it possible.

DISTRIBUTION OF OUTPUT

So the problem of production has, as its solution, the cooperation of individuals within the economic system, specialization, and the exchange of products. Basically, this is true in all economic systems, including the United States, the Soviet Union, and Communist China. The problem of distribution, however, is one that separates the different systems. Going back to our two men on the desert island (who now work together), we can think of at least two totally different ways in which the distribution can be shared. One may argue that the output should be shared equally because they both worked equally hard and both contributed to the production. However, it may be that the other man is much bigger and stronger and has contributed more to the total output and therefore feels that he should get a larger proportion of the output.

There is no clearcut answer to this conflict. Both men have a good moral or ethical argument, and the answer must be decided as part of an ideological framework.

This illustrates the basic difference in ideology between, say, the United States and China. Under the free enterprise system, those who contribute most to the production of goods are said to be entitled to a greater share of the output. A person who works 20 hours a week overtime at his job, it is felt, deserves to take home more money and consume more goods than one who is content to work just a 40-hour week. Similarly, those who make a great contribution to the economic system, such as the original Henry Ford, deserve a larger proportion of the total product than those who contribute nothing but labor each week to production.

Consequently, incomes and wealth are not distributed evenly in the United States, at least partially as the result of the ideology of the economy. In China, on the other hand, it is felt that everyone should work as hard as possible to contribute to production and that everyone should be rewarded according to his needs. That is, if one family has ten members and another only five, the return to each would not be equal but in some proportion to their *needs*.

UNLIMITED WANTS

The first and perhaps the primary objective of any economic system is to utilize resources to meet the needs and wants of its people. Complicating this problem, however, is the fact that these wants are often considered to be unlimited. This is an axiom of economic theory and upon close examination proves to be true, even among the ecologically minded. The vast majority of American families would like to consume more material goods. If they don't have a color television set, they want one; if they have one, they would like to have two. Most families want more than one car, and if they have more than one they would like a newer model more frequently. Even people who reject the material standards of society would like to see resources consumed in a different way. Rather than forests chopped down for wood to build more homes (and second homes) they and their wild animals should be preserved like the clean air and clear waters of nature. But these people are in definite conflict with the consumers who want lumber for their houses and who want the wooded areas open to snowmobiles, dune buggies, and motorcycles. Anyway one views it every economic system has limited resources available for consumption, and there is more demand than there are resources. This problem must be settled in some way.

There are other goals of society aside from the ecological ones that do not emphasize consumption of output. Nationalism is one such goal. Countries spend vast quantities of their resources fighting wars which in no way contribute to the enjoyment of their consumers. These wars are (theoretically) fought for ideals which are more nationalistic than consumer-oriented.

In addition to the consumer and the government, business also demands a share of the resources for goods that it wants to produce in the future. This is known as *investment*. The simplest example might occur back in our very elementary economy with the two men on the island where, instead of consuming all of the vegetables that they produce in one year, they may save some to provide seed for the following year. In this manner, they are foregoing present consumption in order to increase the amount produced in the future. Similarly, a business may take some of its earnings to buy machinery that can increase future production. So all three sectors—consumer, government, business—make demands on the total output of the economy.

CONSUMERS RELATE TO THE OTHER SECTORS

The consumer is not only the ultimate consuming unit but also, in the American economy, owns virtually all of the resources used for production. These resources may be divided into four categories: *land, labor, capital* (that is, machinery and other manufactured goods used for production), and *entrepreneurial ability* (the ability to run an enterprise, to direct the activities of the other three resources in a productive manner). They are leased by the consumer to the business and government sectors in return for appropriate payment.

In figure 2-1, we can see the simple relation between consumer and business. Consumers allow the business sector to use their land in return for rent. They give their labor in return for wages and salaries; they lend their capital, the return on which they are given as interest and contribute entrepreneurial ability in return for profit.

Across the top of figure 2-1 we can see that the consumer supplies business with these four resources and gets a flow of money income in return. The business sector, on the other hand, uses the resources to produce what the consumer ultimately desires—finished goods and services. In order to pay for them the consumer gives back the money income it received from the business sector from the sale of its resources. Thus, we have a circular flow.

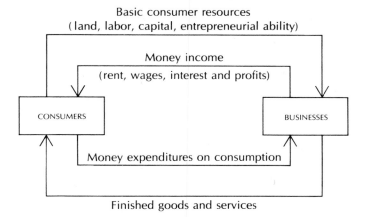

Figure 2-1
Consumers relate to
business in the
economic system

The government sector can be added in this simple model without much loss in clarification. Some consumers sell their resources to the government (postmen, soldiers) and receive money in return, so the top loop is no different with the government added (fig. 2-2). However, in order to pay for services of the government, all consumers are forced to spend some of their money income on taxes. So we merely add the words "and taxes" to the lower money loop and our model is complete.

The circular-flow diagram illustrates the modern economy that has been monetized; it does not show how the system always was. In pre-monetary economy, the consumer and the producer were the same. Our man on the desert island who produces his own food and consumes it does not create a circular flow. Even when there are two men—or

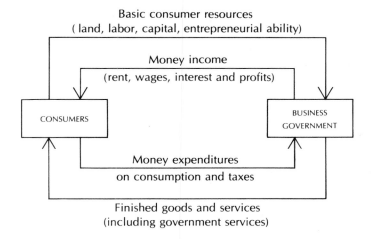

Figure 2-2
Consumers relate to
business and
government in the
economic system

twenty—on our desert island, a monetary economy is not necessary. While economic efficiency dictates specialization in exchange of goods, such exchange need not involve the complications of money; rather it could be in a barter form. The man who hunts can exchange some of his game for the produce of the man who farms. In this case each person is both the consumer and the businessman and the monetary flow is not necessary. However, while barter may work for a society of limited size, it certainly is not most efficient for larger economies. Today, when specialization is the norm, we could hardly imagine a man producing crankshafts in the Chevrolet factory and exchanging his produce at the end of the day with the butcher and the baker, who probably have no need for that crankshaft. In a complex society, the function of money has been to allow specialization and to achieve a unit of exchange acceptable in payment for services by the business sector and for goods by the consumer sector. We will discuss the role of money in greater detail in later chapters.

OBJECTIVES OF THE SECTORS

We have mentioned that there are three primary sectors in the economy: consumer, business, and government. Each has its own objectives, and they often come into conflict. In order to understand the interaction between the three sectors, we must understand their basic objectives.

A. The Consumer Sector

The basic objective of the consumer sector must be said to be the *maximization of utility* or the obtaining of the greatest pleasure or satisfaction. Every family has certain wants and needs as well as certain constraints or limitations. The basic constraint on the family is that of income; it cannot spend more than it earns for more than a short period of time. This does not mean that it cannot borrow and spend more than what is earned in a year, but over several years the family must earn, or be given, at least as much as it spends.

The family's goal is to get the greatest amount of pleasure from spending its income however much it is. The total may vary from year to year, depending on decisions the family may make regarding the choice of occupation, the amount of education, the use of leisure time, the number of children, and the total number of family members who are in the work force. These can alter the income and, consequently, the total utility that a family can enjoy.

B. The Business Sector

While the ultimate objective of the consumer is to maximize his satisfaction or utility, the ultimate objective of business is to maximize profits. Businesses are owned by consumers who wish to get the greatest possible return on the capital they have invested in order to maximize their own utilities. There are some exceptions, which will be discussed later, but basically the objective of business is to make as much profit as possible. There are two basic ways to do this: to produce and sell a higher dollar value of goods and services, and to cut costs and operate more efficiently.

the family as a business   For several reasons, businesses in the United States are run more efficiently than families. This is partly because the science of economics has spent more than seventy years concentrating on business efficiency, partly because people are specially trained in the art. Business decisions are generally made carefully and more or less scientifically, whereas a family often acts on impulse. And yet the decisions in both cases have some very real similarities. *The theme of this book is that the family is a small business*—it is a small decision-making unit. It has income and it has expenditures; it must pay taxes, needs a place to locate, makes investments, saves. These are all matters that concern business too, but are treated on a much more scientific level.

For example, both businesses and families need a location. When a manufacturing company needs a plant, how does it make its choice? It consults the best available experts, often people who do nothing but specialize in plant location, and looks carefully at certain important factors such as the size of the building, the distance to customers, the location of main roads and highways, the governmental services available, and the local tax structure. Most of these considerations are also important when the family chooses its "plant"—that is, decides where it is going to live.

There is also a similarity in capital acquisition. The producer may need a new truck, and his decision as to whether and what kind to buy depends on cost and benefit. The household needs a car for much the same reason—transportation of people and goods. Yet the decision to buy a car may be more the result of color, style, or whim than of practical considerations.

The family, a little business itself, could learn a lot from the accepted scientific criteria business uses to guide its decisions. These criteria will be discussed in subsequent chapters.

C. The Government Sector

The ultimate objective of the government, as stated in the preamble to the American Constitution, is "to promote the general welfare." This implies that the government, in some sense, must try to maximize the utility of all of its people—a most unenviable task. The hope is that the result be policies that reflect the "will of the majority."

The government has certain functions in the economy which become more and more important as our society develops. These can be broken down into the traditional, and the newer or non-traditional functions.

The *traditional functions* performed by government in a (more or less) free enterprise economy are those that business cannot itself perform but are necessary for its success.

There are certain services that a society depends on that cannot be realistically or efficiently rendered by a business. One is national defense. The maintenance of an army, navy, and air force is an expensive and complicated service that presumably benefits everyone in the United States. If the armed services were run by a business and supported only by those who wished to pay, many problems and complications might arise that would result in a less efficient system of national defense. Similarly, other functions such as police and fire protection are best served by a governmental body that can tax all citizens rather than depend only on the support of those who want to pay.

A second traditional and necessary function of government is to create and enforce rules for the operation of business. If there were no such rules, there would be less incentive for one business to deal honestly with another and the entire economy would function less efficiently.

During the past half century, or so, the government has taken on many *new functions* to meet the changing needs and ideals of society. One which has greatly expanded within recent years is the protection of the consumer from business. This protection exists in several areas. First, the government has begun enforcing agreements between the consumer and business, much as it enforces the rules between businesses, specifically in the areas of warrantees and guarantees. It also enforces rules against monopolies, partially for the benefit of the consumer. More recently, the government has begun to protect the consumer from fraudulent advertising and unsafe products put on the market, and most recently has made an attempt to inform the consumer and make him better able to judge the worthiness of a product or service. Unit pricing laws and the Truth-in-Lending legislation are examples of this.

A second major new function of the government is the exercise of control over the economy, practised in earnest since the end of the Second World War, with a commitment to full employment, growth of the economy, and stable prices. These objectives and the means of achieving them will be discussed later in this book.

Another relatively new function of government is to insure a decent level of living for all people, which came into prominence in the 1930s with new Federal programs including minimum wage, social security, and unemployment insurance. The progressive income tax and government assistance programs have also helped make incomes a little bit better distributed. This goal has become more pronounced since about 1960 with the proclaimed war on poverty.

Very recently, the government has taken on a far more active role in the protection of the environment. Actions have included restrictions on industrial production and land development as well as required alterations in automobiles.

SUMMARY

1. The consuming unit, the family, numbers more than 65 million in the United States, which make up the consumer sector of the economy. This interacts with the business, government, and foreign sectors to make up our economy.

2. The objectives of each sector differ, and conflicts may develop between them. In general, the objective of consumers is to maximize utility, while businesses attempt to maximize profits.

3. Consumers in our society own all of the basic resources needed for the production of goods and services. These resources are sold to business and the government for money which consumers use to purchase final goods and services.

4. An important function of an economic system is to effectively utilize limited resources. The formation of individual consumers into an economic unit helps avoid violent conflict over the limited resources. It also helps increase the production of goods through economies of scale.

5. While processes of production are similar in most advanced economies, the process of distribution of output to consumers differs according to ideology. In the capitalist system, each consumer's share of the total output is presumably affected by his contribution to the productive process. In non-capitalist systems, output is more equally shared.

6. The family may best be viewed as a business in that it must make businesslike decisions. Consequently, it is advisable for families to use business criteria to help make the best possible economic decisions.

7. The functions of the government in our economy have been evolving over the years. While still performing the *traditional* functions such as national defense and maintaining the legal system, the government has newer roles in stabilizing the economy, protecting the consumer and the environment, and reducing income inequality.

1. In the past week how have you been economically affected by other consumers? How have you interacted with the business sector? The government sector? The foreign sector?

2. If business and government are made up of consumers, how can their objectives conflict with consumer objectives?

3. Are there consuming units today that also produce the goods that they use? Is this inefficient? Why?

4. Does a hermit, living by himself in the woods, lay any claim to society's scarce resources? In what way?

5. How good a job does our government do in maximizing the total utility of its people? Why do you say this?

6. What types of family financial decisions cannot be handled like business decisions? Why?

7. Are there any government functions that could be performed as well by business? Why is this not done?

TERMINOLOGY

consumer sector
business sector
government sector
self-fulfilling prophecy
foreign sector
production
distribution of output
limited resources
economies of scale
unlimited wants
investment
capital
entrepreneurial ability
rent
barter
maximization of utility
economic constraints

Friedman, Milton. *Capitalism and Freedom.* Chicago: University of Chicago Press, 1962. (A philosophical discussion of benefits of capitalism)

Goldman, Marshall I., ed. *Comparative Economic Systems: A Reader,* Second Edition. New York: Random House, 1971.

Gruchy, Alan G. *Comparative Economic Systems.* Boston: Houghton Mifflin Company, 1966. (Discussion and evaluation of the operations of the different kinds of economic systems)

Smith, Adam. *An Enquiry into the Nature and Causes of the Wealth of Nations:* Representative Selections edited by Bruce Maglish. Indianapolis: Bobbs-Merrill, 1961. (See chapter 1 for a discussion on division of labor.)

Two examples of the simplest forms of economic systems.

Defoe, Daniel. *The Life and Strange Surprising Adventures of Robinson Crusoe.* Boston: Houghton Mifflin Company, 1909.

Wyass, Johann D. *The Swiss Family Robinson,* by Jean Rudolph Wyss. Chicago: Rand, McNally and Company, 1916.

3

THE
FAMILY
IN THE AMERICAN
ECONOMY

Throughout this book we speak of the *consumer*. But who is he? Well, in the first analysis he is everybody. He's you, he's me, the President—he's everybody who earns money or eats or consumes any product.

But how does this help us understand our economy? It doesn't. It is not sufficient to study each individual—this is not totally meaningful. The little baby who sleeps in its crib is indeed a consumer. Every four hours he whines and cries for his bottle of milk (assuming he isn't breastfed) which has to be purchased at the store. However, can we really say that he is making decisions which shape his own future or that of the economy?

The economic unit of analysis, the one which we are most interested in studying, must be larger than each single individual. Consequently, we focus on the family as a consuming decision-making unit and study the family's economic behavior to try to understand our economy.

There is justification for focusing the analysis on the family. After all, the family (which, for our purposes is the insular family, consisting of parents and dependent children) tends to live together. It also tends to pool its incomes, if it has more than one source, and tends to spend the income for the benefit of everyone in the family. As a result, many of the consumption decisions are made jointly rather than by individuals within the family. This is particularly true for large, expensive, durable items (such as the automobile or household appliances) which serve the entire family.

In addition to its consuming function, the family is pretty much the last unit of dependency in our economy. Blood is thicker than water, and all that. Our family (we hope) cares for us when we are sick, it helps us out when we are broke, it feeds us when we are hungry.

Of course, the family today bears only slight resemblance to the idealized family of a century ago. Still, it is the most useful unit analysis and one to which we will refer when we speak of the *consuming unit*.

THE CHANGING ROLE AND STRUCTURE
OF THE FAMILY IN THE MODERN ECONOMY

Some of the major questions of the last two decades asked by sociologists, family counselors, and women's magazines have been "What Has Happened to the American Family?", "Will the American Family Survive?" or "Is the Family Dead?" Many hypotheses are advanced for the observable decline in familial relationships: the increasing divorce rate, the proliferation of children growing up in fatherless or motherless homes, and the lack of responsibility felt by grown children for their own parents. Some of these theories are no doubt familiar to all of you: "The Hollywood movie and the loose living of the Hollywood stars have encouraged this," "The pill and the promiscuity that it has promoted have destroyed the family," or "Franklin Delano Roosevelt and social security and welfare have ruined the family." Unfortunately, readers who subscribe to any of these popular theories are wrong. These factors are effects, not causes, of the decline in the strength of the family. The real culprit is *technology*.

Let's go back to the idealized family, the so-called extended family of 100 years ago. This type of family is not entirely extinct today. It can still be seen in less well developed economies, even to some extent in parts of the United States.

The *extended family* consisted not only of the parents and the dependent children but also included the grandparents, brothers and sisters, cousins, aunts, and uncles—all sorts of blood relations. In a largely agricultural society where nearly everyone had to work the land in order for the society to function, it was natural for children to stay in the same community when they grew up, to marry from the same community, and often to take over the family farm when the parents were no longer around.

FUNCTIONS OF THE EXTENDED FAMILY

The extended family served many important functions. First, it served as *protection*. If a member of the family was endangered, he could depend on his blood relations to come to his aid. If a house caught on fire, all the relatives would drop what they were doing to put it out.

The family also was its own *insurance*. A hundred years ago, the farmer rarely carried life insurance. If he died, his wife and children would be provided for by members of the family. If he took sick, his chores would be covered by other members of the family. There was no need for pension plans or social security. When members got old, they were looked after by younger members of the family.

The family also served as its own *financing* unit. If Uncle Bob's horse keeled over one day while plowing and he was left without a horse, he did not have to go to the money lenders and pay exorbitant rates of interest. The other members of the family would chip in what they had and Uncle Bob would pay it back when he was able.

Similarly, the family provided its own *welfare* or relief. Anyone in temporary trouble did not have to seek the assistance of the government (which didn't offer it anyway in those days), but could turn to his own family for help until he was better able to cope for himself.

THE DECLINE OF THE EXTENDED FAMILY

What has killed this romantic idea of the extended family? The cause as we stated before is basically the increase in technology. At the time of the first United States Census in 1790, 94 percent of the population of this country lived in rural areas. In those days, nearly everyone farmed for a living. Within a century, the proportion of the population living on farms had been cut in half and today is less than 10 percent. As a result of the industrial revolution, and particularly its contribution to agricultural technology, fewer people were needed to produce the same amount of food. In technical terms, *productivity,* or output per worker, increased in agriculture. This freed more people to go to the cities and the factories and produce other goods. As opportunities and incomes increased in the cities, many people were attracted to leave their farms.

Also, with an expanding population, there really was no opportunity for everyone in a family to earn a living on the farm, and since it was possible to work the land with fewer and fewer people, more and more members of the family found it necessary to leave the land and journey to the cities to earn a living. This was the first step in the separation of the extended family.

But now we must answer an important question: although the movement from the farms to the cities made the cohesiveness of the extended

family less convenient, why did they not tend to stay together in the cities? One answer is that the need for *occupational mobility* has forced the family to split apart. The modern economy needs people with many skills. Craftsmen of many varieties are needed—carpenters, metal workers, plumbers, electricians—as well as professional people such as lawyers, accountants, and teachers. Even in cases where the extended family initially managed to hang pretty much together in an urban environment, it would soon separate. A son would grow up and learn a trade—perhaps metalworking. But his birthplace could not be expected to accommodate the growth and skills of all the families; soon there were no longer jobs for metalworkers. But in another city there was a big demand and wages were much higher. First the family visited frequently, then they simply wrote, and before long first cousins in different cities could not recognize each other if they met on the street.

A modern economy depends on the mobility of its resources. Often the growth of industrial cities was tied to the existence of a nearby resource or a new technology. Cities would spring up from almost nothing to places employing thousands within a matter of a few years. The need was great for all types of resources, and they had to come from some place else. If the industry needed coal to smelt steel, the coal had to be shipped from the coal producing regions. Industry also needs human resources—people who can make the non-human resources work. And these people had to come from someplace also.

DIMINISHED ECONOMIC FUNCTIONS OF THE FAMILY

So we see that the extended family was almost forced to dissolve by the diminished need for agricultural labor and the increased need for labor mobility in the growing economy. But with the dissolution of the extended family came the withdrawal of many of the functions that the family had previously performed. The ironworker who left his parents and brothers and sisters in Podunk to work in the steel factories of Gary was now on his own. Who would provide for him if he got sick? Who would take care of him when he got old? Who would lend him money when he needed money? It was necessary for a substitute institution to assume these economic functions formerly performed by the extended family.

And so this has slowly come to pass. For example, the government provides social security for nearly every working person. When this was first proposed by President Roosevelt in the 1930s, many people looked at it as socialism. "Why shouldn't the family take care of itself?" they asked. But others were more realistic and recognized the changing times. According to Professor Robinson,

Whatever the philosophical objection to a social security program may have been, certain hard facts of life were undeniable. Nearly four out of five income-receivers were dependent upon paid employment for their livelihood. There were many hazards to the continuity of income, some of which seemed to be increasing in severity as the economy became more specialized. Income interruptions included being laid off, getting sick, being injured on the job, getting too old to meet the demands of modern industrial life, and of course, death.[1]

In the last analysis, you don't have more than just your immediate family to fall back on. The Survey Research Center has found that the amount of money families give to help out each other is so small that it is almost insignificant. Furthermore, when people are asked if they feel they have a responsibility to take care of their aged parents, fewer and fewer respond positively. In 1960, two-thirds of the family heads responded that relatives should be responsible for old people in need; by 1970, this had diminished to less than two-fifths.[2]

Other functions have also been picked up by the government. Welfare, formerly handled by the family or the church, is now handled by the government. Similarly, unemployment insurance is generally available to workers to protect them in the event they are out of work and unable to support their families.

Some family functions have been picked up by labor unions in the guise of pension plans, and in the early days particularly, a kind of welfare for widows of workers who were killed on the job.

Still other functions have been picked up by business, which operates them largely on a profitmaking basis. Two of the most important are *life insurance* and *consumer finance*.

While the worker at one time knew that in the event of his sudden death, his family would take care of themselves, he is now forced to depend on third parties to insure their survival and protection. Consequently, it is almost mandatory that wage-earners have life insurance against catastrophe. When one has to borrow money for a period of time, he usually can no longer turn to his family. Lenders—banks, finance companies, and credit unions—have arisen to fill this gap. (Of course much lending is no longer for emergencies or necessities but for the enjoyment of luxuries. This will be covered more fully in later chapters.)

[1] Ross M. Robertson, *History of the American Economy.* 2nd edition, (New York: Harcourt, Brace & World, Inc., 1955), p. 612.

[2] Nancy A. Baerwaldt and James N. Morgan, "Trends in Inter-Family Transport," in Lewis Mandell, *et. al., Surveys of Consumers 1971-72.* (Ann Arbor, Michigan: Institute for Social Research, University of Michigan, 1973), pp. 206–207.

THE OBJECTIVES OF THE FAMILY

The insular family of today must make many critical decisions in new areas. The objective of the family, as a consuming unit, is to use its resources to maximize the total utility or total enjoyment of the entire family.

The resources of the family are basically the skills and strengths that members of the family have that can earn income. The income is, in turn, used for expenditures that result in utility for the family. So the decisions made by the family unit are largely in two areas—*income* and *expenditures*. These decisions form the basis of the following chapters.

SUMMARY

1. The family is the ultimate consuming unit in our society. This is so because the family tends to live together, to pool its income for the benefit of all members. The family is also the last unit of dependency in our economy.

2. The family of today is the *insular* or *core* family consisting of, at most, parents and dependent children. The larger or "extended" family, consisting not only of the core family but also of grandparents, uncles, aunts, cousins, and so on, has virtually disappeared as an important economic entity in our society. This decline accompanied the movement of the population from the farms to the cities, the increasing need for occupational specialization, and the increased mobility of the labor force.

3. The extended family performed many economic functions such as insurance, financing, old age security, and so on. These functions have had to have been assumed by "third party institutions," such as the government, banks, finance companies, and insurance companies.

4. The objectives of the insular family of today are to use their resources to maximize the total utility of all the members.

QUESTIONS

1. Is the insular family, which seems to be prevalent today, the final form that the family will take, or will it further decompose into a set of individuals? Or, perhaps, will the trend reverse and the extended family re-emerge? Why do you say this?

2. Within recent years there has been much experimentation with "communal living." A group of largely unrelated individuals is merged together to form a "superfamily" which resembles, in many ways, the extended family of the old days. Do you feel that groups of this sort will be successful over the long run? Why do you say that?

3. Which former economic functions of the extended family have been picked up by the Federal, state, and local governments? Which functions have been picked up largely by profit-making organizations and which by non-profit organizations?

insular family
extended family
durable goods
productivity
occupational mobility

4

THE DETERMINATION OF FAMILY INCOME

There was once an imaginary (but very believable) distinguished professor of economics who was being honored at the end of a long and highly productive career of research and teaching. At this very gala occasion, the old professor was approached by a reporter who asked him a very standard question.

"Tell me, Professor, can you sum up all that you have learned in your studies of economics in one sentence?"

"Yes," said the professor, "I should have gone to medical school."

LABOR INCOME OF INDIVIDUALS

Table 4-1 shows what the professor meant when he regretted his career. On the average, physicians make almost twice as much as economists, with pretty much the same amount of training.

So the choice of occupation is an important determinant of labor income. Yet it is only one of many factors that influence the money you make by working, some of which you can affect and some of which you cannot. Among the background features important in determining the amount of money that a person makes at his job are his *education,* his *race,* his *age,* his *sex,* and his *domicile.*

TABLE 4-1

Income Differences Among Occupations

Occupation	Median	Mean
Physicians	$25,000	$30,538
Dentists	23,031	25,103
Lawyers and Judges	19,466	22,734
Physicists and Astronomers	15,937	15,545
Aeronautical Engineers	15,477	15,383
Economists	14,194	15,499
Geologists	13,887	15,089
Psychologists	13,644	14,849
Civil Engineers	13,102	13,682
Managers and Administrators	12,805	14,513
Chemists	12,302	12,524
College and University Teachers	12,215	12,715
Accountants	11,639	12,537
Biologists	11,232	11,506
Electricians	9,813	9,853
Secondary School Teachers	9,646	9,789
Plumbers	9,448	9,536
Elementary School Teachers	8,991	9,095
Clerical and Kindred Workers	8,279	8,461
Radio and T.V. Mechanics	7,983	7,889
Carpenters	7,577	7,580
Clergymen	6,599	6,974
Laborers (except farm)	6,076	6,089
Farm Laborers	3,354	3,736
Private Household Workers	2,690	3,304

Income figures are for all workers in each category who worked in 1969.

Source: 1970 Census of Population. Subject Reports Earnings by occupation and education. U.S. Department of Commerce. Bureau of the Census.

Some of these variables obviously cannot be changed regardless of how willing the person is. You are stuck with your race and your sex and your age. However, you may be able to change the amount of education that you have, and you certainly can move from one place to another in order to increase your earnings.

THE EFFECT OF EDUCATION

Social scientists have long noted the strong correspondence between edu-

TABLE 4-2

Labor Income of the Family Head for Males in the Labor Force, 1971

Group	Mean Income
A. Education	
0–5 grades and trouble reading	$ 4,396
0–5 grades and literate	4,885
6–8 grades	5,591
9–11 grades	6,618
High School	7,554
High School plus non-academic degree	8,361
College, no degree	8,900
B.A.	12,064
Advanced degree	13,855
B. Age of Family Head	
Less than 25	$5,049
25–34	7,655
35–44	9,180
45–54	8,291
55–64	7,743
65–74	5,121
C. Race	
White	$8,190
Black	5,831
D. Size of Community	
500,000 or more	$9,241
100,000–499,999	8,327
50,000–99,999	7,334
25,000–49,999	7,895
10,000–24,999	5,988
E. Region	
Northeast	$8,749
North Central	8,416
South	6,749
West	7,864

·cation and income. Table 4-2 part A shows that more education tends to result in more income. Men with college degrees tend to make about three times as much as men with less than an elementary school education and nearly twice as much as high school dropouts. Why is this so? Do professional men who sit behind their desks all day work harder than ditchdiggers and truck drivers? Hardly.

An educated person has what economists call *human capital,* which is the training he has that enables him to perform services that could not be performed by someone without it.

Returns to Human Capital

In chapter 2 we discussed the analogy between the family and business. One of the respects in which the family is very much like a business is that they both have certain amounts of capital, that is, assets that yield a return. In addition these assets can be increased by both the family and the business. In the case of the business, if it wants to increase sales and profits, it may increase its capital by buying more machines, another plant, more trucks, and so on. In the case of the family, individual members increase their earnings by increasing their stocks of human capital.

A person increases his human capital by acquiring skills or education that make him more valuable and hence worth more on the market. The returns to investment in human capital are additional wages or salary. The approximate magnitude of these returns can be seen in table 4-2 part A. Persons who have dropped out of school before completing high school make less than high school graduates, while high school graduates make less than college graduates, who make less than people with advanced degrees.

Now the question may be asked: if more human capital leads to more income, why doesn't everyone get a Ph.D., or three or four of them? This can be answered by looking at the business that acquires more capital. At some point, the cost of acquiring an additional truck is greater than the additional revenues that would accrue. Therefore, it would not be a wise business decision to purchase that truck. Similarly, in the case of people, additional increments of human capital may result in additional income, but acquiring human capital has a cost just as acquiring a truck has. At some point the cost of acquiring additional human capital may be more than the additional income a person would make over his lifetime from having that capital, in which case a person's education should most profitably come to a conclusion.

This means that one must look at the costs and benefits of human capital before deciding to acquire more of it.

benefits of human capital   First, what are the benefits of human capital? The most obvious benefit—as we have just discussed—is the additional income that accrues to people who have more training or education.

The additional training or education not only equips people with the skills or knowledge needed to perform certain higher-paying jobs, but also helps them past barriers that restrict hiring. For example, the Ph.D.

degree has long been referred to by cynics as the "union card" to get into college teaching.

A second advantage is that people with more education or training also tend to enjoy their work more, even apart from the higher pay they get, because of the nature of their work.[1] A third benefit is that better-trained people have different lifetime earning patterns than those who must use their physical capital to earn a living. They are more likely to find work in jobs that engage their minds, and they often find their salaries keep increasing during most of their working lives. People who depend largely upon their bodies generally find their earnings peaking at some point well before retirement age.

A fourth return on investment in human capital may be nonmonetary. This is the value of the education which does not translate itself directly into higher wages. Three such benefits may be seen. First, many people enjoy getting their education. They look back on their college days as the best period of their lives and feel that they enjoyed the time more than if they had been working at a paying job during those years. Technically, this portion of their education is not an investment in human capital but rather consumption or enjoyment. Practically, however, it is difficult to separate the two components.

A second nonmonetary return, similar to the first, is that education often sets the stage for a fuller, more enjoyable life. For example, a person may learn about classical music during college and thereby appreciate and enjoy good music for the rest of his life. Similarly, literature courses may expose the student to authors and writing styles that will enrich his whole life.

A third nonincome benefit of human capital was discussed in the first chapter. This is the fact that part of one's education may equip him to deal with economic decisions in a capable manner. Courses in economics or accounting or other such subjects may make a person able to utilize his income more wisely and thereby raise his standard of living.

the costs of acquiring human capital The acquisition of human capital in the form of education or training is often fairly expensive. There are at least three costs that we can associate with the acquisition of additional human capital. The first, and most obvious, is in the form of tuition or fees for training or education. The person going to college may pay $2,000 or $3,000 a year in tuition as well as additional sums for books, lab fees, and other expenses.

A second monetary cost of acquiring additional human capital is even larger than the tuition cost: the income bypassed while acquiring educa-

[1] Stephen B. Withey, *et. al., A Degree and What Else?: Correlates and Consequences of a College Education.* (New York: McGraw Hill, 1971), Table 38, p. 89 and p. 130.

tional training rather than having a full-time job. An individual coming out of high school who decides to go to college is foregoing a fairly sizeable income, perhaps $7,000 or $8,000 a year, in order to continue his education. Over four years this may amount to some $30,000 not earned.

A third cost of acquiring human capital is nonmonetary and this is any unpleasantness associated with the educational training. While the net experience of one's college years may be positive, few people finish training or education without taking courses which are dull, distasteful, or more demanding than they anticipated. Many people do not enjoy going to school, and to someone coming out of high school, the idea of four more years of education, particularly at the expense of a fair standard of living which could be afforded a single individual entering the labor force, is often more than sufficient to dissuade him from increasing his human capital. Unfortunately, several years later when that person is married and finds that his income from unskilled labor is not sufficient to support a family in any decent sort of style, the costs of returning to school are generally prohibitive.

calculating costs and benefits of acquiring additional human capital   Bill is a college senior majoring in business administration with a tough decision to make. Having looked around the job market, he found that he could start at a bank for $9,500 per year. However, according to the personnel manager of the bank, if Bill had an MBA (Master's of Business Administration) he could start at $1,000 more.

Bill found that a local college offered an MBA program that he could complete in 12 months, if he went full time. The cost of tuition, fees, and books would be $3,500.

If we just consider the case on monetary grounds, would Bill do well to take the extra year of school? In order to decide this, we must know the full monetary costs and benefits of the decision.

First the costs: Bill has two types of costs, out of pocket or *explicit* costs and hidden or *implicit* costs. His explicit costs have already been mentioned. They are tuition, fees, and books, which come to $3,500.

However, Bill's *implicit* costs are even greater. Remember that he could earn $9,500 by working next year instead of going to school. That $9,500 is his implicit cost of obtaining the additional education. Adding the implicit and explicit costs, Bill will pay $13,000 for his MBA.

Is this worthwhile? We can't say unless we calculate the benefits of the education and compare them to the costs. Bill's MBA will add $1,000 per year to his income. If we assume that this differential doesn't change over time (in other words, he will always make $1,000 more than if he didn't have the MBA degree) we can calculate how much the MBA is worth.

Bill is currently 21 years old. If he went to school for his MBA, he would be 22 when he began work. If he retires at age 65, he will have worked for 43 years. Therefore, over his working career, he will make an extra $43,000 as the result of his MBA.

However, in making the decision of whether or not to continue his schooling, Bill should *not* compare the $13,000 in cost with the $43,000 in added revenues. The reason is that the $43,000 will come in over a long period of time, while the $13,000 must be spent right away. Comparing the two is like comparing apples and oranges.

In order to make the cost and benefit of the MBA comparable, we must ask how much the extra $1,000 per year over 43 years is worth *today*. This is called the *present discounted value of a stream of future payments.*

Why isn't $1,000 per year over the next 43 years worth $43,000? Let's ask this another way. Would you pay someone $43,000 if he guaranteed to pay you $1,000 per year for the next 43 years? Of course not! He could put the money in the bank and earn interest on it which he would keep since he must return only your original $43,000 to you.

We must *discount* the amount we get in the future by the rate of interest that we could earn if we had the money now. Suppose that the rate of interest were 6 percent, and I promised to give you $1.00 a year from today. How much would you give me now? You would give me an amount such that the interest on it added to the amount would equal $1.00 in a year. In actual fact, this would be about 94.3 cents.

While we need not go into the mathematics of it, the present discounted value of future payments can be calculated or, more easily, read from a table such as the one that we have on the following page for an interest rate of six percent.

Returning to Bill's case, we see from table 4-3 that at six percent interest, the present discounted value of $1.00 per year for 43 years is $15.31. Multiply this by 1,000 and the value to Bill of an extra $1,000 per year for 43 years at 6 percent interest is $15,310. Comparing this to his cost of education of $13,000, we see that Bill makes a relatively small monetary gain by attending school for an extra year.

It may be interesting to note that if the interest rate were 8 percent instead of 6 percent, the extra $1,000 per year for 43 years would be only $12,043 and Bill would be advised to skip the extra schooling.

THE EFFECT OF AGE ON INCOME

Age is another important factor affecting labor income. Although there isn't much that you can do about your age (except getting a brain transplant or lying), knowledge of what you can expect your future income to be can help you in your plans.

Although table 4-2 part B shows that labor income, on the average, peaks before age 45, this is somewhat misleading. For one thing, older people tend to have less education than younger folks since each succes-

TABLE 4-3

Present Discounted Value of $1.00 per Year at Various Interest Rates

Number of Years	Interest Rate			
	4%	6%	8%	10%
1	0.9615	0.9434	0.9259	0.9091
2	1.8861	1.8334	1.7833	1.7355
3	2.7751	2.6730	2.5771	2.4869
4	3.6299	3.4651	3.3121	3.1699
5	4.4518	4.2124	3.9927	3.7908
6	5.2421	4.9173	4.6229	4.3553
7	6.0021	5.5824	5.2064	4.8684
8	6.7327	6.2098	5.7466	5.3349
9	7.4353	6.8017	6.2469	5.7590
10	8.1109	7.3601	6.7101	6.1446
11	8.7605	7.8869	7.1390	6.4951
12	9.3851	8.3838	7.5361	6.8137
13	9.9856	8.8527	7.9038	7.1034
14	10.5631	9.2950	8.2442	7.3667
15	11.1184	9.7122	8.5595	7.6061
16	11.6523	10.1059	8.8514	7.8237
17	12.1657	10.4773	9.1216	8.0216
18	12.6593	10.8276	9.3719	8.2014
19	13.1339	11.1581	9.6036	8.3649
20	13.5903	11.4699	9.8181	8.5136
21	14.0292	11.7641	10.0168	8.6487
22	14.4511	12.0416	10.2007	8.7715
23	14.8568	12.3034	10.3711	8.8832
24	15.2470	12.5504	10.5288	8.9847
25	15.6221	12.7834	10.6748	9.0770
26	15.9828	13.0032	10.8100	9.1609
27	16.3296	13.2105	10.9352	9.2372
28	16.6631	13.4062	11.0511	9.3066
29	16.9837	13.5907	11.1584	9.3696
30	17.2920	13.7648	11.2578	9.4269
31	17.5885	13.9291	11.3498	9.4790
32	17.8736	14.0840	11.4350	9.5264
33	18.1476	14.2302	11.5139	9.5694
34	18.4112	14.3681	11.5869	9.6086
35	18.6646	14.4982	11.6546	9.6442
36	18.9083	14.6210	11.7172	9.6765
37	19.1426	14.7368	11.7752	9.7059
38	19.3679	14.8460	11.8289	9.7327
39	19.5845	14.9491	11.8786	9.7570
40	19.7928	15.0463	11.9246	9.7791

sive generation in this century is better educated than the one before. While a grade school education was the norm for our grandparents and our parents did well to finish high school, the current generation of youngsters finds over half of high school graduates going on for higher training. Therefore it is not surprising to find younger people, with their extra human capital, earning more money than their elders.

Yet this doesn't tell the full story either. While human capital is one factor that makes a worker more valuable (and able to earn more), *experience* is another factor that affects income, but it affects it differently in different occupations.

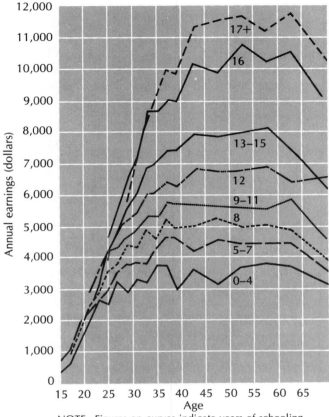

Fig. 4-1
Age profiles of earnings of white, nonfarm men, 1959 (annual earnings classified by years of age, for indicated schooling groups)

NOTE: Figures on curves indicate years of schooling completed.

Source: Jacob Mincer, *Schooling, Experience and Earnings*, (New York: Columbua University Press for NBER, 1974).

People whose occupations require physical strength, such as football or construction, will often find experience to be of limited value. Income often declines as their physical strength deteriorates. People whose occupations do not rely primarily on physical strength but where continued experience is valuable, such as law or medicine, often find that their income continues to increase almost to the age of retirement.

Figure 4-1 shows the patterns of interaction between education and age (which is similar to experience). Men with less than high school education (grades 0–11) tend to peak in earnings at almost age 35. High school graduates peak in earnings at about age 40 while college graduates (16 years of education) peak at age 50, and those with more than a college education do not reach their highest earnings until they are almost 60.

Consequently, a person considering a job should look at the return over an entire lifetime rather than the return merely in the first year of work.

A person's human capital, that is his "machinery" that he can use to earn money for himself, may be said to consist of two parts—the body, and the mind. Just as capital used by businesses, such as trucks and machinery, depreciates with age, so does the human body.

Experts in gerentology (the study of aging) have advanced a hypothesis that aging is the process of random shocks to the system which tend to deteriorate organs. Over a period of many years, when enough organs have been damaged, the body breaks down. This is similar to a car, which, when it is new, may have an occasional malfunction which is readily cured in the shop. However, as time wears on, other functions go bad to the point where one day the entire machine collapses. Therefore, a person who is selling his *physical* capital to earn his living, such as a construction worker, a ditch digger, or a truck driver, finds that his strength and reflexes deteriorate after the age of 30 or 35. It is apparent that the employer who is buying physical strength may replace him when he can no longer perform as well as a younger person.

EARNING POWER FROM
PHYSICAL LABOR

People who use the mental portion of their human capital often fare much better in the course of a lifetime. Whereas the physical body *deteriorates* over time, the mind often *appreciates* in value due to the experience built up and retained. This accounts for the fact that professional people and others who depend largely upon their minds in their occupations find their incomes increasing over most of their working lives.

EARNING POWER FROM
WHITE COLLAR WORK

People who live and work in or around large metropolitan areas tend to earn more than their counterparts who live some distance from these areas (table 4–2, part D). This is true for two reasons. First, within a large metropolitan area, there are more job opportunities and therefore employers must pay somewhat higher amounts to attract employees to work for them. In rural areas, where there are few employers, there is little or no competition for employees and wages tend to be lower. Secondly, the cost of living is often higher in larger metropolitan areas so that workers there would have to be paid more to enjoy the same standard of living as their counterparts elsewhere.

The region of the country is also related to labor income. Table 4-2 part E shows that workers in the Northeast are highest paid while workers in the South earn the least. This is accounted for not only by differences in urbanization, but also genuine differences in economic development and cost of living. Incomes are lower in the South for at least two reasons: the South has relatively less industry and consequently less better-paying industrial employment; and the cost of living is lower in the South (due to the milder climate which requires less heat and fewer heavy clothes in the winter as well as the lower food costs due to the longer growing season), which means that people can enjoy a higher standard of living for less money.

EFFECTS OF DISCRIMINATION: RACE AND SEX

Labor income is strongly affected by two background variables that, unlike education and location, cannot be altered: race and sex.

Income differentials on the basis of race and sex are well known. Whites make substantially more money than blacks, and men earn more than women. According to table 4-2 part C, white males make over $2,000 more than black males. Even larger differences are found when incomes of men are compared with women.

Are these differences in income the result of discrimination? Partly. Economists are careful to use the term *discrimination* when difference in income cannot be explained by difference in ability. For example, white males make more money than black males, but also, on the average, have more education. Therefore, if part of the income differential is due to differences that affect job ability and performance, only the remainder may be ascribed to discrimination.

A statistical technique exists that allows the researcher to isolate the effects of discrimination from other background variables. The use of this technique, after controlling for non-racial variables, reveals that black males earned $.50 per hour less than white males.[2] We must conclude, therefore, that racial discrimination in employment accounts for a large proportion (over half) of the income differential between white and black males.

Using a similar technique, researchers at the Survey Research Center found that after controlling on factors such as education, tenure, race, age, region, and occupation, women with full-time jobs still earned about $1.00 per hour less than men with full-time jobs. It appears that sexual discrimination is even greater than racial discrimination.[3]

Of course, some may legitimately argue that economic discrimination, as we measure it alone, understates the true effects of discrimination on income. Women and blacks may have less education than their opposites *because* of discrimination in education and hiring practices, and true effects on income may be even larger than the amounts reported above.

NONMONETARY COMPONENTS OF LABOR INCOME

While background characteristics are important in determining the amount of money income, the choice between several jobs or occupations may hinge on other reasons. What are some of these?

[2] Katherine Dickinson, "Wage Rates of Heads and Wives," in Morgan, *et. al., Five Thousand American Families.* (Ann Arbor: Institute for Social Research, 1974), p. 166.

[3] Ibid.

Fringe Benefits

The value of fringe benefits paid to workers in this country has been continually increasing during recent decades. Social security contributions of the employers, pension plans, hospitalization plans, dental plans, life insurance, unemployment insurance, and other such things add more than 12 percent to the average salary. Pay for leave time including vacations, holidays, and sick time boosts the average fringe benefit package to 22 percent of money income.

Consequently, when considering the choice between jobs, the individual must consider the fringe benefit package as well as the pure money income. Anyone who has had to pay his own hospitalization insurance realizes this alone may amount to a substantial portion of his salary.

Risk and Stability

A second important factor in considering the choice of a job is stability of the income. People who work in the construction business often find their incomes fluctuating greatly from month to month (depending on weather) and year to year (depending on business conditions). Although these people may have relatively high earnings, this is offset by the risk of being out of work for uncertain periods of time.

An occupation at the other extreme is that of teaching school which has generally been associated with relatively low rates of pay but which has (until very recently) been a reliable and dependable source of income, year after year.[4] Consequently, a person should evaluate the stability and risk of being out of work in addition to the monetary and fringe benefit package of the jobs.

Job Satisfaction

A very important nonmonetary return is the enjoyment that a person gets from his job. In this respect, we observe a rather strange situation. Economic theory states that, all other things being equal, a job that is relatively more unpleasant should pay more to encourage people more to enter such occupations. However, empirical data from the Survey Research Center shows that people who make more money are, on the average, more satisfied with their work than people who make less money.

As it turns out, both pay and job satisfaction are strongly related to the level of a person's education. People with high levels of education get better paying jobs and also jobs that they enjoy. People with relative-

---

[4] Recently, Jacob Benus found that income instability is strongly associated with low income. He concludes: "The poor not only have low incomes, but they also have more unstable incomes." in James Morgan (ed.), *Five Thousand American Families—Patterns of Economic Progress.* (Ann Arbor: Institute for Social Research, 1974).

ly little education often are forced to take boring, monotonous jobs which are also relatively low paying.

In some cases, however, unusual jobs such as underwater diving and test piloting often pay additional money to compensate for the high degree of physical risk.

Control Over Working Hours

An issue that has become important in recent years is the value of control over one's working hours. In the automobile industry, it has been traditional that overtime is non-voluntary, although this has recently been changing. If the plant has to catch up, the foreman can assign overtime to his workers and this cannot be refused. Non-voluntary overtime is often unpleasant for the worker who may have his weekend plans interrupted or who may be forced to work for long stretches of time without rest. Consequently, people who have control over their hours have an advantage—all other things being equal—over those who work fixed hours or whose hours are determined for them by someone else.

THE RELATION BETWEEN MONETARY AND NONMONETARY COMPONENTS OF LABOR INCOME

It is interesting to note that, by and large, the nonmonetary components of labor income tend to be related to the monetary—in other words, jobs that pay better also tend to have better benefits. In a recent study, Greg Duncan of the University of Michigan's Survey Research Center found this to be true of higher status jobs.[5] Duncan also found that when nonmonetary components are included with money income from work, the advantages of education are further increased.

TOTAL FAMILY INCOME

A family's total income is often larger than that of a single worker—more than one family member may work, and there may be sources of income other than labor.

Labor Income of Wives

An important trend affecting the income of families over the recent decades has been the growing proportion of wives who have jobs. Table 4-4 shows that the proportion of married women who work has grown from 17 percent in 1940 to 41 percent in 1970. Since the proportion of

[5] Greg Duncan, in James Morgan (ed.) *Five Thousand American Families—Patterns of Economic Progress.* (Ann Arbor: Institute for Social Research, 1974).

TABLE 4-4

Female Labor Force as Percent of Female Population

(Persons 14 years old and over through 1966;
16 years old and over thereafter)

Year	All Females	Single Females	Married Females		Widowed or Divorced Females
			Total	Husband Present	
1940	27	48	17	15	32
1950	31	51	25	24	36
1960	35	44	32	31	37
1970	43	53	41	41	36

Source: *Statistical Abstract* 1972, Table 346, p. 219.

single, widowed, or divorced females who work has remained relatively constant over this time, the addition of wives to the labor force has increased the proportion of all women who work from 27 percent in 1940 to 43 percent in 1970.

This development has been associated with changing ideas regarding the role of the wife. A half century ago, a working wife symbolized the inability of the husband to provide a decent living for his family. Today, a wife who neither works outside the home nor has small children to care for is often considered lazy.

The contribution from the wife's job added some $3,474 to the average income of families with both a husband and wife, some 26 percent of the total.[6]

Non-Labor Income

Figure 4-2 shows the composition of family income. Labor income in the form of wages, salaries, and fringe benefits accounts for 69 percent of the total. The income of proprietors (people who have their own businesses) adds another 8 percent.

Transfer Payments

Transfer payments are income that the family gets in the form of welfare, veterans benefits, social security, and other payments that are neither earned by current labor nor by current investments. Each year, more

---

[6] Statistics calculated from *Statistical Abstracts of the U.S.*, 1972 ed., Table 534, p. 327.

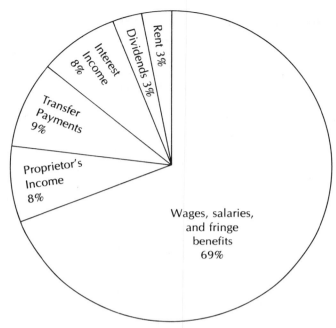

Source: *Statistical Abstract,* 1972, Table 517, p. 317.

Fig. 4-2
Composition of
Family Income 1970

than 40 percent of American families receive some transfer income, but generally the amounts are so small that total transfer income equals only 9 percent.

Interest Income, Dividends, and Rents

Income from savings accounts, stocks, bonds, and real estate is often considered to be capital income since it is a return on an investment (capital). It is the largest part of capital income (8 percent of family income) since three-quarters of all American families have at least one interest-paying savings account. Dividends and rents each only account for 3 percent of family income, but these are particularly important for wealthier families.

Non-Money Income

It is apparent that income earned in the market place is only a part (although generally the largest) of the total income available to the family.

A recent trend in economics, begun by Professor Becker,[7] has been to consider the family's consumption patterns constrained not only by income but also, and perhaps ultimately, by the time available to the family. In other words, each person is ultimately constrained by the 168 hours of the week. Most people work about forty of these hours, and allowing two hours a day for lunch and transportation, may spend fifty hours a week in connection with their jobs. This is less than one-third of the total number of hours. Eight hours of sleep a night adds fifty-six hours per week, which makes 106 hours, leaving some sixty-two hours of the 168 per week over which a person has some discretion. A person may use those hours to produce additional money income by working overtime at a second job, he may produce substitute income by doing non-market work at home, or he may forego income and spend them for leisure or recreation.

non-market home production   The value of a family's home production is often much greater than it imagines. Every job one does at home—mowing the lawn, fixing dinner, vacuuming the floor—saves the family money that it would have to spend to have those services done by someone else. Consequently, when a person chooses to give up some leisure time for home production, as is true in most families, he is really increasing income by saving the money otherwise spent on those services.

In a recent book, Professor Serageldin estimated that the average family saved more than $4,000 a year by home production activities.[8] He also found that wealthier families tended to have less non-market income than less wealthy families. They often purchased services on the market—cleaning, gardening, miscellaneous home repairs—that poorer families could not afford and had to do for themselves.

In a more recent study, Mandell focused solely on those home production activities which are generally purchased on the market.[9] These included automobile repair, home maintenance, and the growing, canning or freezing of foods, but excluded activities such as home cleaning and gardening which most families do for themselves anyway. He found that, on the average, families save $186.00 per year by their home production efforts. He also found that families whose incomes have fallen do not compensate by increasing their amount of home production.

Home production "do-it-yourself" activities offer both benefits and costs. An economist would summarize these as follows:

---

[7] Gary S. Becker, "A Theory of the Allocation of Time," *Economic Journal,* (75), September, 1965.

[8] Ishmael Serageldin, *Non-Market Components of National Income,* Institute for Social Research, 1969.

[9] Lewis Mandell, "Market-Substitute Home Production," (Survey Research Center Working Paper, 1973).

Benefits of Home Production

1. If you do it yourself, you save the out-of-pocket expense of having someone else do it for you. If the painter estimates $100 in labor cost to paint your garage and you do it yourself, you have saved $100.

2. The income tax factor makes your savings even greater. If you elected to pay the painter $100, you would have to earn *more* than $100 to end up with that money. If you are in the 25 percent tax bracket, you would have to earn $133.33 at work in order to come home with the $100 you need to pay the painter.

3. Many people enjoy do-it-yourself activities.

Costs of Home Production

1. Economists would rank *opportunity cost* as the greatest cost of home production (ignoring the cost of materials, which would have to be paid whether you or someone else did it). Opportunity cost is the loss you are taking by not using your time in a more productive manner.

If the man who decided to paint his garage took a week off from work in order to do this, his opportunity cost is the money he would have earned at work. If he would have taken home $150 by working, his opportunity cost is $150.

Of course, one must be realistic when assessing the actual amount of opportunity cost. If a man paints his garage on evenings and weekends, his opportunity cost may be low, depending upon his opportunities to work elsewhere. If he could be earning $6.50 per hour by working overtime at the plant, his opportunity cost is high. However, if there are no part-time, short duration jobs available, his opportunity cost may be next to zero (he could always walk the highway collecting soda bottles for fifteen cents each).

2. Lack of efficiency is another cost of home production for most people. The professional may be able to paint the garage in 20 hours while it may take the owner twice that long.

3. Lack of quality may be another cost of home production. Unless a person is skilled, a do-it-yourself job may end up looking like it.

4. Home production also involves equipment cost. You cannot paint a house without the proper ladders and brushes which must be purchased or rented. Money sunk in expensive tools and equipment could be in the bank (or elsewhere) yielding interest. So whether you buy or rent your equipment, the charges must be added in figuring the true cost of home production.

LEISURE

What is left over from the 168 hours after work, sleep, and home production are taken out is often called leisure. Of course, a person may use

his so-called leisure time to increase his human capital (by taking a class or teaching himself accounting at home), in which case he would be investing rather than enjoying leisure.

Most people tend to use their leisure time for rest and enjoyment. It is not at all certain that leisure time is wasted time even for a family wishing to maximize its income. Leisure in the form of physical activity and exercise is important for the maintenance of the human capital of the body. Medical studies show that people who do not get a sufficient amount of exercise find that their vital organs deteriorate more rapidly than those people who exercise regularly. Also, although there is not nearly enough evidence to make it conclusive, it appears that relaxation, whether in the form of watching a ball game or reading a book for pleasure or just sitting out on the lawn watching the clouds go by, may be important for the healthful functioning of the body. Relaxation aids the physical plant in the body, which is given a chance to rejuvenate itself, and also the mental plant, which may need a rest after concentrated hours of difficult activity.

SUMMARY

1. Labor income is generally the most important component of total family income. An individual's labor income is determined by many factors, including education, race, age, sex, and geographic location.

2. More education generally means more money. Much of this difference is due to improved human capital—skills or knowledge needed to perform certain high-paying jobs. Education also helps to overcome barriers to hiring in the first place.

3. The costs of acquiring human capital include income foregone from not working, as well as tuition, books, and other expenses connected with education or training. Other, nonmonetary costs may also keep individuals from acquiring additional human capital.

4. The costs of acquiring additional human capital are borne within a few years, but the benefits accrue over the lifetime. In order to see whether the benefits are worth the cost, it is necessary to calculate the present discounted value of the stream of future benefits.

5. While discrimination is still an important determinant of earnings, in economic terms it is measured as the difference in earnings between two persons who have all of the same qualifications but who differ only by factors such as race and sex.

6. Aside from the pay check associated with the job, there are nonmonetary components of income, and they tend to vary directly with money

income: fringe benefits, stability of employment, job satisfaction, and control over working hours.

7. Calculation of a family's total income includes the labor income of all members of the family and nonlabor income such as proprietor's income, transfer payments, interest income, dividends, and rent.

8. Nonmonetary income is becoming increasingly important to American families. This includes do-it-yourself activities and other forms of home production. The benefits of home production must be calculated carefully in order to be sure that they outweigh the costs.

1. Why do people with more education tend to have higher incomes? Does education account solely for the difference? Does it ever work in reverse?

2. Very few medical doctors also have Ph.D.s or law degrees. Why do they stop their education when they get their medical degree? What can be said about the small number of people who acquire additional degrees?

3. Why is it that people with substantial amounts of education often see their incomes rising until retirement, while those with little education often see their incomes peak half-way through their working lifetimes?

4. Is it economically advantageous to live in a northeastern city? Explain.

5. At what stages of life is a person most likely to receive transfer payments?

labor income
human capital
discrimination
job satisfaction
income stability
transfer payments
capital income
nonmarket home production
opportunity cost
leisure

QUESTIONS TO THE CONSUMER ADVISOR

Dear Consumer Advisor:

I am an eighteen-year-old high school graduate who is working for an insurance company for $6,500 per year. My boss told me that if I went to a junior college for two years full-time, I could become a computer technician and make an extra $1,000 a year. The nearby community college costs $1,800 per year for tuition, fees, and books. Do you think it's worth it to go to school for two more years?

Potential Student

Dear Consumer Advisor:

I am a 6 foot 10 inch college basketball player in my junior year. Recently, I have received some offers to drop out of college and play professional ball. While I think I am good enough to play with most professional teams, I don't think that I am big enough or quick enough to ever become a superstar. Do you think that it's in my interest to take the offer now or to finish out my senior year and get my degree?

Stretch

Dear Consumer Advisor:

I am a production worker in the automobile industry with many years of seniority. As a result, I can work overtime almost any time I want to and make $6.50 an hour. The trouble is my wife is always on me to do jobs around the house like paint the garage and mow the lawn, which I really dislike doing. I told her that we can hire a teenager down the street for $3.50 an hour, and I would just as soon work the overtime to make that money, but she doesn't see it that way. What do you feel?

Charlie

5

FAMILY NEEDS AND EXPENDITURES

When was the last time someone said to you, "I like my work so much I would do it for free," and said it with a straight face?

In spite of the intrinsic value that people may get from working, most of us work largely or entirely for one reason—the money. There are certain things that must be paid—the rent, the car payment, the grocery bill, and there are other things that we don't really need but want to buy.

Powerful forces are at work urging families to spend every last dollar of their income, and even more. What are the spending habits of consumers in our society, and what are the forces that determine them?

THE DETERMINATION OF FAMILY NEEDS

While the basic biological needs of an American family can be met for a few dollars per week for dried beans, rice, and powdered milk, this definition of "needs" is not useful for an understanding of our economy. Needs are culturally determined and often legally enforced. Although indoor flush toilets are a luxury throughout the world, they are considered a basic necessity of life in the United States and are compulsory in many areas.

The United States Government defines a "lower but adequate" standard of living for a family of four in the

United States (for the purpose of calculating changes in the cost of living). Even this standard, which may be considered a lower limit on the needs of a family, contains an allotment for eating at restaurants, movies, a radio, and a television set.[1] Families living at this "adequate" standard would be considered well-off by more than half of the world's families.

If we are willing to accept the fact that, to a great extent, needs in a wealthy economy are socially determined, we can examine the factors that determine the needs of an individual family.

Family Size and Composition

A major determinant of a family's needs is, of course, its size. Throw aside the myth that two can live as cheaply as one or three can live as cheaply as two or twenty-one can live as cheaply as twelve. It just isn't so.

The larger the family, the more food that must be bought and the larger the house that is needed, among other things. Costs increase with the family size, but not necessarily in proportion with the increasing size of the family. Economies of scale exist to reduce the added cost of additional children.

The term *economies of scale* is used in several areas of economics, most generally in discussion of production, and refers to the fact that the cost of adding another unit is less than the average cost of previous units. In the case of the family, the annual expenses for a childless couple may be $8,000; the average cost is $4,000 per person. If they have a child, their *total* expenses may increase to $10,000. Therefore, the child has added only $2,000 to the family's expenses, which is less than the average expense of the original family members. This increased cost for the last unit is known as the *marginal cost*. A second child would increase total family expenses but would lower the average expense.

Number of Family Members	Total Expenses	Average Expenses
2	$ 8,000	$4,000
3	10,000	3,333
4	12,000	3,000
5	14,000	2,800

Why does the family have economies of scale? There are several possible factors:

1. Housing for the family is a *fixed cost* which does not necessarily change as more people are added. If a childless couple spends $3,000 per year on a three bedroom house, the addition of a child or two

---

[1] U.S. Department of Labor, Bureau of Labor Statistics, *3 Standards of Living for an Urban Family of Four Persons,* Bulletin No. 15, 70–5.

TABLE 5-1

Weekly Food Cost for Families, by Type of Family, 1972

(Based on Moderate-Cost Food Plan)

Type	Cost
Couple 20–35 years old	$25.40
Couple 55–75 years old	21.20
Couple with children	
1 child, 1–5 years old	31.40
1 child, 15–18 years old	36.60
2 children, 1–5 years old	36.80
2 children, 6–11 years old	42.90
2 children, 12–18 years old	47.10

Source: Statistical Abstract, 1973, p. 356.

will not increase housing costs. It spreads them over more family members, thereby lowering the average for each.

2. There are other fixed expenses for the family such as the automobile, stove, television set, and telephone, which cost the same regardless of the number of family members (up to a point).
3. Even average food bills fall when more people are fed at one time. Food can be purchased in larger quantities resulting in frequent savings, and the time and heat necessary to prepare a meal for four is not twice as great as for two.

Unfortunately economies of scale in family size do not necessarily keep occurring for large families. At some point, perhaps when a family has a third child, it is forced to move to a larger, more expensive house, thereby increasing average housing costs. Even with economies of scale, the family can count on greater expenses as it gets larger.

Another factor determining a family's needs is its age composition. Government statisticians have developed needs standards based on the age composition of the family as well as its size. According to table 5-1, food costs increase sharply as children get older and the family gets larger.

The Family's Life Cycle

Students of biology are familiar with the *life cycle* of the butterfly. Beginning as an egg, it goes to a squiggly little larva which then becomes a squiggly big larva, known as a caterpillar. Then it undergoes a remarkable face lifting and comes out as a graceful, beautiful butterfly. The butterfly lays eggs to insure the next generation and then flies off to die.

The family begins when John meets Mary, they fall in love, and tie the knot. The Smith family now exists. But life for John and Mary probably hasn't been altered to any great extent. Instead of living in two housing units, they now live in one, probably a small apartment. Most likely, they both continue to work at jobs they had before marriage, so their incomes have not been altered and their needs may even be smaller than before marriage (if they had each lived alone in their own housing units).

The next step in the family life cycle begins in the maternity ward of the local hospital when Mary gives birth to little Melvin. Right away we know some important things about the family's economic behavior since Mary has probably quit her job, and little Melvin ups the family budget with his doctor bills, food bills, laundry expenses, and babysitters. At this stage, the Smiths begin to feel a little crowded in their small apartment and start driving around on Sundays looking at houses with a yard for little Melvin to play in.

Within a few short years, the stork blesses little Melvin with a baby sister, Cynthia. Expenses increase again since, by now, the Smiths are living in their own house.

Over the years Melvin and Cynthia grow from small children into fine teenagers and start eating the Smiths out of house and home. And then comes college, which increases expenses even more.

But finally, Melvin and Cynthia are married and living on their own and the (original) Smith family finds expenses dropping at last. And so we leave the Smith family, in the golden years of their life cycle, retired, with small expenses, babysitting for their grandchildren until they are called into the world beyond.

For purposes of analysis, economists use the following life cycle stages:

Younger than age 45
1. Unmarried, no children
2. Married, no children
3. Married, youngest child under age 6
4. Married, youngest child age 6 or older

Age 45 or older
5. Married, has children
6. Married, no children, head still working
7. Married, no children, head retired
8. Unmarried, no children, head retired

Analysis of life cycle is valuable for more than just explaining expenditures. It is also helpful in explaining income (since it determines the wife's participation in the labor force), housing, automobile purchase, and debt. We will refer to the concept of the family life cycle frequently in discussing these other aspects of economic behavior.

Location of Residence

A family's place of residence also determines family needs. Table 4–2 shows the cost of living for families in different regions and size places.

Families living in warmer regions can generally meet their needs for less money. Housing is less expensive since they often don't need basements or insulation, and winter heating bills are much lower. Clothing costs are also diminished since much heavy winter clothing is unnecessary, and food costs are often lower because of the longer growing season which diminishes the need to ship food very far.

Even within climatic regions, the cost of living is determined by the size of place of residence. Families living in large cities or their suburbs find that housing and services are generally more expensive.

Housing in cities is more expensive (for the same living area) because land is scarcer and worth more. While land in farming areas outside of the city may be worth $500 to $1,000 an acre, land in the center of the city may go for 50 or 100 times that amount.

Services are often more expensive in urban areas for reasons explained more fully in chapter 4. The demand for all types of services is more broadly based in cities, thereby enabling people to charge more for their services. In addition, those who must live in urban areas where they work have higher living expenses, thus compounding the problem.

DISCRETIONARY EXPENDITURES

The mark of a wealthy economy is not only seen in the increased scope of its definition of needs but also in the gap between a family's needs and its *disposable income* (that is, "take-home pay" or income after things such as taxes, union dues, and social security have been taken out).

This portion of income is often referred to as *discretionary* since its use is at the discretion of the family. It can be put into savings or used to buy things that the family wants such as a vacation or a new car. It can also be used to repay debts.

The importance of discretionary expenditures was first noticed by economist-psychologist George Katona of the Survey Research Center shortly after the end of the Second World War. Katona found three conditions causing the growth of discretionary expenditures. First, a great many families had incomes in excess of their needs, creating discretionary income. Second, a large proportion of families found themselves with sizable *liquid assets* (cash, bank accounts, or other assets that could be turned quickly into money) as the result of the forced savings-bond purchases made during the war. Third, creditors began to see consumers as a lucrative source of business, and consumer credit became widely available.

For the first time in history, a majority of families in the population had some control (or discretion) over what they spent and when they

TABLE 5-2

Indexes of Comparative Costs Based on a Lower Living Standard for a 4-Person Family[1], Spring 1967

(U.S. Average Urban Cost = 100)

Region	Total Budget	Food	Total Housing[2]	Shelter[3] (renter costs)	Transportation[4]	Clothing and Personal Care	Medical Care[5]	Other Family Consumption
Urban United States	100	100	100	100	100	100	100	100
Metropolitan areas[6]	101	101	102	103	94	102	103	104
Nonmetropolitan areas[7]	94	94	90	88	126	92	87	83
Northeast:								
Boston, Mass.	106	105	112	115	95	101	100	106
New York-Northeastern New Jersey	102	107	95	94	83	104	108	106
Nonmetropolitan areas[7]	96	100	86	83	129	95	94	82
North Central:								
Chicago, Ill.– Northwestern Ind.	103	102	111	114	91	103	103	103
Detroit, Mich.	99	102	94	93	99	103	99	106
Nonmetropolitan areas[7]	98	96	104	106	123	95	83	81
South:								
Atlanta, Ga.	95	94	96	93	94	97	93	110
Austin, Tex.	89	94	81	76	91	92	92	101
Washington, D.C.– Md.–Va.	104	99	113	118	101	97	98	105
Nonmetropolitan areas[7]	88	90	83	78	125	86	84	83

TABLE 5-2 (continued)

Indexes of Comparative Costs Based on a Lower Living Standard for a 4-Person Family[1], Spring 1967

(U.S. Average Urban Cost = 100)

Region	Total Budget	Food	Total Housing[2]	Shelter[3] (renter costs)	Cost of Family Consumption Transportation[4]	Clothing and Personal Care	Medical Care[5]	Other Family Consumption
West:								
Honolulu, Hawaii	122	122	140	145	111	99	99	112
Los Angeles–Long Beach, Ca.	107	101	109	113	98	106	133	107
Nonmetropolitan areas[7]	103	100	101	99	132	101	93	85

[1] The family consists of an employed husband, aged 38, a wife not employed outside the home, an 8-year-old girl, and a 13-year-old boy.

[2] Total housing includes shelter, household operations, and house furnishings. All families with the lower living standard are assumed to be renters.

[3] Average contract rent plus the cost of required amounts of heating fuel, gas, electricity, water, specified equipment, and insurance on household contents.

[4] The average costs of automobile owners and nonowners in the lower budget are weighted by the following proportions of families: Boston, Chicago, New York, and Philadelphia, 50 percent for both automobile owners and nonowners; all other metropolitan areas, 65 percent for automobile owners, 35 percent for nonowners; nonmetropolitan areas, 100 percent for automobile owners.

[5] In total medical care, the average costs of medical insurance were weighted by the following proportions: 30 percent for families paying full cost of insurance; 26 percent for families paying half cost; 44 percent for families covered by noncontributory insurance plans (paid by employer).

[6] For a detailed description, see the 1967 edition of the *Standard Metropolitan Statistical Areas*, prepared by the Bureau of the Budget.

[7] Places with population of 2,500 to 50,000.

Source: 3 *Standards of Living for an Urban Family of Four Persons, op. cit.*

spent it. Expenditures or needs were already determined by family size, composition, and location, but what determined discretionary expenditures? Professor Katona had an answer for this. "Consumer sentiment," he said.

Consumer sentiment is almost as hard to explain as it is to measure. Basically, it is a general feeling of how well-off the consumer thinks he is and how he assesses the future. Over twenty-five years of national surveys, Katona has found that when consumers feel relatively well-off, that their condition and the condition of the economy will continue to be good, they are in a buying mood. Conversely, pessimistic feelings will induce consumers to hold off on expenditures that would deplete their liquid assets or put them in debt, so that they can be better prepared to meet the worst—loss of a job or a cut in income.

Take the Smith family, for example. When Mel was just a little tyke, John and Mary decided that it would be nice to replace Old Betsy, their aged, unreliable car with a new model. "If this heap can get us through one more winter," John said, "we'll get a new car in the spring."

Spring came, and with it came a downturn in the economy. The stock market plunged, unemployment rose, and the engineering concern that John worked for had some contracts cancelled.

"What about that new car?" asked Mary on a warm April day.

"I don't really think so," replied John. "Things aren't looking so good in the economy, and some of the guys at work are already being laid off. I think we're better off holding off for a while to see how things go. If I lose my job, we're better off with a few dollars in the bank than we are with a $2,000 automobile loan hanging over us. Besides, Old Betsy is still a mighty fine car."

CONSUMPTION AND INCOME

The consumption behavior of a family is both interesting and important for the economy. A family can do only two things with its income—it can consume goods and services, or it can save. Most families do both—they consume with most of their income and save the remainder.

Now this may appear strange to many people who seem to spend every dollar they get and have virtually no savings in the bank. But not every dollar that we spend is consumption. For example, if we live in our own home and make a mortgage payment of $200 every month, part of that $200 is going to reduce the amount that we owe (amortization) and is really a means by which we save money.

There are other examples of disguised savings. The purchase of an automobile for $3,000 may appear to be $3,000 worth of consumption. However, one does not use all of the services of an automobile in the week, or month, or year of purchase (unless he wraps it around a pole). The automobile, like a refrigerator or T.V. set or other types of *consumer durables,* are *investments* which yield services over a relatively long period of time. Only part of the price is considered consumption—generally the decrease in value during the period of time for which consumption is measured. If your new car depreciates $1,000 in value over the course of a year, you are consuming $1,000 worth of car in that year. The other $2,000 that you laid out for the car is an investment for services in future years.

Families not only tend to use most of their income for consumption, they also have a habit of consuming a large part of any income *increase* that they might get. The seemingly simpleminded observation that people consume part of their income increases (rather than saving it all) constitutes the "fundamental psychological law" that John Maynard Keynes made famous in 1935. "The fundamental psychological law, upon which we are entitled to depend with great confidence both *a priori* from our knowledge of human nature and from the detailed facts of experience, is that men are disposed, as a rule and on the average, to increase their consumption as their income increases, but not by as much as the increase in income."[2]

This law constitutes an important part of the macroeconomic theory that we will examine in part 3 of this book.

Consumption Function Theory

As other economists began to examine the actual behavior of families more closely, they found that Keynes' law, while true, did not tell the entire story. According to Keynes' hypothesis, if John received an increase in pay amounting to $3,000 per year, the Smith family would increase their consumption (by most of that amount) and put a little more into savings. But incomes don't keep increasing every year. When Mary Smith had little Melvin, she quit her job and the family income shrank. In fact, over a recent five-year period, data from the Survey Research Center found that *80 percent* of all American families had at least one year-to-year decrease in income. What does the Smith family do when their income falls by $6,000 as the result of Mary's departure from the labor force? Do they cut their consumption by nearly that amount and greatly reduce their standard of living, as Keynes' law, taken in reverse, would have us believe?

Not if they are typical of most other families. Economists have found that the reaction of consumption to income is not symmetrical. When families experience an increase in income, their consumption generally increases by almost as much (just like Keynes said). However, when families experience a decrease in income, consumption tends to fall by little, if at all.

---

[2] John Maynard Keynes, *The General Theory of Employment, Interest and Money* (New York: Harcourt, Brace & World, Inc., 1935), p. 96.

relative income hypothesis   An interesting explanation for this assymetry was borrowed from the sociologists who had long studied the desire of families to "keep up with the Joneses."[3] The *relative income hypothesis* speculates that when families have an increase in income, they soon adjust their consumption to a higher level by doing such things as moving to a better neighborhood and getting a better house and car. When income suddenly falls, they find it very difficult to return to their former, lower standard of living and try to hold out as long as they can at the higher level of consumption.

When John received his $3,000 raise, he and Mary decided that they could finally afford to buy a house and get out of their cramped apartment. So after a considerable search, they bought an attractive, three bedroom house in a good school district. To go with the house, they had to get kitchen appliances and a fair amount of new furniture. In addition to this, they decided that the car was a neighborhood eyesore, and traded her in on a new one. Before the raise, John was taking home $10,000 a year and spending $9,000 of it. Now he is taking home $12,500 and spending $11,000 of it.

A year after John got his raise, his company lost its main contract and was forced to lay John off. As the result of his good recommendations, he was able to find another job right away, but at his old salary before the $3,000 raise.

Now the Smiths were forced to cope with a $3,000 decrease in income. What could they do? They could sell the house and furniture and move back to the old apartment (and sell the new car and buy the old one back from the junkyard), but such economic behavior is very difficult and hardly ever observed.

Instead, they tightened their belts a little, cutting down on steaks and postponing planned purchases of durable goods, and drew a little bit from savings as well. Consumption was reduced by $500 while disposable income fell by $2,500. If John's income doesn't increase (and Mary isn't tempted to go back to work as many wives do when faced with a decrease in family income), the Smiths will eventually be forced to reduce consumption even further (to John's $10,000 income) since their savings will someday be exhausted.

permanent income hypothesis   A second explanation for the consumption behavior of families takes a longer view. This theory says that consumption should not be expected to change immediately with shortrun changes in income since families have a notion of long-run or permanent income and consume according to this.[4]

---

[3] James Duesenberry, *Income, Saving, and the Theory of Consumer Behavior,* (Harvard University Press, 1949).

[4] Milton Friedman, *A Theory of the Consumption Function.* (Princeton: National Bureau of Economic Research, 1959).

Permanent income is determined by a family's income earning abilities which may be broken down into human capital and non-human capital (or assets such as stocks, bonds, bank accounts, and real estate). A young physician who has a lot of human capital may be unable to work for a year as the result of an illness. His short-term or *measured* income declines to nearly zero. Would we expect his consumption to decline to this level? Certainly not. Our physician realizes that his average annual income over his working lifetime may be expected to be $50,000, so the year of no income decreases his average expected income by only a couple of thousand dollars, at most. The permanent income hypothesis says that he will consume according to his average lifetime income rather than the income in one year.

life cycle hypothesis Perhaps the most interesting and useful explanation of consumption combines the permanent income notion and the life cycle approach to consumption. The life cycle hypothesis says that families have a notion of their lifetime income pattern as well as their lifetime needs or expenditure pattern.[5]

■ **LIFESTYLE**
▭ **INCOME**

By following a "game plan" of income and expenditure patterns, a family can get the greatest utility from their income. This assumes (as is the case for most families) that the family prefers a more consistent standard of living to one of ups and downs.

The Smith family has the following life cycle game plan in mind.

Life Cycle Stage	Income	Expenditures	Savings
Just Married	Both work, high income	Relatively low, no high expenses	High savings
Young children	Only John works, income low	High; new house, furniture, children expenses	Very low, if at all; may spend savings
Older children	John and Mary work, income high	Very high; kids eat a lot, allowances, cars, college expenses?	Some savings, if possible
Children gone	John (and possibly Mary) work; Relatively high income	Relatively low; can move to lower-cost housing	Very high; saving toward retirement
Retired	Low income, pension and social security.	Relatively low	None, or spend savings

5 Franch Modigliani and Richard Brumberg, "Utility Analysis and the Consumption Function: In Interpretation of Cross-Section Data," in K. Duriharu, (ed.), *Post-Keynesian Economics,* (Rutgers University Press, 1954).

This pattern may vary for families with slightly different objectives. Some people want to leave a large estate for their children and save relatively more. Others aim to live as well as they can until they die, and deplete their savings during retirement.

SUMMARY

1. In an advanced economy such as ours, it is useless to distinguish between *needs* and *wants*. The most that can be said is that some needs are biologically determined, but these are relatively small compared to those needs which are socially determined.

2. A family's needs are determined by a variety of factors including size and composition, life cycle, location of residence, and income.

3. A family's consumption is generally strongly associated with income. This relationship is largely due to the fact that consumption is "constrained" by the amount of income that a family has to consume. It has also been found that when a family experiences an increase in income, consumption increases, but by a smaller amount than the increase in income. This relationship was discovered by John Maynard Keynes and underlies much of economic theory.

4. Generally speaking, when a family experiences a sudden decrease in income, consumption will decrease slowly, if at all. Several theories have been advanced for this type of behavior. Most prominent are: the *relative income* hypothesis, which says that people adjust to a certain standard of living and find it very hard to decrease it; the *permanent income* hypothesis, which says that a family's consumption changes only over the long run and that short term increases or decreases in income do not affect consumption greatly; and the *life cycle* hypothesis, which says that people have an economic "game plan" for their lifetime consumption and tend to follow this rather than short run fluctuations in income.

QUESTIONS
FOR
DISCUSSION

1. How little money could you (and your family, if you have one) live on and still maintain your health? What fraction is this of your current monthly expenditures? What accounts for the difference?

2. The cost of living is often higher in the North than in the South as a result of higher heating, home insulation, and clothing costs; yet, Honolulu is the most expensive place to live of the major cities in the United States. Why is this so?

3. As time goes by, is discretionary income as a proportion of a family's gross income increasing, decreasing, or remaining about the same? Why do you say this?

4. The three theories explaining consumption are based on relative income, permanent income, and life cycle. Which of these hypotheses do you feel is most valid? Is more than one valid? Explain.

biologically determined needs
societally determined needs
family composition
economies of scale
fixed costs
family life cycle
discretionary expenditures
disposable income

liquid assets
consumer durables
consumption
relative income
relative income hypothesis
permanent income hypothesis
life cycle hypothesis

Dear Consumer Advisor:

I read in the paper the other day that families on welfare in our state sometimes get more than $300 a month. Now, I'm not opposed to helping out a family that needs some food or a warm place to stay, but the article says that these welfare families get television sets, radios, and things like that. My brother who is in the Peace Corps says that in some countries of the world for $300 a month you can live like a millionaire. Don't you think that we are over doing it with this welfare bit?

Concerned

Dear Consumer Advisor:

My husband and I have always managed to live within our incomes. My husband is a trucker who owns and operates his own rig and generally clears $20,000–$25,000 a year. We live in a nice neighborhood and enjoy a good standard of living. Lately, however, due to the high cost of fuel, my husband's income has dropped by about a third and things are getting very tight around here. I wonder, should we sell the house and move to a cheaper one, or should we borrow some money to see us through these hard times?

Ms. Trucker

SELECTED REFERENCES AND SOURCES OF DATA

The following well-known books discuss three different notions of consumption and its value and effect upon society.

Galbraith, John Kenneth. *The Affluent Society*, 2nd edition. (Boston, Houghton Mifflin, 1969.)

Katona, George. *The Powerful Consumer.* (New York: Mc Graw Hill Book Company, 1960).

Veblen, Thorstein. *The Theory of the Leisure Class.* (New York: The Modern Library, 1934).

6

CONSUMER DEMAND

Any time you spend money in the modern American economy, whether for necessities or for luxury goods, you are faced with a most bewildering assortment of choices. If you need a man's shirt you have a wide choice, from an import for two dollars to a hand-tailored shirt for thirty-five dollars. Even among the two-dollar shirts there are different brands, styles, and colors. When you go shopping for a family necessity such as food, you have numerous choices between different types of proteins—milk, fish, eggs, beans, and meat. Even within one category, such as meat, there are also numerous choices which can be made. A study of consumer demand relates, at least partly, to the study of why people choose one good or one product rather than another, but like a lot of things in our economy, the process is not over when a man chooses a name-brand shirt rather than the cheap import or the expensive hand-tailored one. One consumer does not make up the entire economy, but if many consumers also choose that particular shirt, changes are going to be noted—perhaps in the price of the shirt and eventually in the supply available.

A study of consumer demand is worthwhile not only because it helps us to understand the motivations of the consumer but also because it helps us understand the effects that are felt throughout the economy as a result of these purchase decisions.

DETERMINANTS OF INDIVIDUAL CONSUMER DEMAND

Suppose you go to the supermarket to buy a sirloin steak and there in the butcher's case you find big, fat, juicy steaks marked $1.79 per pound. What factors run through your mind when you decide whether or not you should buy that steak?

Price

One of the primary considerations that influences your decision whether or not to buy steak, of course, is the price. If it is very high, chances are you will buy very little steak, if any at all. If, on the other hand, it is very low, you may end up buying quite a bit of steak within a given period of time.

Suppose you walked into a supermarket and found that same juicy sirloin steak on special at 10 cents a pound. What would you do then? Most people, even those who didn't like steak very well, would probably load up their shopping carts full of steak and buy as much as they could fit in their freezers.

So one thing we can say about price is that, all other things being equal, as it goes up the quantity demanded goes down, and as it goes down, the quantity that the consumer demands goes up. This intuitively obvious statement is known as the *law of demand*. Note that the law of demand speaks of *quantity* demanded, not demand per se. It does not say that if the price goes up demand for the good goes down. It says that the *quantity demanded* goes down. The word *demand* by itself stands for something quite different which we will see in a moment.

It is also important to realize that when we speak of quantity demanded, we always mean quantity demanded *per period of time*. For example, when we say that at $1.79 per pound a consumer would buy only one pound of steak, we mean that he would buy one pound with a certain frequency—say once a week. If we did not specify a time period we would not know whether that one pound would be for a year or every day.

In figure 6-1 we have drawn an illustration of the quantity of steak that a consumer would purchase at different prices. The various prices at which the steak might be sold are listed on the vertical axis labelled "price of steak in dollars." The number of pounds of steak that the consumer buys at each price is on the horizontal axis. Let us consider the first price, 50 cents per pound. "Well, let's see," the consumer would say, "I can eat a pound of steak every day. That makes seven pounds in a week, and I'll have friends over to dinner one night—so I'll need ten pounds." You will note on figure 6-1 that there is a dot corresponding to the coordinates of 50 cents and ten pounds.

Now how about a dollar a pound? How many pounds would our consumer buy if the price were a dollar per pound? "Well," he would reason,

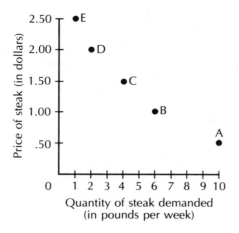

Figure 6-1
Quantity of steak
demanded at each
price

"a dollar per pound is still a pretty good bargain since this type of steak normally runs $1.79 a pound. I believe that I will buy six pounds." So we see in figure 6–1 that there is a dot corresponding to six pounds at a dollar per pound. At $1.50 per pound it is still cheaper than usual but no terrific bargain so our consumer would, say, buy four pounds. At $2.00 per pound it is more expensive than usual and so let us say that our consumer might buy two pounds, and at $2.50 per pound he might decide to only buy one pound and have it one night as a special treat.

Thus figure 6–1 has five dots, A, B, C, D, and E representing quantities of steak that would be bought at various prices.

Demand Curves

Now if we join the dots with a curve in figure 6-2, we have what is called a demand curve or a curve that represents the quantity that the consumer would demand at every possible price. Now the fact that we have drawn a curve through the five points does not necessarily mean that if the price were raised from $1.50 to $1.51 the consumer would cut back his consumption from four pounds to 3.92 pounds. Drawing a curve rather than five unconnected points is a piece of art-work which makes it easier for us to see a relationship.

Once we have our demand curve we can find out what quantity of steak the consumer will buy each week by merely drawing a horizontal line at the right price level. For example, if we want to know how many pounds he would buy at $1.50 we draw a horizontal line at the $1.50 level through the demand curve as we have done in figure 6-2 and then we read the quantity by drawing a vertical line at the intersection down to the horizontal or quantity axis. We see in this case, as we already

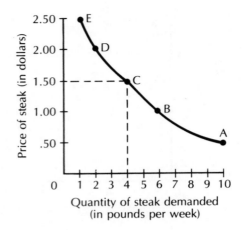

Figure 6-2
Demand curve for
steak

know, that at the price of $1.50 per pound the consumer will buy four pounds per week.

Change In Demand

If a consumer walks into a supermarket and sees steak at a certain price, knowledge of that price alone is not going to tell us how much (if any) the consumer will buy. In order to know how much steak he will buy, we must know other things about him. These things include his tastes, the price of substitute goods, the price of complements, and his income.

tastes A consumer who hates steak may not buy any at any price and will surely buy less per week at every price than the consumer who really enjoys steak. Suppose that he walked into the supermarket and found that they were having a sale on steak at 50 cents per pound. Assuming that he wasn't interested in making a quick buck by buying them all up and selling them for $1.25—let's assume he's just buying for himself—at 50 cents a pound he may buy only four pounds, thinking to have some steak-fancying friends over one night. At $1.00 per pound he may only buy two pounds. At $1.50 a pound he may buy only one pound of steak and at $2.50 he would buy no steak at all. Let's look at this man's demand curve by drawing a curve through points A′, B′, C′, D′, and E′ in figure 6-3. We see by comparison that the demand curve of a steak hater is down and to the left of the person who has a normal taste for steak. Similarly, in that same figure, we see that a person who is particularly fond of steaks would *at every price* buy more steaks than a person who has a normal taste for steaks. The coordinates of the steak lover would be A″, B″, C″, D″, and E″, and his demand curve would be higher and to the right of the person with normal tastes.

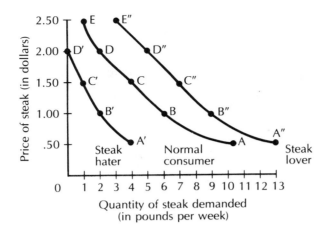

Price	Quantity demanded		
	Normal consumer	Steak lover	Steak hater
$ .50	10	13	4
1.00	6	9	2
1.50	4	7	1
2.00	2	5	0
2.50	1	3	0

Figure 6-3
Demand curves of three individuals for steak

Similarly, for the same individual, a change in taste would cause a shift in the demand curve or a *change in demand*. If the normal consumer in figure 6-3 read that steak caused hardening of the arteries, his demand would decrease and his new curve would resemble that of the steak hater. If, on the other hand, he got a new girlfriend who loved steak, his demand would increase and his demand curve would resemble a steak lover's.

price of substitutes   While a steak fancier may prefer a thick juicy steak to anything else, he may also like a nice piece of roast beef, and if the price of roast beef seemed more reasonable he may end up eating roast beef rather than steak. For most consumers, roast beef is a substitute for steak. There are other substitutes for steak such as hamburger, hotdogs, and fish. Not all of them are as good substitutes as roast beef. If a consumer walked into his supermarket to do his week's shopping and found that while steaks were selling at $2.00 per pound, the supermarket was running a special sale on lean roast beef for 79 cents per pound, he might decide that rather than buy his normal four pounds of steak at $2.00 a pound, he would buy more roast beef than he would

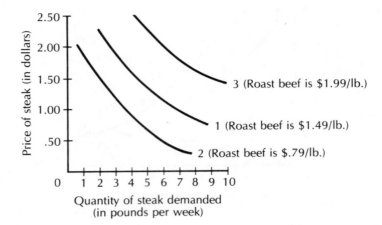

Figure 6-4
Demand curve for
steak shifts with
changes in price of
substitute

ordinarily buy and substitute roast beef for steak. Therefore his demand curve for steak is affected by the price of substitutes for steak. The lower the price, the greater the chance that the consumer will buy a substitute for steak, and all other things being equal, the less steak he will purchase at each given price. What this means is that our consumer's demand curve for steak will tend to shift downward and to the left if the price of roast beef decreases (curve 2, figure 6-4). Similarly, if the price of roast beef were suddenly raised to $1.99 per pound (curve 3), the consumer would substitute steak for roast beef so that at any given price for steak he would buy more steak within a week than he ordinarily would have. So, to summarize, we would say that if the price of a substitute good goes down the demand for the original good goes down, and as the price of a substitute increases, the demand for the original also increases.

the price of complementary goods   Complementary goods are goods which tend to be purchased and consumed together, where the use of one adds to the enjoyment gained from consuming the other. Examples of complementary goods are bread and butter, coffee and cream, and bacon and eggs. If the price of a complementary good changes, the demand for its complement will be affected.

To use our example of steak, during the summer many people like to grill their steaks on an outdoor barbecue. This would make barbecue briquets a complementary good to steaks. If our consumer went to the supermarket and saw a big sign advertising charcoal briquets at a penny per hundred pound bag, it is not at all unlikely that he would be encouraged to buy extra steaks to take home and grill since the cost of the finished product, the charcoal grilled steak, will have decreased. This would mean that at every price for steak a decrease in the price of the complementary good would increase the quantity of steak purchased.

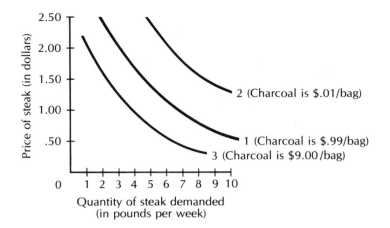

Figure 6-5
Demand curve for
steak shifts with
changes in price of
complements

Similarly, of course, if the price of charcoal goes up to $9.00 a bag, it is not at all unlikely that the demand for steak would fall. (See figure 6-5).

income In chapter 5 we discussed the relation between income and consumption. We found that people with higher incomes tended to spend more money on consumption than lower income families. However, this does not mean that consumption of *every* good will increase. If our steak fancying consumer suddenly got an increase in pay, he might increase his consumption of steak at every given price, thereby implying that his demand curve would move upward and to the right (figure 6-6A). Yet this type of demand curve shift may not apply to other goods. If our consumer uses his increased income to purchase more steak, he is probably eating less of something else. Chances are that he eats less

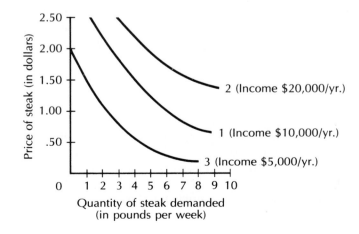

Figure 6-6A
Demand curve for
steak shifts with
change in income

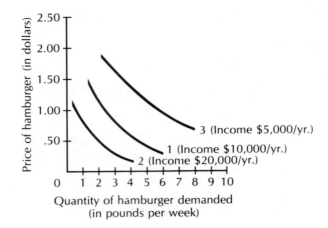

Figure 6-6B
Demand curve for
hamburger shifts with
change in income

hamburger. So if we look at the demand curve for hamburger in figure
6-6B, we may find that an increase in income has shifted the demand
for hamburger downward, so the curve beginning at A may shift downward
to B whereas the demand curve for steak would shift in entirely the
opposite direction.

When an increase in income results in more money being spent on
any good, we say that good is a *superior* good. If, on the other hand,
an increase in income decreases consumption of a particular good, we
say that the good is *inferior*. Luxury goods such as choice cuts of meat,
expensive cars and tailored clothes are generally superior goods, while
less expensive necessities such as hamburger, second hand cars, and mail-
order shirts are often inferior goods.

the effect of expectations   If you expect that the price of steak will
go up 25 percent within a week, chances are that your purchase of steak
this week will be greater than usual in order to beat the price increase.
Therefore, we may say that expectations of a price increase will increase
demand for a product whereas demand falls if prices are expected to
go down.

MARKET DEMAND FOR GOODS

The discussion of consumer demand thus far may appear interesting to
some students and pointless to others. "So you buy less when the price
is high—tell me something I don't know," is a likely reaction. The use
of demand curves to illustrate a relatively simple concept may appear
to merely complicate things.

In fact, the demand curve for any single individual is only of theoretical interest. No matter how weird that individual is, his behavior can affect only himself. If he wants to buy 100 pounds of steak at $2.50 per pound, fine! It's his money and there's plenty of steak for everyone at that price.

The matter becomes more interesting and the effects more important to consumers when you *aggregate,* or add together the demand of each individual to find out *total* or *market demand* that determines the price that the consumer ends up paying.

Let's begin by looking at the individual demand curves of three individuals, A, B, and C (figure 6-7). Of course, the market for any good includes more than three individual consumers. For some goods that are sold nationally (like soap or toothpaste) the market may include all of the families in the United States. Even those who don't use toothpaste are included since they might buy it under the proper circumstances. For other goods (milk) the market may be city-wide and for still others (bakery pastries) the market may only comprise several blocks. A market composed of only three consumers may therefore be a little small, but it is useful for purposes of illustration.

At any given price, each of our three consumers can tell us the quantity of steak that he will buy in any one week. At 50¢ per pound, for example, consumer A would buy ten pounds, consumer B (who isn't as fond of steak) would buy five pounds and consumer C (who loves steak) would buy 15 pounds. The market demand for steak (in our little three consumer market) would therefore be 10 plus 5 plus 15 pounds for a total of 30 pounds per week *at 50¢ per pound.* Similarly, we can add together individual demand at any other possible price to arrive at the market demand at each price.

The *market demand curve* merely illustrates graphically the market demand for steak. In figure 6-7 we have drawn horizontal lines through each of the prices to show that the market demand curve can be made by adding together the quantities demanded by each individual at each price. It becomes evident that the shape of the market demand curve is similar to the shape of the individual demand curve—they both slope downward to the right.

MARKET SUPPLY

Knowledge of market demand is not quite enough information to determine price. Market supply must also be known.

Market supply is determined by all of the sellers who sell to any market. Generally speaking, the higher the price of a good, the *greater* will be the quantity that sellers will supply to any market. This is known as the *law of supply*. Why is this so? In the case of beef, for example, a higher price makes it more worthwhile for the farmer to raise cattle,

Price	Quantity demanded (lbs./week)			
	Consumer A	Consumer B	Consumer C	Total (A + B + C)
$ .50	10	5	15	30
1.00	7	2	9	18
1.50	4	1	6	11
2.00	2	0	4	6
2.50	1	0	3	4

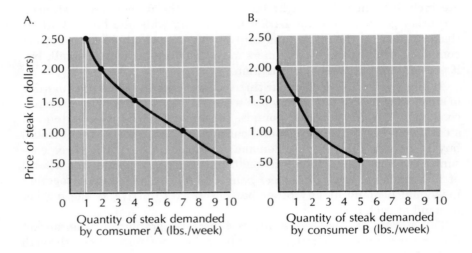

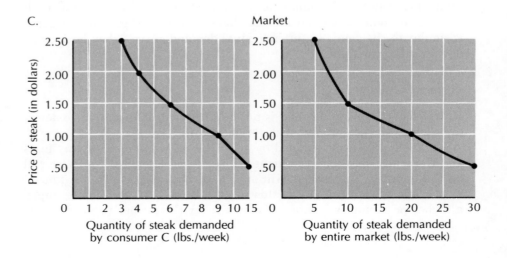

Figure 6-7
Market demand for
steak

and if the price of pork does not show a similar increase, the farmer may use his land and corn to raise more cattle and fewer hogs. Also, a higher price for beef may encourage other farmers (or non-farmers) to raise cattle, thereby increasing the quantity of beef available for the market.

In figure 6-8, the market supply of beef is given. At a price of 50¢ per pound, the price of beef doesn't even cover the cost of cattle feed. Therefore the only beef that would come on the market would be from cattle already slaughtered where the meat would rot if not sold. At 50¢ per pound, only 1,000 pounds would be made available (the farmers eat the rest themselves or give it to their relatives).

At $1.00 per pound, the farmers still aren't breaking even, so only 3,000 pounds would be put on the market. At $1.50 per pound, the farmers are covering their costs and make 7,000 pounds available. At $2.00 per pound, they are willing to slaughter more beef since they are making a tidy profit so they would supply 20,000 pounds, and at $2.50 per pound, they would butcher their whole herds (35,000 pounds) since there is so much money to be made.

Figure 6-8 shows the market supply of beef which slopes upward to the right, reflecting the desire of sellers to supply more at higher prices. In figure 6-9, we have added a demand schedule showing market demand for beef (over a somewhat wider and more realistic market than our three consumer market for steaks).

At a price of 50¢ per pound, consumers would like to buy 30,000 pounds of beef per week. Unfortunately for them, the price is too low to pay farmers to sell much beef and only 1,000 pounds are made available. This would leave an *excess demand* of 29,000 pounds at that price. Since a price of 50¢ per pound would leave many consumers without the beef that they want, there would be upward pressure on prices—consumers would pay more to get more beef.

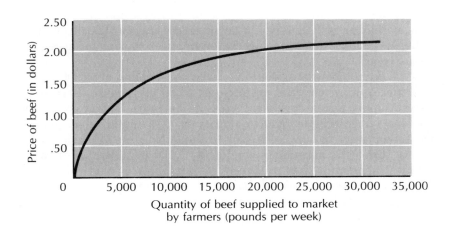

Figure 6-8
Market supply of beef

Price	Quantity Demanded	Quantity Supplied	
$ .50	30,000	1,000	Excess demand = 20,000 lbs.
1.00	15,000	3,000	Excess demand = 12,000 lbs.
1.50	7,000	7,000	Quantity demanded = Quantity supplied
2.00	4,000	20,000	Excess supply = 16,000 lbs.
2.50	2,000	35,000	Excess supply = 33,000 lbs.

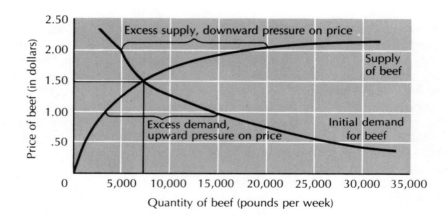

Figure 6-9
Market demand and
supply for beef

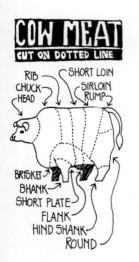

At the other extreme, a price of $2.50 per pound would create similar but opposite problems. This price would be very attractive to farmers who would be willing to make 35,000 pounds available to the market. However, they could not sell it all since consumers would buy only 2,000 pounds at that price. There would be an *excess supply* of 33,000 pounds, and there would be some pressure to lower prices so that farmers could sell more beef.

At $1.00 per pound, there would be an excess demand of 12,000 pounds and further upward pressure on price. At $2.00 per pound, there would be excess supply and a downward pressure on price. But at some price in between, buyers will demand a quantity exactly equal to that quantity which sellers wish to supply. In our example, this *equilibrium* price is $1.50. At this price, consumers would buy 7,000 pounds of beef, which is exactly the amount that producers would supply at that price. Since both consumers and sellers are happy, there is no further pressure on prices to move either up or down and the *price is set for individual consumers and producers.*

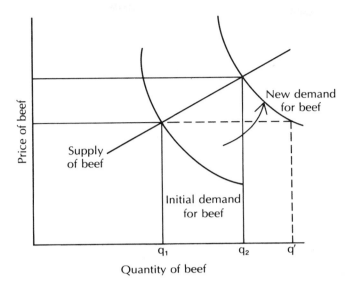

Figure 6-10
Increase in demand
for beef

The diagram in figure 6-9 combines the supply and demand curves on a single set of axes. The intersection of the two curves determines both price and quantity (in this case, a quantity of 7,000 pounds and price of $1.50 per pound). At any price *above* $1.50 per pound (say $2.00 per pound), quantity supplied is greater than quantity demanded and there is downward pressure on price. At a lower price ($1.00 per pound in figure 6-9) there is excess demand and prices are pressured upward.

SHIFTS IN DEMAND OR SUPPLY

Earlier in this chapter we discussed some causes of changes in demand which cause the demand curve to shift. For example, increased consumer income may cause the demand curve for beef to shift up to the right since consumers want more beef at every possible price. When this happens, the price of beef will be forced up. Figure 6-10 illustrates this.

Increased consumer income causes consumers to want more beef at every price. The demand curve shifts upward to the right. But at the old price (p_1) consumers now want a larger quantity of beef (q') than suppliers will sell (q_1). Therefore, *excess demand* is created and prices must increase (to p_2) in order to make everyone satisfied again.

Supply may also shift as the result of factors such as increased costs of production. If the price of cattle feed increases, farmers will supply

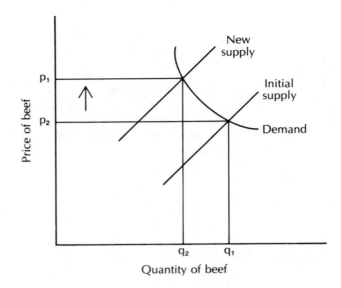

Figure 6-11
Shift in supply curve
due to increased cost
of production

less beef at each price so that the supply curve will shift upwards to the left (figure 6-11).

The result of this shift will be an increase in price (from p_1 to p_2) and a decrease in quantity sold (from q_1 to q_2).

ANSWERS TO IMPORTANT QUESTIONS

While we certainly have not explored every detail of supply and demand, we have sufficient tools to answer several important consumer questions relating to prices.

Question 1: What caused beef prices to increase so much during the last few years?

The recent increase in beef prices is due to factors affecting both supply and demand. On the demand side, increasing consumer incomes have enabled consumers to buy more of everything, including beef. Yet beef is a superior good and consumers will switch to eating more beef (and less of other goods) when their incomes increase. This factor shifts the demand curve to the right (figure 6-12).

But this is not the entire story. Farmers who produce beef have found the price of grain increasing rapidly. This is due in large part to increased foreign demand for American grain. Since the price of grain has increased, the supply of beef (the quantity supplied at each price) has decreased. Both of these conditions acting at the same time have caused a great increase in price.

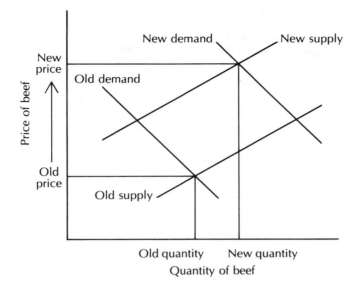

Figure 6-12
Shift in demand curve
with increased
income

Question 2: Can government price ceilings hold down prices?

Many students will remember the attempt of the government to hold down beef prices in 1973 by putting an upper limit or *ceiling* on the prices. As is the case with *all* price ceilings which are below the level at which quantity demanded and supplied are equal, shortages were created. Figure 6-13 illustrates this.

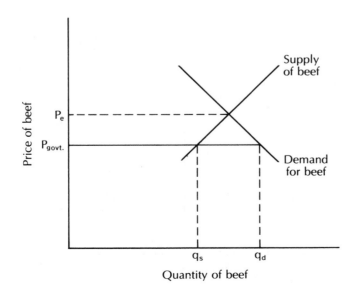

Figure 6-13
The effect of price
ceilings

The government price (p_g) is below the *equilibrium* price (p_e) necessary to equate quantity supplied and demanded. At the government price, consumers demand more beef (q_d) than producers will supply (q_s). Many consumers find that they can't buy the meat they want and would prefer to pay more to get meat.

Shortages are a common result of price ceilings that are below the equilibrium price. It is therefore not clear that price ceilings are in the consumer's interest, although they look like a good deal. Steak at 50 cents per pound is no bargain if there is none for sale.

Question 3: What caused the great increase in gasoline prices in 1973?

The recent energy crisis, like the beef situation, was due to a combination of demand and supply changes. The demand for gasoline kept increasing as the result of several factors including greater fuel consumption by newer, less-polluting automobile engines, and greater fuel consumption by foreign countries. These factors alone probably would have caused a substantial increase in the price of gasoline as indicated in figure 6-14. In this illustration, increased demand has caused the price of gasoline to increase from 35 cents per gallon (hypothetical figure) to 43 cents. The increased price would have resulted in a slight increase in quantity supplied.

However, as most of us remember, the price increase did not end at that relatively low level because of a second complicating factor—the decrease in supply. The shift in the supply curve to the left resulted first from the oil embargo of the Arab countries which cut the supply of crude oil (the raw material used to produce gasoline) and later by a unified action of oil exporting countries (in the Middle East, Africa,

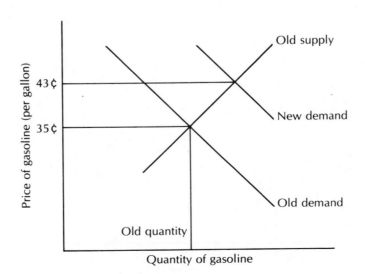

Figure 6-14
Changes in the
demand for gasoline

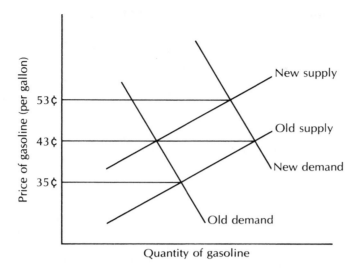

Figure 6-15
Changes in the
demand and supply of
gasoline

and Latin America) to raise the price of crude oil to the oil companies. Figure 6-15 shows that the decrease in supply caused prices to go even higher, in this example, to 53 cents.

Once again, as many of us remember, government efforts to hold prices below the new equilibrium resulted in severe gasoline shortages, long lines, and short tempers. The reasoning behind the government's actions was that with the greatly diminished supplies of gasoline, the equilibrium price needed to clear the market may have been so high (a dollar or more) that lower income families may have been badly hurt. Other government efforts to lower prices, such as the closing of gas stations on Sundays and the lowering of speed limits to 55 miles per hour, were aimed at reducing demand and appeared to have some limited effectiveness.

SUMMARY

1. The quantity of any good that a consumer will purchase within a time interval is inversely related to price. The relation between price and quantity demanded for an individual may be displayed in an *individual demand curve.*

2. An individual's demand curve for any good is affected by other factors such as taste, the price of substitutes, the price of complements, income, and price expectations which can cause the consumer to purchase more or less at every possible price.

3. The market demand for a good consists of summing individual demand for all consumers in a market. The *market demand curve,* like the

individual demand curve, slopes downward to the right to indicate the inverse relation between price and quantity demanded.

4. Generally speaking, the quantity of goods supplied to the market by producers is directly related to price: producers are willing to supply a greater quantity if the price is higher. This relationship is graphically represented by a supply curve. The intersection of supply and demand curves for a good determine the equilibrium price.

5. Efforts by the government to hold prices below the equilibrium level (price controls) are likely to result in shortages of that good.

QUESTIONS

1. Mary became pregnant and developed a terrific craving for pickles. What would happen to her demand curve for pickles? What about the market demand for pickles in her home town? What effect would Mary's pregnancy have on the price of pickles in her home town?

2. One year, American farmers found that the price of wheat was very high compared with the price of corn. As a result, in the next year they planted much more wheat and much less corn. What do you think happened to the prices of wheat and corn? Why?

3. During the recent beef crisis, groups of consumers in many cities decided to boycott beef until the price went down. Who probably benefited by this action and who was hurt? Explain.

TERMINOLOGY

demand
quantity demanded
law of demand
substitute goods
complementary goods
superior goods
inferior goods
price expectations
market demand
quantity supplied
law of supply
excess demand
excess supply
equilibrium price and quantity
shift in supply and demand

For a more detailed theoretical discussion of the supply and demand analysis, see the following books.

Boulding, Kenneth E. *Economic Analysis: Micro Economics.* 4th ed., (New York: Harper and Row, 1966), Chapters 8, 10, and 11.

Henderson, Hubert D. *Supply and Demand.* (Chicago: University of Chicago Press, 1958), Chapter 2.

Katona, George, and Eva Mueller. *Consumer Response to Income Increases.* (Washington, D.C.: Brookings Institute, 1968). (Result of interviews conducted to measure consumer reactions to income increases in 1964–65.)

McConnell, Campbell R. *Economics.* 5th ed. (New York: McGraw Hill, 1972).

Samuelson, Paul A. *Economics.* 8th ed. (New York: McGraw Hill, 1970).

SELECTED REFERENCES AND SOURCES OF DATA

7

INVESTMENT IN CONSUMER DURABLES

In the preceding chapter we examined consumer demand for goods. On a more basic level, let us ask ourselves what the consumer considers before he buys, or what constitutes consumer demand.

A relatively new and very fruitful approach to this question has been suggested by Kelvin Lancaster[1] and is often called the "Lancaster demand theory." He suggests that our demand for any good is based on its components or *attributes*. For example, when a consumer shops for a loaf of bread, he is buying a bundle of attributes including taste, nutrition, packaging, size, and so on. When a woman considers a new handbag, the attributes important to her may include color, material, size, and weight. Certain other attributes, such as durability, may not be of great importance in the case of the bread or the handbag since neither product is expected to last forever.

DURABLE GOODS

There are certain goods, however, for which the attribute of durability is extremely important. These are goods that are expected to yield service to the household for a number of years. Such goods are known as *consumer durables* (or *durable goods*) and include furniture, appliances, and the family automobile. When the Jones family goes to the showrooms to look for a new car, they are certainly going

---

[1] Kelvin Lancaster, "A New Approach to Consumer Theory," *Journal of Political Economy, 74* (April 1966), pp. 132–57.

to consider the attributes of styling, color, size, and horsepower, but they would be very foolish if they did not also consider durability. A car that falls apart after a year would be an unwise purchase, particularly since it is likely that the Jones family would still be paying for it when they no longer could use it. So in the purchase of consumer durables, durability is an extremely important attribute.

Since durable goods (by definition) yield services to the family over more than one year, it is unreasonable to consider their purchase to be ordinary *consumption* like the purchase of a quart of milk or a shirt. Economists prefer to call the purchase of consumer durables an *investment* and speak of "investment in consumer durables" since only a fraction of the good is really "consumed" each year. If, for example, you pay $250 for a washing machine that is expected to last ten years, you are not consuming $250 worth of washing machine services during the first year of purchase but only about $25 worth, and spreading the other $225 over the subsequent nine years. Therefore, when you buy a washing machine, your consumption may be only $25 for the year while your investment is a much larger sum ($225). Seen in this light, it is more reasonable to consider the purchase of a household durable to be an investment than a consumption expenditure.

THE DURABLE AS A CAPITAL ASSET

Since a consumer durable not only lasts longer than most goods but also costs more, the consumer is apt to consider its purchase more carefully. Unfortunately, most consumers lack the appropriate framework for making an intelligent decision about such a product.

Aside from durability and relatively high cost, most consumer durables share another important attribute; *they either save or help earn money for the family.* In business, durable goods purchased for the purpose of earning (or saving) money are known as *capital goods.* For this reason, consumer durables are thought of as the capital goods (or assets) of the household.

The automobile, for example, is an important capital good for many households since it was used by 85 percent of families in 1972 to get the family head to work.[2] In most cases, persons using the automobile to get to work have no alternative form of transportation. Take away their cars and they are deprived of an income.

While the automobile certainly yields more services to the family than simply transportation to work, the value of this service alone far more than compensates for its operating cost. If, for example, a man can earn $8,000 per year by working in a factory to which he must drive a car (and, let's assume he can make no money otherwise), the income would

---

[2] O.E.O. Study of Income Dynamics, Survey Research Center, University of Michigan, unpublished data.

much more than cover the cost of operating the car per year for the average family.

The washing machine (and dryer) in a home saves the cost of having the clothes laundered or dropping quarters into laundromat machines.

The refrigerator saves the time and cost of getting fresh foods each day (or bringing in ice for an ice box). The freezer may enable the consumer to buy foods more cheaply in bulk or on sale.

The durables named above have the common trait of producing or saving money for the family. Yet each of them costs money to own and operate. One useful guide to the desirability of investing in such goods is a comparison of *costs* and *benefits* of the acquisition of the good in a cost-benefit analysis.

THE BUSINESS DECISION

When the businessman considers the acquisition of a capital asset, he examines its yield (generally in dollars per year) and compares it to the total cost of owning and operating the asset (also in dollars per year). If the total yield of a machine (in terms of the value of what it can produce) is greater than the total cost of buying and operating the machine, the businessman will buy the machine because it will yield a profit to him. If, on the other hand, the cost exceeds the yield of the machine, the prudent businessman will reject the purchase, no matter how much he likes the style, color, or salesman of the machine. The purchase of such a good would be a bad capital investment since it would result in a loss for the business.

THE HOUSEHOLD DECISION

Of course, not every household durable is purchased on the same profit/loss basis as the business capital asset since the yield of some household durables such as the television set and the air conditioner are difficult to put into monetary terms. However, a cost-benefit analysis is very useful when you are considering the purchase of a durable solely or largely for the purpose of saving money. Many families have been faced with the question of whether it is cheaper to own a washer and dryer or do the wash in a laundromat, or whether a freezer or a second car is worthwhile buying. For these decisions, a cost-benefit analysis is worthwhile. And the knowledge of how to calculate the true costs of owning and operating a household durable is an important input in the purchase decision of a durable that has no quantifiable monetary yield.

The Cost of a Consumer Durable

In order to be comparable, all costs and benefits of a capital asset must be stated in common terms. Therefore, we will reduce all costs and benefits to *dollars per year.*

Let's consider the dilemma faced by the Morgans. In the Morgan household it is Evelyn who is stuck with doing the wash. After six years of married life, she is sick and tired of dragging the dirty clothes to the laundromat every Tuesday. She doesn't say this to Paul, however, since he prides himself on being a practical-minded individual, so she begins to pitch her campaign for a washer and dryer on the basis of saving the family money.

"Paul," she begins one morning (Tuesday, as it happens) over breakfast, "I see where there is a terrific sale on washers and dryers. I can get both for $400 and save all that money that I chuck into the machines at the laundromat."

"Listen, we've been through this before," came the reply. "When you consider the price of owning the machine, the electricity, gas, hot water, and repairs, you will see that the laundromat is the greatest bargain since the nickel beer."

Without further eavesdropping on the Morgan family argument, let's add up the figures to see who is right. First, what are the likely costs of buying and operating the washer and dryer?

depreciation The initial cost of $400 buys a washer and dryer that last, say, ten years. At the end of that period, let's assume (for simplicity's sake) that the machines are worthless. Therefore, the depreciation (or lessening of value) of the machines *averages* $40 per year ($400 divided by ten years).

It is important to realize that at the end of the first year, you couldn't resell your machines for $360 ($400 price minus $40 for one year's depreciation). Most goods, particularly those used by consumers, actually depreciate much more in early years than they do later. This is due in large part to the desire of consumers to buy things new. However, if the consumer intends to use his washer and dryer over a longer period, it is best to use average depreciation to figure cost per year.

interest A second annual cost of owning a washer and dryer is the *interest* on the purchase price. This is certainly apparent when the consumer makes his purchase *on credit* and borrows all or part of the cost from a bank, credit union, finance company, or the store making the sale. When the consumer buys on credit he must pay interest charges ranging from 9 percent to 18 percent or more.

What many people do not realize, however, is that even when the consumer makes a cash purchase he still must figure on the cost of interest. In this case, interest is called *implicit* and is equivalent to what he could have made on his money by not buying the washer and dryer (and leaving it, say, in the bank). If he left his $400 in the bank at 5 percent interest, he would make $20 interest in a year.[3]

So our consumer has an interest cost whether he finances the machines himself (implicit interest) or through outside credit (explicit interest).[4]

For the sake of our example, and to avoid getting too deeply into a discussion of interest rates which will be covered in chapter 10, let's assume the total interest cost to average $15 per year over the ten years.

operating costs Buying the washer and dryer is only the first outlay of money. In order to operate them, the consumer must pay for water, electricity, and sometimes gas (depending upon the type of dryer). These amounts vary with the usage of the machines as well as local costs for the utilities. Let's assume that these costs would set the Morgans back $50 per year.

repairs Over the ten year life of the washer and dryer, certain repairs must be anticipated. Often, the machines will be on warranty and will be repaired for free during the first year, but in subsequent years repairs become more frequent and more costly.

Many stores will sell a service contract which, for an annual fee, guarantees repairs at no extra cost. However, the price of these contracts is based on the expected repair costs for the average appliance owner, and either way, repair costs must be calculated by the owner.

For our washer and dryer, let's say that $200 over ten years ($20 per year) should cover repairs.

total cost Based on our estimates, the Morgans can expect a washer and dryer to cost them the following amounts per year:

Depreciation	$40
Interest	$15
Operating Costs	$50
Repairs	$20
Total	$125

*IMPLICIT

*EXPLICIT

---

[3] However, the implicit interest cost is *not* $20 per year for ten years since he uses up $40 per year (in depreciation) so that each year the amount that he has invested in a washer and dryer decreases by $40. In the second year, for example, he has only $360 invested in the machines. At 5 percent interest, this would be $18 interest.

[4] When the consumer buys on credit, he generally has both *explicit* and *implicit* interest costs. Most finance contracts would call for repayment of the loan within 3 years which means that he is paying back the $400 purchase price faster than he is using up the machines (in depreciation). At the end of 3 years he owns free and clear machines which still have $280 worth of value [$400–(3 × $40)]. Therefore we must include the *implicit* interest cost of not having that $280 in the bank. At 5 percent interest this would be $14, which is, of course, taxable like other ordinary income.

Benefits

The benefits that the Morgans will gain from owning a washer and dryer are both quantifiable and non-quantifiable in monetary terms.

savings over alternative (laundromat)   The only savings that Evelyn Morgan can demonstrate to her husband is the money that she puts into the laundromat each week. If she spends $3 per week in the laundromat, her annual savings from having a washer and dryer would be $156 (52 x $3) which would exceed the estimated cost of ownership of $125.

gas money   Since the laundromat is only a few blocks away, there is little measurable gain in gasoline savings.

value of time   Of course Evelyn may try to add fuel to her argument by pointing out the fact that she would save two hours per week by not having to go to the laundromat. In chapter 4, we learned that time is worth money and that the *opportunity cost* of doing a nonpaid activity is equivalent to what a person can make in a paid activity. However, Paul is quick to dismiss that argument since it is unlikely that Evelyn would find a paying job for the two hours per week that she would save on the laundry.

It is possible, however, that Evelyn could use the extra hours to engage in market-substitute home production such as sewing clothes that the Morgans would otherwise have to buy or even by painting the garage to save the cost of a professional painter. Yet this type of behavior is not very likely and we would not be wrong in agreeing with Paul that the monetary value of the time that Evelyn saves is close to zero.

better service   A possible argument in favor of owning a washer and dryer is that one's own equipment treats the clothes better and saves money on clothes replacement. This argument is difficult to evaluate in monetary terms.

convenience   In the last analysis, convenience is the most important factor in owning one's own washer and dryer. Therefore, it is useful to find out how much we are paying for convenience. The cost of convenience may be found by subtracting the monetary benefits (savings) from the annual cost. If the cost was $125 per year and the Morgans only spent $60 per year in the laundromat, convenience would cost $125–$60 or $65 per year. However, as we have seen, the monetary benefits actually exceed the cost for the Morgans, so an investment in a washer and dryer would be wise *even without considering the added convenience.*

NON-PRODUCING DURABLES

While calculations similar to the one given above can be made for money-producing or money-saving durables such as a freezer, refrigerator, or automobile, assets that do not produce or save money, such as a television set, may be evaluated in a slightly different manner. The calculation of annual cost is made in the identical manner to that described above. However, the yield is *purely* in terms of convenience, so the cost goes entirely for convenience.

FAMILY DECISION-MAKING

It is quite easy when considering consumer actions to assume a general economic goal exists for the consumer or the family unit. Studies have shown, however, that long-range planning and goals are surprisingly lacking in many instances. The families most likely to have goals are those that are younger or better educated.

Similarly, studies have shown that a large proportion of consumer purchases are bought on impulse. Rational decision-making has been found in various study data to be exercised most likely by better educated, younger, middle income, professional families,[5] as we implied in chapter 1.

Cost of Information

There is an additional cost for purchasing all goods, including durable goods, if the consumer is conscientious in his decision-making. That cost is the cost of gathering information on which he will base his ultimate decision as to whether to buy a good and if so, which model to buy. An example of such cost in specific cases would be the expense of gas and time spent shopping around from store to store. A more general expense of almost all purchases is the cost of subscribing to *Consumer Reports,* or possibly even the expense of taking this course.

PATTERNS OF PURCHASE FOR CONSUMER DURABLES

Since consumer durables are the "capital assets," families tend to acquire them at an early stage of their life cycles. A stove and refrigerator are necessary to the functioning of a modern household and must be purchased (or rented) at the outset of family formation. Other items, such as a washer and dryer, a freezer, and a second car are generally acquired at a later stage when a bigger family makes their purchase worthwhile.

---

[5] Robert Ferber, "Consumer Economics, A Survey," *Journal of Economic Literature,* 11:4 (December 1973), p. 1328.

TABLE 7-1

Purchases of Household Durables by Life Cycle—1969

(Percentage Distribution of Families)

Stage of Life Cycle	Purchased Durable	Purchased Car or Durable
Under Age 45		
Unmarried, no children	31	44
Married, no children	57	71
Married, youngest child under 6	62	70
Married, youngest child 6 or older	54	70
Age 45 or Older		
Married, has children	48	65
Married, no children, head in labor force	48	59
Married, no children, head retired	30	37
Unmarried, no children, head retired	17	22
All Families	45	56

Source: Katona, Mandell, Schmeideskamp, *1970 Survey of Consumer Finances,* p. 80.

Table 7-1 shows the strong relation between family life cycle and the purchase of household durables. The heaviest buyers of household durables are young families with children under six years of age. Older people and unmarried young people are the least likely to buy household durables.

THE AUTOMOBILE—AN IMPORTANT CONSUMER DURABLE

Among those items which are generally considered to be consumer durables, the automobile ranks as the most costly and perhaps the most important to the great majority of American families. In 1971, 83 percent of American families owned at least one automobile and 28 percent owned two or more.[6] This means that there are more automobiles than families.

Table 7-2 shows the special importance of the automobile as an income-producing asset. In spite of the increasing attention paid to public transportation, the private automobile is still responsible for transporting 85 percent of working family heads (who are almost always the chief income producers in the family) to work.

Automobiles are expensive to buy and to operate. In 1969, the average (mean) price of a new car sold in America was $3,690, while the average price for a used car was $1,170. Prices, of course, are up substantially since that time. Among new car buyers, two-thirds were forced to borrow

---

[6] Mandell, *et al., 1971 Surveys of Consumers,* p. 38.

TABLE 7-2

Mode of Transportation to Work, 1972

(Percentage Distribution of Working Family Heads)

Public Transportation	7
Car Pool	4
Drives (by self or with other family member)	81
Walks	4
Other	4
Total	100

Source: Survey Research Center Panel Study of Income Dynamics, 1972. Unpublished data.

money to buy their cars. Among used car buyers, the proportion going into debt was slightly under half.[7]

The cost of operating a car, once you have bought it, is also high, and getting higher all of the time as the costs of gasoline and services increase. There are many misleading reports that result from looking at the cost of owning and operating an automobile in an unsound economic manner. By viewing the automobile as any other consumer durable, in the manner described in this chapter, we can get a clear picture of the types and amounts of costs involved.

Fixed Versus Variable Costs

There are fixed costs of owning and operating any durable good whether it is used or not. In the case of the Morgans, depreciation and interest on their washer and dryer came to $55 per year whether they did one load or five hundred. (Of course, if they took in wash on a commercial basis and kept the machines running around the clock, they would depreciate faster.)

Some costs do vary with the amount of usage. These *variable costs* include electricity, water, and gas for every load of clothes and may also include repairs since a heavier usage causes more frequent breakdowns.

Fixed Costs of Operating the Automobile

The distinction between fixed and variable (or operating) costs is particularly important in the case of the automobile. Variable costs are so high that the difference between driving a car 1,000 miles or 25,000 miles a year is very significant.

Since costs have been changing so rapidly in recent years, the figures

---

[7] Ibid.

used in the following examples are reasonably representative of average car owners and do not represent actual statistical averages. See the Appendix (p.) for tables on actual data. For the sake of simplicity we will use our own figures. Let's go back and look at Paul Morgan, your average, unlikeable person who prides himself on doing everything in a calculated, hardheaded fashion.

Paul trades in his old car for a new car every two years. He tells Evelyn that he read that this was the most economical way to own a car. In actual fact, he hates to be seen in an old car—but he doesn't say this to his wife. With the options that he needs, the car costs him $3,500. He gets $1,800 for his old car and finances the rest. His fixed costs are as follows:

depreciation   The old car depreciated $1,700 over the two years that he owned it. This may seem high to many people, but the average American car loses nearly one-third of its value during the first year, and close to a quarter during the second year. On the average, Paul's car depreciates $850 per year.

interest   Paul borrowed money to finance the purchase of his new car, as most new-car buying Americans do. Therefore, he must pay *explicit* interest to the financing company. Even if he had not borrowed the money, he would have had to figure in the *implicit* value of what his money could be earning. The explicit interest cost to Paul, at reasonable rates, might amount to $150 per year. In addition, he traded in his old car worth $1,800. If he hadn't bought his new car, he could have banked that $1,800 (supposing he could have got that much cash for it), which, at 5 percent would yield some $90 per year. So adding implicit and explicit interest costs, Paul is spending some $240 per year on interest.

insurance   Another fixed cost is insurance. Most states require insurance on automobiles, and every smart person will carry liability insurance whether or not it is required. The cost of insurance does not vary for Paul whether he drives 1,000 or 30,000 miles in a year.[8] Paul has both liability and collision insurance (which the financing company requires him to take) and the premiums come to $200 per year.

licenses   Annual license fee is another fixed cost. In some states, inspections are also required on a regular basis. Let's put Paul's license cost at $20.00 per year.

---

[8] Some insurance companies vary rates slightly by mileage driven per year.

fixed maintenance costs Maintenance costs on an automobile can be divided into fixed and variable costs. Even if the car is used very little, it should be serviced at least twice a year (particularly in cold climates where anti-freeze is used). This cost is $30.00 per year.

other possible fixed costs There may be other fixed costs. In some areas, cars cannot be parked on the streets and garage space must be rented. In New York City, garage space may cost upwards of $100 per month. In other areas, property taxes must be paid on the value of the automobile. However, let's let Paul avoid paying any of these additional costs.

Summary of Fixed Costs

Depreciation	$ 850
Interest	
Explicit	150
Implicit	90
Insurance	200
License	20
Fixed Maintenance	30
Total Fixed Costs	$1340 per year

Even if Paul gets sick and doesn't drive his car for an entire year, the car will still cost him $1340. If he does drive, his costs will be still higher.

Variable (Operating) Costs

gasoline The greatest variable (per mile) cost of operating a car is the cost of gasoline. If Paul's car gets thirteen miles to the gallon and gas costs 50 cents a gallon, the cost per mile is about 3.8 cents. If he drives 12,000 miles per year, which is also about average, gasoline will cost him $456.

other variable costs There are other variable costs such as oil, tolls, parking, tires, and mileage-related repairs which vary so much that it is hard to assign a figure to them. For the sake of our example, however, let's assign a cost of $150 per year for these miscellaneous operating costs.

total variable costs   At 12,000 miles per year,

Gasoline	$456
Other	$150
Total	$606

Average Variable Cost per Mile 5.05 cents

Total Costs

Adding the $1340 per year in fixed costs to the $606 in variable costs, we find that Paul's total annual cost for operating his automobile is $1946. At 12,000 miles, his average total cost per mile driven is 16.2 cents. When you read that the estimated cost per mile of driving a car is 10 cents or 12 cents or 15 cents, the figures refer to *average total cost* which includes fixed as well as variable cost. However, if your employer asks you to drive 100 miles on business, your cost for that trip is only 5.05 cents per mile (the variable costs) since your fixed costs have already been paid for and do not increase with extra miles.

Some Implications

Not everyone spends $1946 per year to operate a car. The greatest part of Paul's expense is in the depreciation on a new car, which costs him $850 per year. If Paul held on to his car for five years, at which time his $3500 car would have declined in value to $700, his total depreciation would be $2800 over five years or $560 per year rather than $850, saving him nearly $300 per year on total cost. Although his repair bills are likely to rise with an older car, they should not average more than $100 per year more, thereby resulting in a net saving of $200 per year.

Then again, if Paul had bought a two-year-old car for $1800 and sold it for $700 three years later, his annual depreciation cost would have been only $367 per year ($1800–$700 ÷ 3). The great expense of owning a newer car is in the depreciation which, we have seen, can amount to nearly half of the total annual expense of operating a car. When car salesmen argue that there is an advantage in trading in a car every two years, they are speaking of *their* advantage. It is cheapest for the consumer to run a car until it literally falls apart (or needs an extremely expensive major repair). New cars may be fashionable, but they are expensive.

The Social Costs of Automobiles

Only part of the cost of an automobile is borne by the family that owns it. These costs, which we have just discussed, may be called internal costs. There are others borne by the rest of society called *external* or *social costs*. These include the air and noise pollution as well as visual pollution of our environment.

The automobile is an important contribution to air pollution, and while the full costs are not completely known, air pollution has been related to several illnesses of the lungs, it discolors clothes and buildings, and it lowers property values. Yet the person who drives through the city each day on his way to work, with his windows closed, breathing filtered, conditioned air, does not pay the costs of the pollutants coming from his tailpipe. These costs are borne by the residents of the city who must also listen to the deafening roar of traffic and see their city divided by ugly strips of concrete highways.

As the result of the increasing social costs of the automobile in the late 1960s, the government decided to act. Consequently, each year's new automobile comes with an increased assortment of hardware designed to reduce harmful pollutants. The expense of this new equipment is borne by the automobile owner in terms of higher purchase price and often reduced gas mileage. However, most experts feel that it is fair to make the polluter pay for reducing the costs he passes on to society.

Mass Transportation

Many people who are concerned with the environment feel that the only solution to the great social costs of the automobile is better mass transportation. If a fast, attractive, and inexpensive system could be created, they argue, people would begin to use mass transit and leave their cars at home.

Unfortunately, the experience of many cities does not make the future look hopeful. Even where public transportation is available, people who have cars tend to use them. A simple look at the economics of the situation will explain why.

Most families—nearly all where the head is in the labor force—own at least one automobile. In most areas of the country it is difficult to function without an automobile these days, since it is often necessary for getting to work, shopping, and taxiing the children.

Yet once a family owns an automobile, it is saddled with the fixed costs of ownership, the largest expense for most families.

Paul and Evelyn Morgan, like most Americans, can't get along without a car. For one thing, Paul drives it each day to his job five miles away. Now suppose that the city in which the Morgans live begins a public transportation system. Paul can take a bus to work for only 35 cents each way. Will he do it?

Probably not. Since Paul pays the fixed cost of owning his automobile whether or not he takes it to work, the ten miles round trip to work costs him only the variable cost for gasoline and the like. This cost is 5.05 cents per mile or 51 cents round trip, a savings over the cost of public transportation.

But in addition to the cost factor, the convenience of traveling in one's automobile is important to most drivers. Paul's car takes him from his door to the parking lot of his business—he doesn't have to walk to the bus stop and wait for the bus. He leaves when he wants to and can stop off on the way or go out of his way if he so desires. Surveys show that, rather than regarding the automobile trip as unpleasant, many drivers look forward to it as the most pleasant moment of the day—a time of solitude free from the pressures of work or home.

For this reason, even free public transportation would be unlikely to attract many additional riders who have automobiles at their disposal. The added cost of driving a car (if any) is just not enough to erase the added pleasures or convenience over public transportation. The only solution would be to greatly increase the *variable cost* of gasoline or downtown parking or by charging high tolls to drive into the city. If society's leaders feel that mass transportation is the answer, they will find that a brief study of the economics of driving will point to a feasible means of achieving an economically viable system of mass transportation.

SUMMARY

1. The *Lancaster demand theory,* a new approach, states that the demand for any product is really the sum of preferences for the different attributes embodied in it.

2. Those consumer goods that are used for a long period of time are called *consumer durables,* and hence their purchase is more an investment rather than consumption since only part of the good is used up in a year.

3. Consumer durables, which either save or help make money for a family, are considered to be *capital goods* or *assets,* and a consideration of the various costs and benefits involved should be made before purchasing them. A *cost benefit analysis* is useful.

4. The costs to be considered in any such purchase include *depreciation, implicit* as well as *explicit interest, operating costs,* and *repairs.* The benefits include savings by not using the alternative commercial services, conveniences, the value of time saved, quality of service. The difference between a business and a private decision in calculating costs and benefits is that, unlike the businessman, the family will consider factors such as convenience, to which it is difficult to attach monetary values.

5. Studies have found that a strong relation exists between purchases of consumer durables and family life cycles in that people in certain age groups tend to purchase more consumer durables than others.

6. Another way of looking at the purchase of a consumer durable is to separate the *fixed* and *variable* costs. Fixed costs are those that occur even if the good in question is used little or more. Variable costs are those that depend on the extent to which the good is used. Total costs include both.

7. A third method is to consider *internal* and *external* costs. The former are borne by the consumer and the latter by society as a whole. An example is the case of owning and operating an automobile. The external costs are the various kinds of pollution the automobile creates that affect everyone.

QUESTIONS

1. In the context of the issues discussed in this chapter, what are the chances that the energy crisis of 1973 might prove to be beneficial to everyone?

2. What are the fixed and variable costs of owning a freezer?

3. What are some of the ways in which opportunity costs are involved when a person decides to buy a sewing machine and make all the family's clothes?

4. Discuss some of the possible consequences of a massive shift to the use of public transportation in this country.

5. Which consumer durables are least well suited for a cost-benefit type of analysis?

TERMINOLOGY

consumer durables
depreciation
implicit interest
explicit interest
capital assets of the family
fixed and variable costs
social costs

SELECTED REFERENCES AND SOURCES OF DATA

Katona, George, Lewis Mandell, and Jay Schmeideskamp, *1970 Survey of Consumer Finances.* (Ann Arbor: Institute for Social Research, 1970).

Lancaster, Kelvin. *Consumer Demand: A New Approach.* (New York: Columbia University Press, 1971).

Mandell, Lewis, ed. *Surveys of Consumers, 1971-72.* (Ann Arbor: Institute for Social Research, 1972).

Nader, Ralph. *Unsafe At Any Speed; The Designed-in Dangers of the American Automobile.* (New York: Grossman, 1965).

Netzer, Dick. *Economics and Urban Problems; Diagnosis and Prescriptions.* 2nd and enl. ed. (New York: Basic Books, 1974). (See chapter 7 on transportation.)

Thompson, Wilbur R. *A Preface to Urban Economics.* (Baltimore: Johns Hopkins Press, 1965). (See chapter 9)

U.S. Department of Transportation, Federal Highway Administration, *Cost of Operating an Automobile—Suburban Based Operation.* 1972.

Before purchasing expensive consumer durables, it is best to seek advice from the following non-biased sources:

Consumer Reports. A monthly publication by Consumer's Union, 256 Washington Street, Mount Vernon, New York 10550.

Consumers' Research. A monthly publication by Consumers' Research, Inc., Washington, New Jersey 07882.

CHAPTER SEVEN
APPENDIX

Source: L. L. Liston and G. L. Grauthier, *Cost of Operating an Automobile.* U.S. Department of Transportation, Federal Highway Commission, Office of Highway Planning, April 1972, pp. 8–11.

Automobile Operating Costs — Bases for Estimates

Item	Standard Size Automobile	Compact Size Automobile	Subcompact Size Automobile
Automobile Description	1972 model 4-door sedan. Equipped with: V-8 engine, automatic transmission, power steering and brakes, air conditioning, tinted glass, radio, clock, whitewall tires, and body protective molding.	1972 model 2-door sedan Equipped with: 6 cylinder engine, automatic transmission, power steering, radio, and body protective molding.	1972 model 2-door sedan. Equipped with: standard equipment plus radio and body protective molding.
Repairs and Maintenance	Includes routine maintenance such as lubrications, repacking wheel bearings, flushing cooling system, and aiming headlamps; replacement of minor parts such as spark plugs, fan belts, radiator hoses, distributor cap, fuel filter, and pollution control filters; minor repairs such as brake jobs, water pump, carburetor overhaul, and universal joints; and major repairs such as a complete "valve job."		
Replacement Tires	Purchase of 7 new regular tires and 4 new snow tires during the lives of the cars was assumed.		
Accessories	Purchase of floor mats the first year, seat covers the sixth year, and miscellaneous items totaling $2.00 per year was assumed.		
Gasoline	Consumption rate of 13.60 miles per gallon was used.	Consumption rate of 15.97 miles per gallon was used.	Consumption rate of 21.43 miles per gallon was used.
Oil	Consumption was associated with gasoline consumption at a rate of 1 gallon of oil for every 186 gallons of gasoline.	Consumption was associated with gasoline consumption at a rate of 1 gallon of oil for every 166 gallons of gasoline.	Consumption was associated with gasoline consumption at a rate of 1 gallon of oil for every 135 gallons of gasoline.
Insurance	Coverage includes $50,000 combined public liability ($15,000/$30,000 bodily injury, and $5,000 property damage), $1,000 medical payments, uninsured motorist coverage, and full comprehensive coverage for the 10-year period. Deductible collision insurance was assumed for the first 5 years ($100 deductible).		
Garaging, Parking, and Tolls	Includes monthly charges of $10.00 for garage rental or indirect cost of the owners garaging facility; plus parking fee average of $54.00 per year, and toll average of $6.94 per year, both of which were assigned in proportion to annual travel.		
Taxes	Includes Federal Excise taxes on tires (10 cents per pound), lubricating oil (6 cents per gallon), and gasoline (4 cents per gallon); plus the Maryland tax on gasoline (7 cents per gallon), titling tax (4 percent of retail price), and registration fee ($20.00 for 3,700 pounds or less shipping weight, or $30.00 for vehicles over 3,700 pounds).		

TABLE 1

Estimated Cost of Operating a Standard Size 1972 Model Automobile[1]

(Total costs in dollars, costs per mile in cents)

Item	First Year (14,500 miles) Total Cost	Cost per Mile	Second Year (13,000 miles) Total Cost	Cost per Mile	Third Year (11,500 miles) Total Cost	Cost per Mile	Fourth Year (10,000 miles) Total Cost	Cost per Mile	Fifth Year (9,900 miles) Total Cost	Cost per Mile
Costs Excluding Taxes:										
Depreciation	1,226.00	8.46	900.00	6.92	675.00	5.87	500.00	5.00	376.00	3.80
Repairs and Maintenance	81.84	.56	115.37	.89	242.65	2.11	296.09	2.96	275.54	2.78
Replacement Tires	17.90	.12	16.05	.12	23.72	.21	44.40	.44	43.95	.44
Accessories	3.21	.02	3.08	.02	2.96	.02	2.83	.03	2.82	.03
Gasoline	286.75	1.98	257.16	1.98	227.58	1.98	197.72	1.98	195.83	1.98
Oil	11.25	.08	11.25	.09	12.00	.10	12.00	.12	12.75	.13
Insurance[2]	164.00	1.13	156.00	1.20	156.00	1.36	147.00	1.47	147.00	1.49
Garaging, Parking, Tolls, etc.	208.36	1.44	199.22	1.53	190.08	1.65	180.94	1.81	180.33	1.82
Total	1,999.31	13.79	1,658.13	12.75	1,529.99	13.30	1,380.98	13.81	1,234.22	12.47
Taxes and Fees:										
State:										
Gasoline	74.62	.51	66.92	.52	59.22	.52	51.45	.51	50.96	.52
Registration	30.00	.21	30.00	.23	30.00	.26	30.00	.30	30.00	.30
Titling	177.15	1.22	–	–	–	–	–	–	–	–
Subtotal	281.77	1.94	96.92	.75	89.22	.78	81.45	.81	80.96	.82
Federal:										
Gasoline	42.64	.30	38.24	.30	33.84	.29	29.40	.30	29.12	.30
Oil[3]	.22	–	.22	–	.24	–	.24	–	.26	–
Tires	1.38	.01	1.24	.01	1.82	.02	3.42	.03	3.39	.03
Subtotal	44.24	.31	39.70	.31	35.90	.31	33.06	.33	32.77	.33
Total Taxes	326.01	2.25	136.62	1.06	125.12	1.09	114.51	1.14	113.73	1.15
Total of All Costs	2,325.32	16.04	1,794.75	13.81	1,655.11	14.39	1,495.49	14.95	1,347.95	13.62

Item	Sixth Year (9,900 miles)		Seventh Year (9,500 miles)		Eighth Year (8,500 miles)		Ninth Year (7,500 miles)		Tenth Year (5,700 miles)		Totals and Averages for Ten Years (100,000 miles)	
	Total Cost	Cost per Mile	Total Cost	Cost per Mile	Total Cost	Cost per Mile	Total Cost	Cost per Mile	Total Cost	Cost per Mile	Total Cost	Cost per Mile
Costs Excluding Taxes:												
Depreciation	259.00	2.61	189.00	1.99	121.00	1.42	85.00	1.13	48.00	.84	4,379.00	4.38
Repairs and Maintenance	292.54	2.95	397.56	4.19	171.82	2.02	244.33	3.26	29.17	.51	2,146.91	2.14
Replacement Tires	45.44	.46	50.69	.53	62.79	.74	52.80	.70	42.11	.74	399.85	.40
Accessories	8.57	.09	8.30	.09	7.65	.09	6.97	.09	5.79	.10	52.18	.05
Gasoline	195.83	1.98	188.03	1.98	168.13	1.98	148.22	1.98	122.71	1.98	1,977.96	1.98
Oil	13.50	.14	13.50	.14	13.50	.16	12.00	.16	6.75	.12	118.50	.12
Insurance[2]	116.00	1.17	116.00	1.22	116.00	1.37	116.00	1.55	116.00	2.04	1,350.00	1.35
Garaging, Parking, Tolls, etc.	180.33	1.82	177.89	1.87	171.80	2.02	165.71	2.21	154.74	2.71	1,809.40	1.81
Total	1,111.21	11.22	1,140.97	12.01	832.69	9.80	831.03	11.08	515.27	9.04	12,233.80	12.23
Taxes and Fees:												
State:												
Gasoline	50.96	.52	48.93	.51	43.75	.52	38.57	.52	29.33	.51	514.71	.51
Registration	30.00	.30	30.00	.32	30.00	.35	30.00	.40	30.00	.53	300.00	.30
Titling	–	–	–	–	–	–	–	–	–	–	177.15	.18
Subtotal	80.96	.82	78.93	.83	73.75	.87	68.57	.92	59.33	1.04	991.86	.99
Federal:												
Gasoline	29.12	.29	27.96	.30	25.00	.29	22.04	.29	16.76	.29	294.12	.30
Oil[3]	.27	–	.27	–	.27	–	.24	–	.14	–	2.37	–
Tires	3.50	.04	3.90	.04	4.84	.06	4.07	.06	3.24	.06	30.80	.03
Subtotal	32.89	.33	32.13	.34	30.11	.35	26.35	.35	20.14	.35	327.29	.33
Total Taxes	113.85	1.15	111.06	1.17	103.86	1.22	94.92	1.27	79.47	1.39	1,319.15	1.32
Total of All Costs	1,225.06	12.37	1,252.03	13.18	936.55	11.02	925.95	12.35	594.74	10.43	13,552.95	13.55

This estimate covers the total costs of a fully equipped, medium priced, standard size, 4-door sedan, purchased for $4,379, operated 100,000 miles over a 10-year period, then scrapped. Baltimore area prices, considered to be in the middle range, were used.

[2] Previous editions of this study used insurance rates designated for Baltimore city. The rates shown above are for the Baltimore suburbs, and consequently are less than the rates presented in the previous study. If the Baltimore city rates had been used in this study, the insurance costs would have been higher. (For example, the first year would have been $232).

[3] Where costs per mile were computed to be less than 1/20 cent, a dash (–) appears in the column.

TABLE 2

Estimated Cost of Operating a Compact Size 1972 Model Automobile[1]

(Total costs in dollars, costs per mile in cents)

Item	First Year (14,500 miles) Total Cost	Cost per Mile	Second Year (13,000 miles) Total Cost	Cost per Mile	Third Year (11,500 miles) Total Cost	Cost per Mile	Fourth Year (10,000 miles) Total Cost	Cost per Mile	Fifth Year (9,900 miles) Total Cost	Cost per Mile
Costs Excluding Taxes:										
Depreciation	674.00	4.65	519.00	3.99	394.00	3.42	305.00	3.05	243.00	2.46
Repairs and Maintenance	79.41	.55	107.14	.83	170.61	1.48	218.90	2.19	240.27	2.43
Replacement Tires	15.30	.11	13.71	.11	12.13	.11	34.27	.34	33.93	.34
Accessories	3.21	.02	3.08	.02	2.96	.03	2.83	.03	2.82	.03
Gasoline	244.25	1.68	218.97	1.69	193.68	1.69	168.39	1.68	166.78	1.68
Oil	10.50	.07	10.50	.08	11.25	.10	11.25	.11	12.75	.13
Insurance	155.00	1.07	147.00	1.13	147.00	1.28	140.00	1.40	140.00	1.41
Garaging, Parking, Tolls, etc.	208.36	1.44	199.22	1.53	190.08	1.65	180.94	1.81	180.33	1.82
Total	1,390.03	9.59	1,218.62	9.38	1,121.71	9.76	1,061.58	10.61	1,019.88	10.30
Taxes and Fees:										
State:										
Gasoline	63.56	.44	56.98	.44	50.40	.44	43.82	.44	43.40	.44
Registration	20.00	.14	20.00	.15	20.00	.17	20.00	.20	20.00	.20
Titling	109.86	.75	–	–	–	–	–	–	–	–
Subtotal	193.42	1.33	76.98	.59	70.40	.61	63.82	.64	63.40	.64
Federal:										
Gasoline	36.32	.25	32.56	.25	28.80	.25	25.04	.25	24.80	.25
Oil[2]	.21	–	.21	–	.22	–	.22	–	.26	–
Tires	1.17	.01	1.05	.01	.92	.01	2.61	.03	2.59	.03
Subtotal	37.70	.26	33.82	.26	29.94	.26	27.87	.28	27.65	.28
Total Taxes	231.12	1.59	110.80	.85	100.34	.87	91.69	.92	91.05	.92
Total of All Costs	1,621.15	11.18	1,329.42	10.23	1,222.05	10.63	1,153.27	11.53	1,110.93	11.22

Item	Sixth Year (9,900 miles) Total Cost	Cost per Mile	Seventh Year (9,500 miles) Total Cost	Cost per Mile	Eighth Year (8,500 miles) Total Cost	Cost per Mile	Ninth Year (7,500 miles) Total Cost	Cost per Mile	Tenth Year (5,700 miles) Total Cost	Cost per Mile	Totals and Averages for Ten Years (100,000 miles) Total Cost	Cost per Mile
Costs Excluding Taxes:												
Depreciation	194.00	1.96	152.00	1.60	103.00	1.21	73.00	.97	39.00	.68	2,696.00	2.70
Repairs and Maintenance	268.81	2.72	412.04	4.34	177.27	2.09	78.95	1.05	31.10	.55	1,784.50	1.79
Replacement Tires	38.45	.39	36.89	.39	61.53	.72	54.29	.73	41.27	.72	341.77	.34
Accessories	8.57	.09	8.30	.09	7.65	.09	6.97	.09	5.79	.10	52.18	.05
Gasoline	166.78	1.68	160.06	1.69	143.11	1.69	126.43	1.69	96.03	1.68	1,684.48	1.68
Oil	12.75	.13	12.75	.13	12.75	.15	12.00	.16	6.75	.12	113.25	.11
Insurance	114.00	1.15	114.00	1.20	114.00	1.34	114.00	1.52	114.00	2.00	1,299.00	1.30
Garaging, Parking, Tolls, etc.	180.33	1.82	177.89	1.87	171.80	2.02	165.71	2.21	154.74	2.72	1,809.40	1.81
Total	983.69	9.94	1,073.93	11.31	791.11	9.31	631.35	8.42	488.68	8.57	9,780.58	9.78
Taxes and Fees:												
State:												
Gasoline	43.40	.44	41.65	.44	37.24	.44	32.90	.44	24.99	.44	438.34	.44
Registration	20.00	.20	20.00	.21	20.00	.23	20.00	.26	20.00	.35	200.00	.20
Titling	–	–	–	–	–	–	–	–	–	–	109.86	.11
Subtotal	63.40	.64	61.65	.65	57.24	.67	52.90	.70	44.99	.79	748.20	.75
Federal:												
Gasoline	24.80	.25	23.80	.25	21.28	.25	18.80	.25	14.28	.25	250.48	.25
Oil[2]	.26	–	.26	–	.26	–	.24	–	.13	–	2.27	–
Tires	2.93	.03	2.81	.03	4.69	.06	4.15	.06	3.15	.06	25.07	.03
Subtotal	27.99	.28	26.87	.28	26.23	.31	23.19	.31	17.56	.31	278.82	.28
Total Taxes	91.39	.92	88.52	.93	83.47	.98	76.09	1.01	62.55	1.10	1,027.02	1.03
Total of All Costs	1,075.08	10.86	1,162.45	12.24	874.58	10.29	707.44	9.43	551.23	9.67	10,807.60	10.81

[1] This estimate covers the total costs of a medium priced, compact size, 2-door sedan, purchased for $2,696, operated 100,000 miles over a 10-year period, then scrapped. Baltimore area prices, considered to be in the middle range, were used.

[2] Where costs per mile were computed to be less than 1/20 cent, a dash (–) appears in the column.

TABLE 3

Estimated Cost of Operating a Subcompact Size 1972 Model Automobile[1]

(Total costs in dollars, costs per mile in cents)

Item	First Year (14,500 miles)		Second Year (13,000 miles)		Totals and Averages For Ten Years (100,000 miles)	
	Total Cost	Cost per Mile	Total Cost	Cost per Mile	Total Cost	Cost per Mile
Costs Excluding Taxes:						
Depreciation	310.00	2.14	285.00	2.19	2,064.00	2.07
Repairs and Maintenance	76.15	.53	114.59	.88	1,775.71	1.78
Replacement Tires	13.98	.10	12.53	.10	312.29	.31
Accessories	3.21	.02	3.08	.02	52.18	.05
Gasoline	181.84	1.25	163.02	1.25	1,255.15	1.25
Oil	10.50	.07	9.75	.08	103.50	.10
Insurance	145.00	1.00	140.00	1.08	1,251.00	1.25
Garaging, Parking, Tolls, etc.	208.36	1.44	199.22	1.53	1,809.40	1.81
Total	949.04	6.55	927.19	7.13	8,623.23	8.62
Taxes and Fees:						
State:						
Gasoline	47.32	.33	42.42	.33	326.62	.33
Registration	20.00	.14	20.00	.15	200.00	.20
Titling	84.57	.58	–	–	84.57	.08
Subtotal	151.89	1.05	62.42	.48	611.19	.61
Federal:						
Gasoline	27.04	.18	24.24	.19	186.64	.19
Oil[2]	.21	–	.19	–	2.07	–
Tires	.94	.01	.84	.01	20.90	.02
Subtotal	28.19	.19	25.27	.20	209.61	.21
Total Taxes	180.08	1.24	87.69	.68	820.80	.82
Total of All Costs	1,129.12	7.79	1,014.88	7.81	9,444.03	9.44

[1] This estimate covers the total costs of a low priced, subcompact size, 2-door sedan, purchased for $2,064, operated 100,000 miles over a 10-year period, then scrapped. Baltimore area prices, considered to be in the middle range, were used. Since cost data for American made subcompacts does not exist past the second year, only the first, second, and estimated ten-year totals are shown.

[2] Where costs per mile were computed to be less than 1/20 cent, a dash(–) appears in the column.

8

THE ECONOMICS
OF FAMILY
PLANNING

When we speak of household durables, most of us think of automobiles, refrigerators, and television sets. Few of us would include children in this category, yet many economists are now beginning to view them as such. And, in fact, following the distinction between yielding and non-yielding durables made in the last chapter, we must put most children in the category of non-yielding durable goods, like television sets and air conditioners.

The primary economic difference is that children cost more than other durables. Even the best color television set is available for less than $1,000. A child may well cost more than 100 times that amount from the time he is conceived until you finally get him out of the house and on his own.

The Yield on Children

A century ago, when the majority of American families still lived on farms, the child was a good investment. At the age of 4 or 5, he could be out feeding the chickens; at 9 he could be milking the cow, and at 12, working beside the adults in the fields. By the time the child left the farm to begin his own family, he probably had contributed an amount of work equal to or greater than the cost of feeding, clothing, and housing him.

Even after he moved away, he was usually not too far

and could be counted on to help his parents. Eventually, when the parents were no longer able to maintain their own farm, they likely moved in with one of their children. So children were a source of cheap labor, insurance for emergencies, and eventually an old age pension. It is therefore not surprising that farm families tended to have large numbers of children.

In underdeveloped, largely agrarian countries today, we see the same thing happening. India, which is severely overpopulated, has seen birth control campaigns impeded by the fact that children are a useful asset which cost nothing to acquire and little to maintain.

But, as we have observed before, conditions in the United States today are far different from those in India—or in our own country a century ago. Few families live on farms, children contribute little or nothing to their families, and parents neither could nor should expect their grown children to help them out very much. This function has been assumed by the government.

Furthermore, children nowadays are a good deal more expensive to maintain. Food and clothing are no longer homegrown and homemade but must be purchased through a series of middlemen who greatly increase the farm price of the materials. Teenagers who used to spend their hours plowing the fields now must be given allowances to help entertain themselves.

Since the cost of children is so high, and since they usually yield no economic return, it is not unreasonable to view them as consumer durables like the television set. True, the emotional returns and entertainment from children are somewhat different from the entertainment of television, but this does not negate the fact that both children and television must compete for the same limited family resources. If a child does, in fact, cost a family $100,000, how many trips to Europe or new cars or years of early retirement does that mean? These are real considerations which should be thought of by the consumer before he decides upon family size. The purpose of this chapter is not to encourage or dissuade people from having children. Rather, it is to examine the economics of children and family size so that the consumer can make the best possible decision here as with the other economic problems he faces.

KID, WE THE MEMBERS OF THE COMMUNITY WISH TO PRESENT YOU WITH THIS GIFT...

Social Implications of Children

In the last chapter we spoke of the external or social costs of the automobile, such as pollution, which are not borne alone by the family. In the same way, we must also look at the social costs of children, since the family does not pay all their costs, either.

The most obvious external costs of children are borne by the taxpayers who provide free public education, which is itself an economic decision of society. The human capital given to all children by society increases their productivity and provides society with their taxes in the years hence. Yet at the time of education, the costs must be paid by current taxpayers who may not live to enjoy the returns 20 years in the future.

Taxpayers also pay for parks where children can play and even for the sustenance of children whose families cannot adequately support them. Yet these social costs, however high they may appear, are not the only ones. Children are extra people in an already crowded world. They also have the ability to grow up and produce more children, thereby further draining the world's resources. While the United States may be physically capable of holding a population three or five or ten times its present size, such an increase may not be socially desirable. Current population related problems such as pollution, crime, and depletion of natural resources, would only get that much worse. So the family that chooses to have a large number of children imposes a cost on society that greatly exceeds the very high cost that the family itself must bear.

Social Benefits of Children

While children are admittedly of little economic benefit to their parents, this is not to say they are not of great benefit to society as a whole. While rapidly increasing population puts a tremendous burden on society, a great fall-off in the production of children may also have a great social cost. An economy needs working people to produce the goods and services. Fewer children now means that later, when the rest of us are about to begin our well-earned retirement and become nonproductive citizens, we may not have enough young productive people to keep the show going. As in many other aspects of economics, extremes in population changes in either direction may have undesirable effects.

The Cost of Children to the Family

In making a correct economic estimate of the family's cost of raising children, one must include both explicit or *out of pocket* costs, as well as implicit or *opportunity* costs, which may be equally high or higher.

As we did with durables, let's estimate costs by looking at the behavior of a more or less typical family that is blessed with its first child. Some readers might object to some of the expenses that we mention, exclaiming "Allowance! I never got an allowance and my kid won't either. He'll get up at 4 A.M. to deliver papers just as I did." This type of behavior, while perhaps exemplary, is not characteristic of most families. And although each reader will find that his own observed or intended behavior differs from that of our model family to some degree, an enumeration of the types of expenses that must be borne (and are often overlooked) can only be instructive to all readers.

Helene Schwartz met Horace Levy when she was out of college six months working as a computer programmer in San Francisco. Horace, who was three years older, was transferred to Helene's division as a systems analyst. Let us skip the boring details of courtship, fights, and reconciliations in order to get to the more interesting economic aspects of their relationship. It suffices to say that the following June they were married and moved into a nice one-bedroom apartment ($160 per month). Having no good reason to do otherwise, they both continued to work at their jobs (he made $12,000 a year, she made $9,000) and traveled to work together, thereby allowing them to dispose of one car.

After a year they decided to begin their family, and some months later Helene confided to her mother that it looked as if she would finally have the grandchild she had been demanding since Helene's marriage. In her seventh month of pregnancy, she requested and got a leave of absence knowing full well that she would not return to work until her child had begun school. Two months later, a daughter, Eyli Anna, was born, a beautiful little redhead with blue eyes.

Let's look at some of the costs associated with little Eyli Anna.

childbirth The first cost was the $15 lab fee to determine whether Helene was pregnant. After that, she arranged a package deal with her obstetrician for prenatal care and delivery which amounted to $300. Vitamins and other medication cost an additional $25 and the hospital bill for the four days of confinement during and after childbirth, which included fees for the delivery room, the nursery, and medication, came to $850. Although some people may have insurance to cover a portion of these costs, the Levys had to pay the full amount themselves, so even before little Eyli could come home, she had cost her parents a total of $1,190.

But where was Eyli going to sleep? Of course, she could sleep in a dresser drawer and it probably wouldn't matter to a four-day old baby whether she slept in a drawer or an antique mahogany crib, but what would Helene's mother say when she had to open the right drawer just to see her first grandchild? So another $200 was shelled out for baby furniture, clothes, bottles, and a carriage, running the start-up expenses to $1,390.

medical care Over the next 18 years, Eyli will have many medical expenses. In her first years, there are regular visits to the doctor. When she gets bigger, she also begins to visit the dentist and perhaps the orthodontist as well. And she may need glasses. Let's assume that her medical and dental bills average only $100 per year—over 18 years, this will total $1,800.

food The amount of food that a child consumes depends on age, as we have seen in chapter 5. Initially, the cost of the child's food may be less than $5 per week, but as an active teenager this may go up to $15. At an average of, say, $10 per week, or $520 per year, food costs for 18 years will amount to $9,360.

clothing The costs of clothing a child can vary greatly, depending upon climate, style, variety, and the amount of clothing that can be made at home. Averaging the costs for a teenage girl with those for a youngster, a figure of $200 per year does not seem out of line. This adds another $3,600 to the bill over 18 years.

other out-of-pocket (explicit) expenses Raising children may mean other expenses. As they grow older, they need different furniture. They need money to buy school supplies; many receive allowances; some take music lessons, art lessons, ballet lessons. Also, don't forget the baby sitter. Athletically minded youngsters need sports equipment. Lumping all of these things together and averaging the 18 years at home, ten additional dollars per week does not seem unreasonably high. This adds another $9,360 to the total.

total explicit expenses Thus far, we have the following explicit expenses for the first 18 years of Eyli's life:

Childbirth and Related Expenses	$1,390
Medical Care	1,800
Food	9,360
Clothing	3,600
Other Expenses	9,360
Total	$25,510

Implicit Costs

As we said earlier, these explicit costs are only part of the total expense. Other implicit or opportunity costs may amount to even more money.

foregone income of wife Perhaps the greatest cost of Eyli to the Levy family is the income the family loses when Helene drops out of the labor force for several years. Recent studies have shown that even after adjusting for all other factors, women with children under school age are far less likely to be employed than other wives.[1]

If Helene has no other children and returns to the labor force at the

---

[1] See, for example, Dickenson & Dickenson, "Labor Force Participation of Wives: The Effects of Components of Husbands' Income," in Mandell, *et al., Surveys of Consumers 1971–72*, p. 250.

end of five years, she has lost five years' pay. Even assuming (which is very unlikely) that her salary would have stayed the same during that period, the Levy family would be deprived of $9,000 times five years or $45,000 in income.

Had she received increases or promotions during that five year period, the loss would be that much higher. And if we bear in mind that when she returns to work in five years it will likely be at her old salary, the loss becomes higher still since each additional year that she works will be at a lower salary than she would have been making had she remained at her job and gained five years' more experience.

To carry this one step further, it is not at all certain that she could even get her old job back after five years of professional inactivity. In her rapidly changing field, she may have fallen behind the technology and be forced to undergo additional education to be as valuable as she was before she left her job. Many persons who leave the labor force for several years find that much of their human capital has become obsolete and must be reacquired.

But let's be satisfied with the low estimate of a $45,000 loss, and move on.

housing   Little Eyli Anna was first brought home to her parents' pleasant one-bedroom apartment. After the initial excitement, however, the Levys decided that three's a crowd in a one-bedroom apartment, so they looked around for something bigger. In their own apartment complex, they found a two-bedroom apartment for $220 a month, $60 more than they were already paying. If they took this, they would be paying an extra $720 per year ($60 times 12 months) or $12,960 over the next 18 years. However, if the Levys are like most families, the odds are excellent that they will look to buy a home, ostensibly in order to have a yard for Eyli and room for her to move around.

Maintaining a house that approximated the style of living that the Levys enjoy in their current apartment might well cost more than the extra $60 per month for a larger apartment. But let's continue our modest tack and bill them only for the additional $12,960 that the larger apartment would cost.

total costs thus far:

Explicit Costs	$25,510
Implicit Costs	
Wife's Income	45,000
Housing	12,960
Total	$83,470

other costs   Before we begin to consider the expenses of higher education, we should touch upon other possible implicit costs. One that is hard to quantify is the opportunity cost of diminished occupational mobility. A parent who has a child in school is often less likely to move in order to get a higher paying job.

In addition, the time demands of children may inhibit parents from taking additional jobs or jobs that require them to be away from home for long periods of time. All of these factors may cost the family money.

higher education   Surveys reveal that the vast majority of American parents aspire for their children to have a college education; in fact, more than half of all high school graduates at least begin some form of higher education. (Since you, reader, are already in college, it is very likely that your children will also go to college, so start saving.)

Recent estimates place the total cost of a year in college, including room, board, tuition, books, lab fees, allowance, clothing, and so on at figures that can approach or exceed $5,000. If we send Eyli away to a private college, we have set the Levys back an additional $20,000 for four years. Of course, she could stay at home and go to a local state-supported college for $2,000 a year, but then again, she could go to medical school after college for an *additional* outlay of $20,000. So let's settle on $20,000 for her education.

total costs   You will notice that we have not been extravagant in bringing up Eyli. We did not give her a car, nor did we send her to Europe or even to summer camp. Furthermore, we did not add in the cost of her wedding which, according to the customs of our society, the Levys must bear. Yet even so, our total cost comes to $103,470. Even without college, she costs more than $80,000.[2] As we said earlier, this money could make a great difference in the Levys' standard of living.[3]

Economies of Scale—the Number and Spacing of Children

While the cost of a second child is not like a penny sale where you pay full price for the first item and only one cent for the second, additional children are nevertheless cheaper than the first. As a family ac-

---

[2] These figures are supported and in fact shown to be somewhat conservative in an article entitled "The High Cost of Child-Rearing," *U.S. News & World Report,* January 17, 1972. For even more costly estimates, see "The High Cost of Childhood," *Esquire,* March 1974.

[3] One must bear in mind the fact that these costs are spread out over the next 18 or 20 years, and the *present discounted value,* or the cost at the time the decision to have the child is made, is a great deal less. If the $83,470 is spread evenly over 18 years, the annual cost is $4,637 and at 6 percent, the present discounted value is $50,219. (Table 4-3) The $103,470 spread over 21 years would have a present value of $57,943.

quires more children, the average cost per child tends to drop, thereby implying that there are *economies of scale* in children.

Why do additional children cost less? For the most part, explicit costs are the same for each child. Few obstetricians give quantity discounts or reduced rate discounts for the next child, and although some savings may be achieved in handing down furniture and clothing, this probably doesn't amount to much. There may be some savings in food as the result of buying and cooking larger amounts but again, this saving is relatively small. Of the $25,510 in explicit costs for the Levy's first child Eyli, perhaps $1,000 or so can be saved on their second child, Kilgore.

The real savings comes in the implicit costs. The additional housing expenses associated with the first child will generally not be matched by those associated with the second child. If the family had purchased a house, the extra bedroom is likely there already. If they had moved to a larger apartment, the second child could share a room with the first, at least for several years.

The Economies of Spacing

But by far the greatest economies are realized in the opportunity cost of the wife's foregone salary. If the Levys have only one child, Helene will be out of work for five years—until Eyli begins school. If they have a second child a year later, Helene will be out of the labor force for only one additional year for the second child. This means that the added or *marginal cost* of the second child, in terms of lost salary, is only $9,000. If the children are spaced two years apart, Helene must be out of the labor force for a total of 7 years, so the additional child will cost $18,000. If they are five years apart, there is no savings since Helene must be out of the labor force for a total of ten years, five for each child.

Therefore, a family which plans several children can save thousands of dollars by spacing them economically. The greatest cost savings is obtained when the children are spaced closest together—quintuplets are very economical for a family that wants five children.

However, it is not certain that bunching children close together has no harmful effects. Children may be deprived of sufficient parental attention during their formative years and if, as some economists (Hill and Stafford)[4] believe, the objective of parents is to raise the highest quality child, and if time spent with children contributes to their quality, having children close together may have inefficiencies that compensate, in a negative direction, for the dollars of saving.

---

[4] C. Russell Hill and Frank P. Stafford, "The Allocation of Time to Children and Educational Opportunity," Discussion Paper, Institute Public Policy Studies, University of Michigan.

SUMMARY

1. In this country, the roles and functions of children have changed radically. A century ago, and even now in some underdeveloped countries, children were a source of cheap labor and acted as insurance for their parents against emergencies and old age. Factors like the break-up of the extended family, urbanization, and increasing governmental participation in such matters as old age pensions and unemployment benefits mean that children need not be viewed as necessities anymore.

2. The costs of bringing up children is rising continuously. Even though most of us do not view children as consumer durables, the fact remains that they do have to compete with such products for the limited resources of each family. Therefore, it is important that people have more knowledge of the factors to be considered when making decisions on their appropriate family sizes.

3. The costs of bringing up children can be divided into external and internal costs, the former borne by the taxpayers who provide free services, notably, free education. Another such cost arises from the fact that the earth's resources are finite and more children mean faster depletion. Pollution of various kinds is also a by-product of overpopulation. On the other hand, an extreme decrease in population might also involve social costs.

4. The internal costs are implicit as well as explicit. The explicit costs are of course the direct costs of providing the various goods and services children need, while the implicit costs consist of the income foregone by the act of bringing up children, as well as the time and money spent on them which could have been spent in other ways. The most important of these is the earnings lost where wives have to stop working and stay home. Another is the income spent on children rather than invested and earning interest.

QUESTIONS

1. Compare and contrast the arguments for and against population decreases in the United States and in India.

2. Why is the concept of free public education an important economic decision of society?

3. Do you agree that children can be viewed and considered like any other consumer durable? Give reasons for your answers.

4. What types of costs are involved in producing a "higher quality" child?

TERMINOLOGY   economies of scale
economies of spacing
human capital

SELECTED REFERENCES AND SOURCES OF DATA

Journal of Political Economy. "New Economic Approaches to Fertility," Proceedings of a conference June 8–9, 1972. Sponsored by N.B.E.R. and the Population Council. Theodore W. Schultz, ed. LXXXI, No. 2, Part I. (March/April 1973).

Landsberger, Michael. "An Integrated Model of Consumption and Market Activity: The Children Effect," *American Statistical Association. Social Statistics Section. Proceedings.* 197, pp. 137–42.

Morgan, James N. *Five Thousand American Families. Patterns of Economic Progress.* Vol. I. (Ann Arbor: Institute for Social Research, 1974), Chapters 10–11.

Peck, Ellen. *The Baby Trap.* (New York: Bernard Greis, 1971).

9

THE HOUSING DECISION

Immediately following the birth of their first child, the Levys began to ponder their choice of housing. Their initial solution, as we saw in the last chapter, was to move to a larger apartment. But even here, they were not completely satisfied.

For one thing, they anticipated further expansion of their family in a year or two, and this would cramp even their expanded quarters. Furthermore, as their daughter grew old enough to seek the companionship of other children, the Levys noticed that few such children lived in neighboring apartments. Also, as the child became more active, the advantages of a fenced yard on a quiet street began to weigh more heavily in the utility function of the parents.

It is not surprising that the difficult housing decision— single family versus apartment, owning versus renting— presented itself to the Levys at this exact time. Statistical data clearly show that the transition from apartments to single family housing most frequently occurs in the years following the birth of the first child. Table 9-1 shows that while a third of young single people live in single family housing, this proportion increases to only 45 percent of childless young married couples. The birth of a child boosts that figure to 70 percent, and by the time that child is six years old it goes up to 86. If we include mobile homes as single family houses, the figure is even higher.

Although most young people begin their adulthood in multiple family housing, once they make the transition

TABLE 9-1

Type of Housing by Life Cycle, 1971

(Percentage Distribution of Families)

Life Cycle Stage	Single family house	2-4 family struc- ture	Apart- ment, 5 or more unit	Trailer	Total
Under Age 45					
Unmarried, no children	33	24	36	7	100
Married, no children	45	19	23	13	100
Married, youngest child under 6	70	19	4	7	100
Married, youngest child 6 or older	86	8	4	2	100
Age 45 or Older					
Married, has children	87	9	3	1	100
Married, no children, head in labor force	80	10	7	3	100
Married, no children, head retired	82	8	5	5	100
Unmarried, no children, head in labor force	65	17	14	4	100
Unmarried, no children, head retired	65	10	21	4	100
All families	71	14	11	4	100

Source: Mandell, *et al., Surveys of Consumers 1971-72,* p. 30.

to a single family home, they are loath to return to an apartment—even after the children have left home. This leads to the charge by many experts that old people are "overhoused"—that they pay for more housing than they need. Certainly the data in table 9-1 show that only a small proportion of older, childless people give up the house, but additional input—such as the true costs and benefits of such housing—is necessary before we can evaluate the adequacy of housing for old people.

Mobile homes have become increasingly popular in the United States as the cost of housing has increased, yet table 9-1 shows that they are most frequently used by married, childless couples—particularly younger couples. Apparently the birth of children induces many families to move to more permanent housing.

Own Versus Rent

The decision concerning the type of housing is strongly related to housing ownership. Simply stated, most people who live in apartments pay rent, while those who live in single family houses generally own them.

While it may be possible to rent houses in some areas, most families

TABLE 9-2

Housing Ownership by Life Cycle, 1971

(Percentage Distribution of Non-Farm Families)

	Own[a]	Rent	Other[b]	Total
Under Age 45				
Unmarried, no children	15	78	7	100
Married, no children	42	54	4	100
Married, youngest child under 6	62	35	3	100
Married, youngest child 6 or older	76	22	2	100
Age 45 or Older				
Married, has children	79	17	4	100
Married, no children, head in labor force	87	12	1	100
Married, no children, head retired	78	20	2	100
Unmarried, no children, head in labor force	61	39	*	100
Unmarried, no children, head retired	67	26	7	100
All Families	66	31	3	100

[a] Includes trailer owners

[b] Includes families who receive housing as compensation for employment or as a gift.

* Less than 0.5 percent

Source: Mandell, et al., Surveys of Consumers 1971-72, p. 28.

must buy. Table 9-2 shows that patterns of ownership correspond closely to patterns of housing type over the life cycle. Ownership is infrequent for unmarried young people (15%), rising steeply with marriage and children. All told, two-thirds of Americans own their houses.

When the Levys were considering the purchase of a house, they took a sheet of paper and listed all of the advantages of home ownership on one side, and the advantages of renting on the other. The relative monthly cost of each was deferred for later consideration. Their sheet looked like the following:

Advantages of home ownership	Advantages of Renting
Freedom of use	Flexibility
Hedge against inflation	No risk of loss of capital
Savings in "do it yourself"	Adjust easily to family needs
Tax benefits	No maintenance
Forced savings	Shared facilities

The arguments were as follows:

Advantages of Home Ownership

freedom of use   When you own your own house, you are the boss. There is no landlord to tell you to get rid of your cat or that you can't put a television antenna on the roof or paint the kitchen chartreuse.

hedge against inflation   When prices go up, house values generally keep pace (or do even better). If you rent, your rent will often be increased as prices rise. However, if you own your house, your monthly mortgage payments do not increase. Owning a home protects you against inflation. Table 9-3 shows that over time, the prices of both new and existing homes generally have kept up with consumer prices in general, although there have been year-to-year decreases in house values, largely as the result of a shortage of mortgage funds.

Of course deflation (falling prices) could have the opposite effect. Yet long periods of deflation are not nearly as likely as long periods of inflation, for reasons we will go into in chapter 17.

savings in do-it-yourself   If you are handy or enjoy home maintenance and improvement, you can save money by owning your home. When you rent, part of your monthly payment includes the cost of painting, repairing the plumbing and leaks in the roof, and perhaps even cutting the grass or shoveling snow.

By doing these things yourself on your own home you realize the double savings discussed in chapter 4. You save the cost of having someone else do them, and you save the income taxes on that money. If, for example, $15 of your monthly rent went to cover maintenance labor, and you are in the 25 percent tax bracket, you would have had to earn $20 extra per month (25 percent of $20 is $5 which goes for taxes) to pay for that labor. By doing it yourself, you save $20 per month.[1]

tax benefits   Homeownership has been referred to as the "tax loophole of the middle class." The primary tax savings of homeownership is far more substantial than that from do-it-yourself activities.

According to law, all interest charges and real estate taxes are tax deductible for Federal income tax. Since these comprise a large part of the payments made by most homeowners, savings may be substantial.

---

[1] Of course this is true only if you couldn't be making money elsewhere in the time that you spend in this activity. See chapter 4 for a review of opportunity cost and the value of home production.

TABLE 9-3

House Prices as a Hedge Against Inflation

Year	Purchase Price of New Homes	Purchase Price of Existing Homes	New Home Price as Percent of 1965	Existing Home Price as Percent of 1965	Consumer Goods as Percent of 1965
1965	$25,100	$21,600	100	100	100
1966	26,600	22,200	106	103	103
1967	28,000	24,100	112	116	106
1968	30,700	25,600	122	119	110
1969	34,100	28,300	136	131	115
1970	35,500	30,000	141	139	123
1971	36,300	31,700	145	147	128
1972	37,300	33,400	149	155	133
1973	37,100	31,200	148	144	141

Source: *Federal Reserve Bulletins:* Housing prices of homes sold with conventional first mortgages. Consumer prices calculated from the consumer price index.

To illustrate this briefly, let's consider the alternative of a rented apartment for $250 per month versus purchasing a house with mortgage and pro-rated real estate taxes also of $250 per month. In both cases, we will assume that the occupant is responsible for all utilities (heat, water, electricity, gas) and maintenance.

In a recently purchased house, nearly all of the monthly payment goes toward payment of interest and real estate taxes (and only a small proportion goes toward *amortization* or repayment of the loan—a concept we will discuss shortly). If $200 of the $250 payment is for interest and taxes, and if the potential renter/buyer is in the 25 percent tax bracket, he will save $50 per month by buying the home (25 percent of $200) and nothing by renting. Buying is, in this respect, far more advantageous than renting.

forced savings Few American families manage to voluntarily save money on a regular basis, that is, other than the commitments of a contract such as a mortgage or life insurance policy. As a result, they have little to fall back on later.

By buying a house, a family generally obligates itself to repay a large mortgage over a period of years. Monthly payments, after interest and taxes, reduce the amount of borrowed money which is outstanding, meaning that the homeowner's *equity* (house value less outstanding mortgage) gradually increases. Equity can be converted to cash by selling the house or by borrowing against it with a new or second mortgage.

The equity that families have built up in their houses has helped millions of families to an easier retirement, to get out of emergencies, or even to send children to college. It is tantamount to money in the bank.

Advantages of Renting

In spite of the advantages of homeownership, renting is not without its attractions.

flexibility   A great advantage of renting is the flexibility it gives to the family. If a better job offer comes through in another city, the family can move without the additional expenses of selling one house and buying another. Also, if a neighborhood declines or another neighborhood appears more attractive, the family can move with relatively little expense.

no risk of loss   While recent decades have seen the continued rise of most house values, this movement is by no means universal. Cities have declined, neighborhoods have grown out of fashion or deteriorated, and many families have seen the values of their houses drop precipitously.
   A homeowner runs the risk of losing money on his house, of selling it for less than he paid; or worse, not being able to sell it at all for any reasonable amount. Renters can leave an undesirable area on relatively short notice without the risk of losing their investment.

no maintenance   Some people prefer to rent because they don't want to be bothered with the day-to-day maintenance or worry about leaky faucets and dry-rot in the front steps. Of course these people pay for the service as part of their rent, but it is worth the price to many people for the savings in time.

shared facilities   A last advantage of renting, which most often occurs in larger apartment units, is sharing facilities such as a swimming pool and a laundry room. While most families of moderate income cannot afford their own pools, many apartment houses provide them. As in the case with any good that has high fixed costs and low variable costs, the more use the good (pool, washer, dryer) gets, the lower the (average) cost for each user.

Costs of Home Ownership

Having discussed many of the benefits of home ownership that are non-quantifiable (in monetary terms), we must consider those that are quantifiable. The costs of renting are easier to calculate than those of home ownership.
   Consider the Murphys who are currently paying $250 a month for

their comfortable two bedroom apartment outside of St. Louis. Rent, in their case, covers heat, water, and sewer as well as maintenance and other traditional services. It does not include electricity or gas for appliances.

Last weekend the Murphys looked at a house that they really liked. The asking price was $26,900, but the realtor told them that they could get it with an offer of $25,000. Furthermore, they could get a mortgage with a $5,000 down payment and the balance of $20,000 to be paid over twenty years at 8 percent interest. Monthly mortgage payments to the bank (for interest and principal) would be only $167.29—"less than you pay now for rent," the realtor pointed out, "and don't forget those tax benefits!"

Let's calculate the Murphys' probable costs to see whether it is, indeed, cheaper to buy.

interest—explicit The explicit interest is what the bank gets each month—initially, 8 percent of $20,000. This is $1,600 per year or $133.33 per month. Since the monthly mortgage payment is higher than this ($167.29), the difference is *amortization* which reduces the *principal* of $20,000 each month. Initially, the principal reduces very slowly, but as the years go by and the principal slowly becomes smaller and the monthly payment pays more on the principal and less interest, equity builds up (see table 9-4).

But within the first several years, monthly interest charges will stay about $133 per month. Of course it pays to shop around for a loan. Table 9-5 shows us that after 20 years at 8 percent, the Murphys will have paid back *twice* what the house cost. If their loan were only one-half percent less, they would save nearly $1,500 over the life of the loan.

interest—implicit The money that the Murphys put into their house could be earning interest for them. They take $5,000 from their bank (where it earns 6 percent interest) for a down payment. This costs them $300 per year, or $25 per month.

As the Murphys amortize their house over the years and build up equity, more and more of the value of the house is paid for by *their own money*. This means that while explicit interest falls as the loan is repaid, implicit interest grows (but not as fast: explicit interest is higher because banks must make a profit). Therefore the total interest falls slightly over the years. However, implicit interest is a very real cost which is often overlooked by people contemplating the purchase of a home.

property tax Owners of real estate in the United States pay an annual tax based on the value of their property. This tax is generally used to support the activities of local government and, most particularly, to support local schools.

TABLE 9-4

Approximate Annual Interest and Amortization on a 20 Year Loan of $20,000 at 8% Interest

Monthly Payment $ 167.29
Annual Payment $2007.48

Year	Interest	Amortization	Year End Mortgage Balance	Owner's Equity
1	$1,587	$ 420	$19,580	$ 420
2	1,547	460	19,120	880
3	1,507	500	18,620	1,380
4	1,467	540	18,080	1,920
5	1,427	580	17,500	2,500
6	1,367	640	16,860	3,140
7	1,327	680	16,180	3,820
8	1,267	740	15,440	4,560
9	1,207	800	14,640	5,360
10	1,127	880	13,760	6,240
11	1,067	940	12,820	7,180
12	987	1,020	11,800	8,200
13	907	1,100	10,700	9,300
14	807	1,200	9,500	10,500
15	727	1,280	8,220	11,780
16	607	1,400	6,820	13,180
17	487	1,520	5,300	14,700
18	347	1,660	3,640	16,360
19	227	1,780	1,860	18,140
20	147	1,860	0	20,000

Many banks and other mortgage lenders require monthly payment of real estate taxes into an *escrow* account which ensures that the full amount will be available at tax time. Unfortunately for the house buyer, few lenders pay interest on the escrow account, so that the bank has use of the borrower's tax money for free. Many banks also require prepayment of insurance into the escrow account as well.

repairs and maintenance Repair costs are often called "lumpy" by economists since they are often infrequent, unexpected, and expensive. There may be no repairs needed for three years and all of a sudden a pipe will burst or the furnace will quit. Over the years, however, these costs can be averaged, and when we include the commoner ones, they work out to about one percent of the purchase price each year. For the Murphys, this amounts to $250.

insurance Every house should be insured for fire damage, at a minimum. Generally, if the buyer has a mortgage on the property, he will

TABLE 9-5

Differences in Monthly Payments, Total Payments Over Entire Life of Mortgage, and Total Interest Payments for a $20,000 Loan for 20 Years

Interest Rate (%)	Monthly Payment	Total Amount Paid	Total Interest Paid
6	$143.20	$34,390	$14,390
6½	149.12	35,789	15,789
7	155.06	37,214	17,214
7½	161.12	38,669	18,669
8	167.29	40,150	20,150

be compelled to take out such insurance to cover the lender's stake in the property until the loan is repaid. Homeowners' insurance (which covers more than fire, but which is most common) will run about one-quarter percent of the value of the home per year. This adds $62.50 to the Murphys' cost.

heat Once they own, the Murphys must pay for their own heating and hot water; $250 per year should cover these (at least normally.)

water and sewer These costs amount to $40 per year for the Murphys.

depreciation Houses, like any other physical structure, undergo physical deterioration over time. Floors sag, foundations weaken, plaster cracks. However, the attendant loss in value since the Second World War has been more than offset by rising real estate prices (table 9-3). So we will charge the Murphys nothing for depreciation at this time.

TABLE 9-6

Total Costs.

	Annual Costs (early years)*
Explicit interest	$1,587.00
Implicit interest	300.00
Property tax	750.00
Repairs & maintenance	250.00
Insurance	62.50
Heat	250.00
Water & sewer	40.00
Total	$3,239.50 per year or $269.96 per month

* Total costs will decline slightly over time as explicit interest decreases and implicit interest (which is lower) increases. This assumes no inflation.

Tax Savings

Earlier, we mentioned that explicit interest and property taxes are deducted from Federal income taxes. If the Murphys are in the 20 percent marginal tax bracket, they save 20 percent of $2250 or $467 per year in taxes. Subtracting this from their annual costs of $3,239.50 gives us $2,772.50 per year or $231.04 per month in actual costs.

Is it cheaper for the Murphys to buy? According to our calculations, it is, since their total costs of $231.04 per month are less than their rent charges of $250 per month. This isn't always the case, but if the decision for the Murphys hinges on cost, they would be well advised to buy.

SUMMARY

1. Just as in the case of ownership of consumer durables, there is a strong relation between family life cycles and home buying: most families with children in the United States tend to buy and live in their own houses.
2. There are different advantages and disadvantages to renting and to buying houses. Anyone considering the purchase of a house should compare the costs and benefits of buying or renting.
3. We are dealing with a family's limited resources and their alternative uses. The purchase of a house is a matter that should be subjected to a careful cost benefit analysis before any decision is made.

QUESTIONS

1. Discuss why owning your house can be considered a "tax loophole."
2. Suppose a family inherits a large sum of money and immediately decides to buy a house with it. Do you think they should evaluate the costs and benefits associated with this purchase? Why?

TERMINOLOGY

amortization
home owners equity
tax loophole
escrow account
principal
inflation hedge

Katona, George, Lewis Mandell and Jay Schmeideskamp. *1970 Survey of Consumer Finances.* (Ann Arbor: Institute for Social Research, 1970).

Lansing, John B, Robert W. Marans and Robert B. Zehner. *Planned Residential Environments.* (Ann Arbor: Institute for Social Research, 1970). (Discussion of factors affecting neighborhood satisfaction.)

Mandell Lewis, *et. al., Surveys of Consumers 1971/72.* (Ann Arbor: Institute for Social Research, 1972). (See Chapter 2, pp. 21–30.)

Troelstrup, Arch W. *The Consumer in American Society.* 4th ed. (New York: McGraw Hill, 1970). (Chapter 10, pp. 289–324.)

United States Savings and Loan League. Savings and Loan Fact Book Annual Ed., *What You Should Know When You Buy a Home,* Latest ed., Chicago.

Wren, Jack. *Home Buyers' Guide.* (New York: Barnes and Noble, Inc., 1970).

SELECTED REFERENCES AND SOURCES OF DATA

10

CONSUMER DEBT

The area causing consumers the greatest amount of grief is, not coincidentally, the area of greatest misunderstanding—that of consumer debt. Owing money, like most other things, is not entirely evil in and of itself. It can be very useful at times, provided the costs and benefits of *consumer debt* are understood.

What is Consumer Debt?

Consumer debt is borrowing money for non-business needs. Generally speaking, we exclude the mortgage that one has on his house, which is considered an investment rather than an expenditure. Money he owes on almost anything else, however, is included: This would include the car, home improvements unless part of the mortgage, television set, refrigerator, or a trip to the Samoan Islands. Also included is the debt owed on credit cards. It used to be fashionable to refer to consumer debt as installment debt, that is, to be paid off in equal monthly amounts or *installments*. With the advent of charge accounts and credit cards, installment debt is no longer the only type we might encounter.

The Growth of Consumer Credit

Widespread consumer borrowing is a relatively recent phenomenon. In the period from 1950 to 1970, total consumer indebtedness rose sixfold from 21 billion dollars to 126

TABLE 10-1

Consumer Credit

(millions of dollars)

| Year | Total | Installment | | Noninstallment Total |
		Total	Automotive	
1939	1,222	4,503	1,497	2,719
1945	5,665	2,462	455	3,203
1950	21,471	14,703	6,074	6,768
1955	38,830	28,906	13,460	9,924
1960	56,141	42,968	17,658	13,173
1965	90,314	71,324	28,619	18,990
1970	126,802	101,161	35,490	25,641

Source: *Federal Reserve Bulletin,* September 1972, p. A-56.

Note: Noninstallment debt includes single payment loans, charge accounts and service credit.

billion dollars and shows little sign of slowing down (see table 10-1). What factors account for this huge postwar increase in consumer borrowing?

continued decline of the extended family   In chapter 3 we discussed the impact of the decline of the extended family on the institutions that provide them substitute services. Although this was taking place throughout much of the twentieth century, the Second World War and the rapid economic growth that followed added greatly to this movement. Before increased industrialization and its need for mobility destroyed the extended family, the need for consumer credit was handled largely internally. If George needed a horse and couldn't afford it, it was very likely that his brother Fred would lend it to him at no interest. The separation of the extended family meant that the insular family was forced to seek commercial sources of credit.

growth in discretionary incomes   Consumer credit could only become big business when there were enough people who were able to borrow. The ability to borrow implies the ability to repay. Those who spend their entire incomes on necessities could not be expected to repay loans easily.

The economic boom following World War II found the majority of families, for the first time in history, with some discretionary income—that is, income left over after necessities are met. Consumers used this discretionary income to begin purchasing cars, appliances, and other "luxury" goods that had been unavailable for so long. This attracted lenders to compete for the privilege (and profits) of lending the consumer money.

changing attitudes toward consumer debt   From biblical times, lending money to consumers at interest has been at least frowned upon if not entirely prohibited. In earlier times this was understandable, since the consumer borrowed only when he absolutely had to—for example, to keep his family from starving.

Changing economic conditions which made borrowing desirable under some circumstances for reasons other than survival did not have an immediate impact upon the general views toward borrowing. Many people who might have benefited refused to do so, and others had to cope with feelings of severe guilt since, to most people, borrowing should only be done out of the most dire necessity. Even today, when almost everyone borrows some, most feel that consumer debt is a bad thing. Recent studies at the Survey Research Center reveal that only 36 percent of Americans feel that installment debt is okay.[1]

Furthermore, the anti-consumer lending or anti-usury sentiment often constrained lenders from making funds available. State legislatures are still considering usury laws that would greatly restrict the amount of lending. In other words, attitudes have not caught up to the reality of consumer debt.

Who Has Installment Debt?

Table 10-2 gives us a clearer picture of who has installment debt and how much they have. Families with very low incomes are not very likely to be included. This is not because they would not like to have such debt, but rather because no one wants to lend to them because they are considered poor risks. It is a sad but true axiom of credit lending that the only ones who can borrow easily are those who don't have to borrow at all.

Families with low incomes are considered poor risks for several reasons. First, as we saw in chapter 5, low income families must spend their entire incomes just to survive. It is very unlikely that a family earning $3,000 a year can put aside any money each month to repay debts.

Low income families also often have unstable incomes. The type of work available to those who lack skill or education is frequently temporary, seasonal, or susceptible to lay-offs. Through no fault of their own, these individuals are often out of work, which makes them even less likely to be able to meet their repayment obligations.

According to table 10-2, only 19 percent of families with incomes of less than $3,000 have installment debt. For families in the upper-middle class range ($10,000 to $14,999 income per year), this figure is 65 percent.

---

[1] Lewis Mandell, "Consumer Knowledge and Perception of Consumer Credit," Institute for Social Research, lithograph, 1971.

TABLE 10-2

Amount of Installment Debt Outstanding

(Percentage distribution of families)

Category	Have Debt	Amount of Debt				
		$1–199	$200 –499	$500 –999	$1,000 –1,999	$2,000 or more
All families	49	8	8	9	11	13
Annual family income						
Less than $3,000	19	10	5	1	2	1
$3,000–$4,999	31	9	7	5	5	5
$5,000–$7,499	52	10	10	12	11	9
$7,500–$9,999	61	9	9	13	15	15
$10,000–$14,000	65	9	10	10	17	19
$15,000 or more	49	4	6	8	11	20
Age of family head						
Younger than 25	59	5	10	10	13	21
25–34	67	9	10	11	15	22
35–44	63	10	12	14	14	13
45–54	56	11	8	10	13	14
55–64	36	7	7	7	8	7
65–74	14	8	3	*	2	1
75 or older	6	3	1	1	1	*

This may contradict the general notions that consumer debt is associated with lower incomes. Upper middle income families are better credit risks, and therefore can borrow more money.

Many families in the top income range are not as likely to borrow, although nearly half of them do. Obviously they don't have to, but it is interesting to note that when they do, they tend to borrow a lot. Twenty percent of high income families have at least $2,000 in debt outstanding.

Borrowing and the Family's Life Cycle

The ability to borrow is only one factor that explains whether or not a family will have any debt. The need or desire to borrow is another. Borrowing is related to the family's life cycle stage (which determines need) as well as to its income.

In chapter 5 we examined a family's needs and expenditures as related to life cycle. Young families see their expenditures increase as children come and as the need for more housing, furniture, appliances, cars, and many other goods increases. In chapter 4 we saw that when the family's

TABLE 10-2 (cont'd)

Amount of Installment Debt Outstanding

(Percentage distribution of families)

Category	Have Debt	Amount of Debt				
		$1–199	$200 –499	$500 –999	$1,000 –1,999	$2,000 or more
Life cycle stage of family head						
Younger than age 45						
Unmarried, no children	41	4	6	8	12	11
Married, no children	63	4	6	17	19	17
Married, youngest child under age 6	71	11	13	11	15	21
Married, youngest child age 6 or older	71	11	10	13	15	22
Age 45 or older						
Married, has children	57	11	7	10	13	16
Married, no children, head in labor force	43	7	6	9	11	10
Married, no children, head retired	15	6	4	*	2	3
Unmarried, no children, head in labor force	29	8	9	5	5	2
Unmarried, no children, head retired	14	10	1	1	2	*
Any age						
Unmarried, has children	53	9	15	11	9	9

* Less than 0.5 percent

Note: The term "no children" means no children younger than age 18 living at home. Unemployed people and housewives age 55 and older are considered retired; unemployed people and housewives younger than age 55 are considered to be in the labor force.

Source: Katona, G., Mandell, L. and Schmeideskamp, J., *1970 Surveys of Consumer Finances,* Ann Arbor: Institute for Social Reserarch, 1971, pp. 23–24.

needs are at their highest, income is not at its peak since the earners are still relatively young and inexperienced. This situation often creates a need for more funds, and a large proportion of these families consequently borrow.

In table 10–2 we can see that families headed by persons between 25 and 35 years of age are most likely to have consumer debt, and older families less likely. More significantly, younger families with children are most likely to be in debt: 71 percent are, a large proportion owing at least $1,000.

BENEFITS AND COSTS OF CONSUMER DEBT

While many people approach the issue of consumer debt in an emotional manner ("It's immoral" or "You can't live without it"), the sophisticated consumer approaches it as he does any other decision with an open mind, balancing the costs and benefits. Let's consider the benefits first.

The Benefits of Consumer Debt

The idea that many people have of consumer debt is expressed in those famous advertising inducements to "buy now and pay later" or "fly now and pay later." In other words, indulge yourself now in something that you can't afford and worry about paying for it some other time.

While this motivation is certainly prevalent in our society, it is not the only reason why someone would want to borrow. A consumer may be just as practical and hard-headed as a businessman when it comes to borrowing.

borrowing for measurable yield—the business decision   Unlike consumer debt, business debt is fully accepted in our modern society. Businesses borrow to increase earnings and profitability, and so there are clear-cut criteria: will the additional income from borrowing more than offset its cost?

How does this work? A baker may find that the demand for his bread is greater than he can deliver with his existing delivery trucks. If he buys another truck, which costs $4,000, he can increase sales and profits by $1,000 per year, even after the full costs of the new truck (as we measured in chapter 7) are paid.

Unfortunately the baker doesn't have $4,000 available at the moment. Should he borrow the money or wait until he can save it up?

Clearly, if his costs of borrowing it are less per year than the added income, he benefits. The truck is a *capital good* of the business: it is used to produce income. In economic terms, if a businessman finds that the *marginal efficiency of capital* (that is, the additional income produced by a capital good, expressed as a percentage of its cost) is greater than the interest he must pay on the loan, he should borrow. If the baker finds that the purchase of the $4,000 truck nets him an additional $1,000 per year after meeting all non-interest expenses of operating the truck, the marginal efficiency of capital would be 25 percent ($1,000 of $4,000). If the cost of borrowing the funds is less than 25 percent, it would pay him to borrow.

Many consumer loans are not as easy to decide, since the return is not completely measurable in dollars and cents. There are, however, instances where business logic can help the consumer decide.

Businesses have capital goods that yield income in some way, and households, we have seen, do too. One is the automobile. Lacking means of transportation, many people could not get to work at all and others would have to settle for lower paying jobs.

Take the example of a one-car family where the car is used by the husband to get to work. The wife, whose youngest child has just entered school, feels that she would like to go back to work and increase the family's income. She has been offered a job at $7,000 per year but needs an automobile to get the job. Should she buy it even if the family doesn't have the money?

It seems clear in this case that the additional income will more than offset the costs of the car, including a loan. Therefore, a hardheaded business decision to borrow the money could be made.

Other examples of consumer borrowing (considered in chapter 7) that may yield a real dollars and cents return might include loans for a washer and dryer which could save money spent in the laundromat, and perhaps other consumer durables.

the life cycle view of borrowing   Earlier in this chapter we saw that consumer borrowing bears a strong relation to the family's life cycle. Families with young children and big expenses are more likely to be in debt than older families. While the purchases may not yield a dollars and cents return, there may still be some economic justification for them.

As explained earlier, many young families find life expensive since they have certain nonrecurring expenses connected with family formation, such as the purchase of a house. They also find that income is lower than it will be in the future since the bread-winners are just beginning to advance in their positions. Income may also be temporarily depressed if the wife is out of the labor force for a few years.

A family in this situation may reasonably borrow against expected future gains to ease itself over the current tight situation. The costs of such borrowing may be more than overcome by the convenience to the family of having some of their future income used to to help alleviate their present needs.

An example of borrowing as related to life cycle is illustrated in figure 10-1. In this hypothetical case, two young people marry, continue to work, and even save a little money in spite of expenses connected with setting up a household.

With the birth of the first child, the wife quits her job, greatly reducing family income at a time when expenses have increased. At this stage, the family must decide whether or not they will borrow to maintain their standard of living; if not, their expenditures must drop with their income. However, since their future income appears to be robust, lenders will be willing to allow them to borrow for the "lean" earning years and repay the debt during the forthcoming "fat" years.

In this example, the family decides to borrow until the wife returns

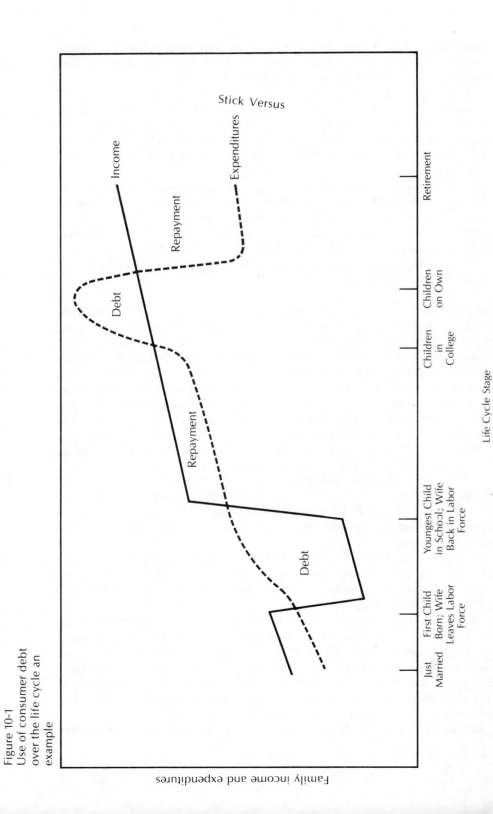

Figure 10-1
Use of consumer debt over the life cycle an example

Family income and expenditures

Life Cycle Stage

Just Married

First Child Born; Wife Leaves Labor Force

Youngest Child in School; Wife Back in Labor Force

Children in College

Children on Own

Retirement

Income

Expenditures

Repayment

Repayment

Debt

Debt

Stick Versus

to work, when they can afford to pay back at least part of the debt.

Unfortunately, expenditures go way up when the children reach college age. Here again, the family opts for debt, since it will be able to repay when the children graduate and are no longer a drain on the family income.

other reasons for borrowing   Aside from the pleasure of enjoying a good earlier than would be possible if the consumer had to save for it, and aside from loans made for true emergency reasons, there are other reasons for borrowing. The Survey Research Center[2] found that many people who borrowed to buy an automobile actually had enough money in savings accounts. Since the rate of interest charged on the automobile loan was far greater than the rate that they were getting on their bank deposit, this seemed illogical.

These consumers explained that if they paid cash for the automobile, their spending habits were such that they would never be able to build their bank accounts back up. In other words, they knew that they would spend their monthly income each month and not be able to save. By signing an installment note, they would be compelled to make the monthly payments and would be able to pay off the car without touching their savings. While this reasoning is obviously expensive to the consumers, they did understand their own motivations and were prepared to pay the cost necessary to preserve their valuable savings accounts. They were also preserving some "liquidity," an asset whose value will be explored further in chapter 12.

The Cost of Consumer Debt

The use of consumer debt may have more costs than most consumers realize.

interest   Interest on a loan—the most obvious cost of consumer borrowing—may be a good deal higher than most consumers realize, often more than twice what they think they are paying.[3] Later in the chapter, we will explain what interest is and exactly how much it costs—and it can be expensive!

insurance   Many lenders protect their money by requiring borrowers to take out special life insurance to cover the loan, often more expensive than other types. It is also true that commissions on this insurance can mean great additional profits for the lender.

---

[2] See George Katona, *The Mass Consumption Society,* (New York: McGraw-Hill, 1964), pp. 235ff.

[3] Lewis Mandell, "Consumer Perception of Incurred Interest Rates: An Empirical Test of the Efficacy of the Truth-in-Lending Law," *Journal of Finance,* Vol. XXVI, No. 5, 1971, pp. 1143–1154.

budget commitment   The consumer who must make payments on an installment debt each month has less flexibility in his budget, another cost of borrowing not measurable in dollars and cents. He has less money to cope with an emergency if it arises and may find himself borrowing even more and becoming more heavily committed.

risk of insolvency   Consumers who are heavily in debt may find that the next emergency is enough to sink them. Lenders who are not paid regularly become rather nasty and may even sue to repossess goods or to have the borrower's wages or salary garnisheed (that is, an amount is taken out by the employer each month for the creditor). In particularly acute difficulties, consumers may even be driven to declare personal bankruptcy, which relieves them of their debt obligation but also may take away almost all their possessions.

Studies at the Survey Research Center have found that the two greatest predictors of serious debt difficulty are a ratio of very high loan repayment to income (20 percent or more of take home), and very small liquid savings.[4] Families with 20% or better repayment ratios have inflexible budgets and can be pushed over the brink by an emergency, particularly if they don't have any liquid assets that can be used to get them by.

buying on impulse   Studies have shown that many consumers feel that borrowing makes it easy to buy goods they may not really need or want. This is particularly easy with the credit cards. The ability to spend "someone else's money" removes an important constraint and may make such expenditures appear less real and less costly by deferring the payments.[5]

paying more   Another disadvantage is that people who buy goods on installment sometimes end up paying a higher price than they would buying for cash. This is particularly true of poorer people who often find that without the installment plan they could not consume many goods at all. Caplovitz documents this in his well-known book entitled *The Poor Pay More*. A person with cash can shop around and look in many different stores and compare prices and features. A person who must buy on installment debt is often very limited in the places he can go in order to buy.

---

[4] George Katona, *et al., 1968 Survey of Consumer Finances.* (Ann Arbor: Institute for Social Research, 1969), p. 154.

[5] Lewis Mandell, *Credit Card Use in the United States.* (Ann Arbor: Institute for Social Research, 1972), p. 50.

UNDERSTANDING INTEREST

The first disadvantage of borrowing money is that no one is going to lend it to you for free with the possible exception of your mother. People lend money to make a profit from the interest you pay. Interest is the amount that you pay, over and above what you borrow, for the privilege of borrowing it. Many people feel that interest is unsignificant; they should realize a few facts. For example, a car bought at an interest rate of 15 percent for 36 months costs half again as much as the initial price by the time it is paid for. People who buy a house on a 25 year mortgage often pay back twice the amount that they borrowed by the time the loan is repaid.

What's In It for the Other Guy?

Lending the consumer money is big business in America. Banks do it, credit unions do it, finance companies do it, loan sharks do it, department stores do it, everybody, it seems, wants to help the consumer buy now and pay it off a little bit at a time. The first thing we ought to understand is that there aren't many "nice guys" in the world of consumer lending. Almost all the lenders—with the possible exception of the credit union—are out to make as much money as they can. Now how does the lender make money? Suppose that you have to borrow $100 until payday which is a month away. Your friend Al says, "I can loan you a hundred dollars," and you say to your friend Al, "Well, I'll tell you what. I'll take the hundred dollars until payday but since I'm using your money when you could be using it yourself, I'll give you $5.00." Well, that sounds okay to Al so you borrow the hundred dollars, and a month later you pay back $105 to Al. You have had the use of the money when you needed it and Al makes $5 for lending you his money. That $5 is interest you are paying. Now, let's suppose that Al says, "Gee, that was a pretty good deal. Maybe I ought to go into business and I could make a lot of money doing that." Well, Al is pretty limited because all he has is that hundred dollars so the most income he could make would be $5 a month which isn't really enough to keep a man in business. So, in order to lend out money, Al is forced to borrow it from somebody. Al knows a very rich fellow by the name of Jim, and he says to Jim, "Listen, how about lending me $10,000 so that I can lend it out to other people." Jim isn't going to give Al his $10,000 for nothing so he says, "Okay, I'll give you my $10,000 but every month you will have to pay me $250 in interest." Al thinks it over and says, "Well, $250 on $10,000 comes to $2.50 on a hundred dollars. That's what I would have to pay to Jim in order to borrow his money. However, I can turn around and lend my money and get $5 for a hundred so I can make a profit by using someone else's money."

This is basically the way any lending institution operates. A bank, for example, may give you an automobile loan at 15 percent per year. However, the bank must get its money from people who deposit with the bank. Well, people who deposit must be paid something for *their* money. In the case of a savings account, they may be paid 5 percent. In the case of a checking account, the banks do not pay interest to the depositor, but the services that they give in processing checks and keeping records is of value to the customer and substitutes for interest.

A financial institution, let us say a local bank, may get money from depositors at 5 percent and lend it to the borrowers at 15 percent. The difference between 15 and 5 percent represents profit for the bank. Is this all pure profit? The answer is no. Banks have *administrative expenses*—rent on buildings, salaries, and advertising. They also must bear *bad debt loss*—they may not get their money back on some loans. As we saw earlier, many people borrow more than they can repay. A bank that may make thousands of loans in a year should expect that a few will not be repaid. This can amount to a sizable expense. After subtracting for bad debt loss and the administrative costs of running the bank, the difference between the 5 percent the bank must pay for the money it lends and the 15 percent that it gets for lending is profit.

The consumer should notice that if a bank charges 15 percent for its automobile loans, the local finance company may be charging 25 percent. Why is this the case? Well, different consumers are different kinds of risk. As we said, one of the costs that a lender must cover is the amount of loss that he expects from consumers who borrow and do not repay. The probability of repayment often differs with characteristics of the consumer. For example, if you had $100 and two friends of yours, Irving and Robert, both asked to borrow the money for several months, how would you make a decision as to whom it would be safer to lend your money? Irving has a job paying $20,000 a year that he's had for a long time. He has a nice house that is mostly paid for and no other debt. Robert, on the other hand, works off and on, rents an apartment and owes $2,000 on a car, $300 on a color TV set, and $700 on a trip to California. If both of them offered you the same amount of interest, to which would you lend your money? The answer is obvious.

If both Irving and Robert came to a bank and wanted to borrow money, the bank would see Irving as being almost a riskless loan, whereas Robert would have a high probability of not being able to repay. If the bank charges 15 percent interest, it would likely loan to Irving and not to Robert.

Where can Robert now turn in order to get a loan? The answer is to a high-priced lender such as a finance company, which charges a much higher rate of interest in turn for issuing a loan to a high risk.

There are many types of lending institutions that tend to specialize in certain types of people. Low cost lenders such as the banks and credit unions lend money largely to people with secure jobs and little debt. On the other hand, high-priced lenders such as finance companies tend to lend to people who are somewhat more likely to default.

The Annual Percent Rate of Interest

Frank has been shopping around for an automobile for a long time and finally comes up with a car that he wants. It has all the features, and it is a good price—$3,000. Frank doesn't have $3,000, so he must borrow at least part of the price of the car. The dealer offers him what he says is a good deal—all Frank has to do is pay $500 down and then just $125 a month for 24 months. But Frank has heard in several places that the dealer very often charges a higher interest rate than banks, so he decides before accepting the dealer's deal to go visit a couple. The first one says that if he can put $1,000 down on a $3,000 automobile he can pay off the balance at a rate of only $100 a month for 30 months. Another bank says that he doesn't have to put so much money down— only $100—and then pay off the loan at the rate of $140 per month for 36 months. Which is the best deal for Frank? *Given only this information,* it is very difficult to tell. Loans vary by amount of down payment, amount of monthly payment and total number of payments. It is very seldom that you will find two loans that are exactly alike. In order to tell which loan is the best deal, a uniform manner has been developed for calculating a loan's cost. This uniform manner is known as the *annual percent rate of interest.* The annual percent rate of interest tells you what proportion of the money that you have outstanding on a loan in the course of a year must be paid to the lender as interest. The annual percent rate offers the borrower a chance to compare loans in a uniform manner. This is very similar to the batting averages used in professional baseball to evaluate the hitting ability of various players. For example, if player A has been at bat 185 times and has gotten 60 hits, is he a better baseball player than player B who has only been at bat 100 times and has gotten 33 hits? The answer is no. The first player bats just about 300 while the second player bats approximately 333. The batting average is expressed as a percentage or as a proportion of a perfect average. Similarly, the annual percent rate helps the borrower compare loans differing in terms of down payment, monthly payments, and amounts.

To gain an approach to the tricky problem of annual percent rate of interest, consider the following question:

Suppose you needed $1,000 to buy a car, and you found a bank which said that you could borrow $1,000 and repay the loan over a year's time in equal monthly installments. Their interest charge for this loan would be $60. What percent rate would you be paying?

Many people will see that as an easy problem. Sixty dollars interest on a $1,000 loan is 60/1000 or 6 percent, right?

Wrong. The actual interest charge is closer to 12 percent. Why is this so?

Installment loans generally call for repayment in a series of equal monthly payments (which also include interest). Each payment you make reduces the amount that you are borrowing from the bank. Therefore, the $60 that you pay in interest does *not* allow you to borrow $1,000 for the full year. Since you pay about 1/12 of that back each month, you only have use of the $1,000 for one month: when you make your first payment, you only have about 11/12 of the $1,000, and at the end of 6 months you only have about half of that amount. At the end of 11 months, you have only 1/12 of the original $1,000 left.

If the bank had given you $1,000 on September 15 of one year, and you returned the $1,000 in one payment on September 15 of the following year, with an additional $60 in interest, you would be paying 6 percent interest.

But if you are forced to repay the principal as an *installment loan* over the course of the year, *on the average* you have the use of only about half of the $1,000 for the full year. If you pay $60 on about $500, your annual percent rate of interest is closer to 12 percent than to 6 percent.

Without going into tedious numerical examples, we can summarize the interest rate paradox as follows: when you borrow money and pay it back in monthly installments during the year, you get the use of the full amount borrowed for only a short time and, averaging through the months, get the use of only about half the amount borrowed for the entire year. Therefore, to convert from dollars of interest per $100 borrowed per year to annual percent rate, multiply the dollars of interest by 2, and you will not be far off.

Truth-in-Lending Law

Repeated studies find that few consumers can convert from dollars per year to percent rate of interest, so the Federal Government decided to help by passing the Truth-in-Lending Law which requires lenders to tell prospective borrowers the interest they are paying both in terms of annual percent rate and dollar amount. As we mentioned before, knowledge of the annual percent rate is critical when shopping for loans. Not only does it enable the buyer to choose the lowest cost loan when loans differ in terms of amount borrowed, number of payments, and monthly payment, but it also gives the buyer a sense of perspective. In survey after survey, a large proportion of the population says that 6 percent is the rate that they must pay on a loan.

Although the law itself was well motivated, data collected before and since it was implemented have not shown an improvement in the public's understanding of interest rates. There are two possible causes for this memory lapse:

First, the Survey Research Center has found after years of studies that to most borrowers, the sole important criterion in selecting a loan is the size of the monthly payment.[6] If a repayment schedule can be accommodated within a consumer's monthly budget, the consumer is all too likely to look no further. To cater to this, automobile loans have been expanded from two to three years and are now being expanded to four years. Stretching out the loan lowers the monthly payments, which the consumer likes, but greatly increases the amount of interest payable over the life of the loan, which the consumer is not aware of.

A second, not unrelated, cause of ignorance of prevailing interest rates results from the lack of understanding of what an interest rate is and what it does or can do. Many consumers assume that all rates are the same; others feel that if they know the dollar amount they need not know the annual interest rate. Until consumers are made aware of the reasons they should *want* to know the annual percent rate of interest, they will not be motivated to care enough about the rate to remember it.

Components of the Interest Rate

Institutions which lend money (banks, credit unions, finance companies) charge a rate of interest which must cover certain expenses which may include:

cost of money The money that the bank or credit union lends to you largely comes from their depositors, both consumers and businesses. The role of the bank is that of a financial *intermediary*—taking the money depositors have available and lending it to those who want to use it.

Part of the bank's cost is what they must pay their depositors. If the interest rate is 5 percent, one might take that to be the bank's cost of money. Yet this is not quite correct. When the bank lends money to Joe Jones to buy his new car at 12 percent, the true cost of money for that loan is the interest that the bank *could have* realized by lending its money to a *riskless* borrower. This is the *opportunity cost* of the loan and the concept is similar to the opportunity costs we discussed in earlier chapters when we considered the loss of the family's income when the wife did not work and the loss of bank interest resulting from investment of savings in a consumer durable.

Practically speaking, if the bank hadn't loaned its money to Joe Jones

---

[6] George Katona, *op cit.,* p. 240.

at 12 percent, it could have bought government securities (short-term Treasury bills or notes) which are riskless. Joe Jones may not pay off his loan, but the government will. If Treasury bills are paying 7 percent interest, *that* is the true cost of money (the base rate) to the bank.

Another type of riskless loan is one made to a big corporation. Since it is secured by billions of dollars in assets, it is considered nearly impossible that a bank will lose money on it. The interest rate charged to such large companies is known as the *prime rate* and is pretty much the same for banks all over the country. Since this prime rate is for the most risk-free borrowers, it sets the floor for other loans with greater risks. If the prime rate is 7 percent, the biggest companies in the country such as A.T.&T., IBM, U.S. Steel and Xerox can borrow at this rate. Smaller companies in sound financial condition can usually borrow at a slightly higher rate. Consumers in good financial shape pay somewhat more than this, and consumers in not such good financial shape pay a good deal more, if they can borrow at all.

risk of loss   As we have just seen, borrowers pay different rates of interest based on their degree of risk. Generally speaking, the best consumer loans cost a few percentage points more than the prime rate. Even the most reliable consumer has the potential for loss. He may lose his job, or someone in the family may be stricken by an incapacitating and expensive illness during the time that the loan is outstanding.

Every lending institution encounters a certain proportion of bad debts in the course of a year. In order to insure that they are compensated for any losses resulting from failure to repay, the institution will charge an extra amount (above the low-risk prime rate) to build up a pool to cover losses. If a bank finds that over a year it loses 3 percent of the money it has loaned to a certain class of borrowers, it will, in the future, charge at least 3 percentage points more to that type of borrower than to a prime rate borrower. Over time, the bank becomes capable of evaluating the expected loss rate from any type of borrower and adjusts the cost of the loan accordingly.

Criteria used to establish the credit-worthiness of the consumer (which, in turn, establishes the rate he must pay) include the size of the income, the stability of that income (length of time the consumer has held his job), the size of the monthly payments he must already pay (for housing and other loans), the assets that he owns which could be used to repay the loans, and perhaps most importantly his loan history. If he has failed to repay debts in the past or has been late in paying, this information is almost invariably recorded on his credit record and will be uncovered during the credit check which preceeds the loan.[7]

---

[7] Under the recent Fair Credit Reporting Act, consumers who are turned down for credit can examine their files to see whether incorrect information exists and can force such information to be corrected.

The best credit risk is a consumer with a large and steady income who has always repaid loans promptly, who owns his own house, who has no debts outstanding save a mortgage, and who owns other attachable assets (bank accounts, securities, land). Such a consumer can probably come up with a loan at a rate just a few percentage points above the prime rate. Others who do not measure up to this ideal will generally have to pay higher rates.

administrative costs As we have seen, a bank or any other financial institution has certain administrative costs that must be covered by the (interest) charges. Such costs include employee salaries, cost of operating the premises (rent, electricity), advertising, and so on. Aside from these relatively *fixed* costs, there are other administrative costs that vary with the type of loan. Another reason for the low interest charge made to *prime borrowers* (the prime rate) is that they generally borrow very large sums and *economies of scale* come into play to save the bank money.

It takes the same (or less) time for a bank officer to lend $1,000,000 to General Motors as it does to lend $2,000 to Joe Jones to buy his car. Therefore, *per dollar lent,* it takes much less time and effort to lend to G.M. than to individuals. Since time is money, consumer loans cost more to administer and must be charged accordingly. In addition, they often involve more record keeping over the course of the loan, as monthly payments are billed and recorded.

profit Most financial institutions are in business for profit. These include banks, finance companies, and stores that offer their own customer credit. Other institutions, notably credit unions, do not make a profit.

The goal of profit-making institutions is, naturally enough, to earn a profit for its owners (or stockholders). The interest rates must be high enough to cover more than expenses. So consumers who are eligible to borrow from a nonprofit lender often find their rates somewhat lower.

THE STRUCTURE OF THE CONSUMER CREDIT MARKET

Borrowers differ in the kinds of loans they need and in ability to repay, so it is not surprising to find specialization among financial institutions.

Banks

The term *bank,* although used by the public to represent many financial institutions, refers technically to *commercial banks* which offer checking accounts to their customers. Until recently (the past two decades), banks loaned primarily to businesses. With the rapid growth of consumer credit following World War II, they became more oriented to the individual in order to reap some of the big profits.

Credit Unions

Credit unions are nonprofit institutions that accept deposits from and lend to members who are generally grouped by the employer, church, or social organization. Since groups are often closely linked in terms of economic status and background or, as employees of a cooperating organization, can have loan repayments deducted from their paychecks, the risk of severe loss is generally lower than it would be for other consumers. Combining this factor with their nonprofit status makes credit unions among the most economical of lenders.

Finance Companies

Many consumers find that they cannot borrow from low-cost financial institutions. Finance companies specialize in serving these higher risk consumers, and naturally charge higher rates for their service to cover greater expected loss and higher collection costs of the loans. Because of this they have come under attack for *usurious* practices. In some instances, usury laws have been passed that set a low maximum rate that they can charge.

While many consumers and consumer groups feel that such laws are in their interest (why pay 15 percent for a loan when we can pass a law which gets it for us at 6 percent?), most economists and a good deal of history show that this is not necessarily so. All lending institutions have costs which must be covered, and if the ceiling rate on interest does not allow for the coverage of these costs, loans will not be made. In instances where states have passed low interest rate ceilings, poor risk consumers (often members of minority groups) were denied legitimate loans and forced into the hands of loan sharks at much higher rates.[8] If the 20 percent rate charged by the finance company seems high, it is much lower than the 200-plus percent rate charged by some loan sharks.

Credit Cards and Revolving Credit

In recent years, the "closed-end" type of installment credit that we have been discussing has been replaced to a growing extent by "open-ended" or revolving credit. Closed-ended loans are the traditional installment loans which have a fixed amount, a fixed time period, and a fixed monthly payment, all of which are agreed upon when the loan is made. Virtually all automobile loans today are still closed-ended loans.

Open ended or revolving credit loans have no fixed time, amount, or

[8] This statement was made by Paul Samuelson, "Statement before the Committee of the Judiciary of the General Court of Massachusetts in Support of the Uniform Consumer Credit Code, January 29, 1969," unpublished.

monthly payment. They are flexible arrangements the lender has with the borrower to allow him to borrow when and how much he wishes (within certain established limits depending on his credit rating) and to repay the loan on pretty much his own terms. Such arrangements are most convenient for the consumer who need not apply for credit each time he wishes to borrow money. Furthermore, since he can control the size of the monthly payment (above some minimum proportion of the outstanding balance), he has greater budget flexibility than with the traditional closed-ended installment loan.

credit cards A customer entitled to use a revolving credit plan is, with some exceptions, given a *credit card* to identify him as a participant in the plan and which is used to expedite purchases.

Half of all American families use at least one credit card (table 10-3). Higher income families are the most frequent users because of their higher level of spending as well as their superior ability to be granted a card (they are generally more credit worthy than lower income families). Other frequent users include families in early life cycle stages who are also large spenders and often require revolving credit.

There are several different types of institutions that issue credit cards.

stores The most widely used cards are those of retail stores—either the large national chains such as Sears, Penneys, and Wards, or local stores and chains. More than a third of all families use a store credit card.

bank About 28 percent of families use bank credit cards. At one time there were dozens of such cards, but now two large bank card plans dominate the market. Bank card users can not only charge goods in thousands of retail establishments (and rent cars, buy plane tickets, and so forth), but they can also obtain an immediate cash loan which is charged through their card to their revolving account.

travel and entertainment Among the best-known travel and entertainment cards are American Express, Diners Club, and Carte Blanche. These cards cost $15 to $20 a year, while the others are generally free.

Finance Charges on Revolving Credit

Since the amount owed on credit cards and revolving credit plans may vary from month to month, interest is calculated on a monthly basis. Generally, the revolving credit rate is 1½ percent per month on the unpaid balance. This works out to 18 percent per year, making it considerably higher than that charged for ordinary installment credit. For this reason,

TABLE 10-3

Use of Credit Cards Within Specific Groups

(percentage distribution of families)

Category	Use Credit Cards	Don't Use Credit Cards[a]	Total	Number of Families[b]
All families	50	50	100	2576
Annual family income				
Less than $3,000	17	83	100	353
$3,000–$4,999	24	76	100	304
$5,000–$7,499	39	61	100	404
$7,500–$9,999	54	46	100	412
$10,000–$14,999	67	33	100	631
$15,000–$19,999	74	26	100	277
$20,000–$24,999	84	16	100	94
$25,000 and over	81	19	100	101
Age of head				
Under 25	42	58	100	257
25–34	61	39	100	471
35–44	57	43	100	488
45–54	60	40	100	514
55–64	46	54	100	426
65 and over	31	69	100	420
Life cycle stage of family head				
Under age 45				
Unmarried, no children	39	61	100	183
Married, no children	64	36	100	169
Married, youngest child under age 6	60	40	100	496
Married, youngest child age 6 or older	65	35	100	261
Age 45 or older				
Married, has children	58	42	100	324
Married, no children, head in labor force	58	42	100	380
Married, no children, head retired	35	65	100	246
Unmarried, no children, head in labor force	46	54	100	150
Unmarried, no children, head retired	23	77	100	197
Any age				
Unmarried, has children	27	73	100	170

TABLE 10-3 (cont'd)

Use of Credit Cards Within Specific Groups

(percentage distribution of families)

Category	Use Credit Cards	Don't Use Credit Cards[a]	Total	Number of Families[b]
Education of head				
0–5 grades	15	85	100	136
6–8 grades	28	72	100	460
9–11 grades	40	60	100	449
12 grades	54	46	100	483
12 grades plus other non-college training	66	34	100	273
College, no degree	60	40	100	412
College, degree	81	19	100	209
College, advanced degree	83	17	100	138
Occupation				
Professional, technical and kindred workers	80	20	100	303
Managers, officials	72	28	100	179
Self-employed businessmen	53	47	100	99
Clerical-salesworker	67	33	100	287
Craftsmen, foremen	57	43	100	373
Operatives	42	58	100	360
Laborers and service	36	64	100	252
Farmers and farm managers	35	65	100	61
Housewives under 55, students, armed forces	37	63	100	193
Retired; housewives over 55, permanently disabled	29	71	100	469

[a] Credit card use includes the use of any of the following types of credit cards: gasoline cards, bank cards, travel and entertainment cards and cards good at specific stores.

[b] Excludes 16 families for whom education of head is not ascertained.

Source: Lewis Mandell, *Credit Card Use in the United States.*

it is worthwhile for the consumer to consider other, lower-cost lenders, particularly if he must borrow large amounts or for long periods of time.

One reason for the higher cost of using credit cards is that the cost of administering the system is high. Each time a shopper makes a purchase on his credit card, slips must be filled out and transmitted, accounts must be updated, and customer statements grow longer. Adding this to the usual cost of money, administration, and risk of loss substantially increases the lender's expenses, which he must pass on to the customer (or lose money).

Most credit card companies do not charge interest on balances paid within a certain period of time, and this increases their costs. Since half of all cardholders always pay their charges on time,[9] the burden of their credit card expense falls on those who don't.

In addition to finance charges, several credit-card operations, including banks and travel and entertainment plans, also derive revenues from merchants who accept credit cards. Stores and restaurants generally pay between 2 and 6 percent of credit-card purchases to the issuing companies for the privilege of extending this service to their customers. Some critics feel that since those who use credit cards and those who don't are generally charged the same price, there is discrimination in favor of the card holder: he is getting an extra, expensive service for free. In addition, they argue, stores and restaurants may be forced to raise their prices to cover the cost of the credit card discounts, thereby increasing costs to everyone—card users and nonusers alike. Recently, some credit card companies have begun to allow merchants who accept their cards to give cash discounts to customers who do not use credit cards for payment.

SUMMARY

1. Cost-benefit analysis can also be successfully used with *consumer debt,* which is borrowing for nonbusiness purposes such as the purchase of a car and vacation expenses. Consumer debt also includes what one owes on credit-card accounts.

2. This kind of debt is of recent origin and naturally became big business only when people had *discretionary income*—that is, reasonable levels of income and the ability to repay loans.

3. Since the amount of borrowing depends not only on one's ability to borrow but also on the need for extra money, a family's borrowing is closely related to its life-cycle stage.

4. Business loans depend mostly on the marginal efficiency of capital. While the benefits from a consumer loan cannot be completely measured in the same terms, a knowledge of the benefits and costs involved can be of great help to the consumer.

5. The most important cost of borrowing money is the amount of interest one pays, and it is crucial that consumers be aware of the explicit as well as the implicit costs involved. The concept of *annual percent rate of interest,* which allows one to compare loans, is of great help.

---

[9] Lewis Mandell, *Credit Card Use in the United States, op cit.,* p. 77.

6. The enactment of the truth-in-lending law by the Federal government, which requires that borrowers be told of the real costs of loans, is one method that helps the consumer learn about the annual rate of interest. In spite of this, however, it has been found that most consumers are concerned only with the size of the monthly payment.

7. Banks, credit unions, and finance companies all deal in consumer debt. The use of credit cards, which is an open-ended or revolving kind of loan, is of recent origin and involves much higher annual percent rates of interest than apply to installment buying.

QUESTIONS

1. Why do you think consumer debt became more important in recent times in this country?

2. Is consumer debt good or bad in itself? Give reasons.

3. Borrowing for business purposes depends on the marginal efficiency of capital. This might not be true in the case of consumer loans. Why not?

4. When the prime rate is 9%, will the interest rate on consumer loans be higher or lower? Why?

TERMINOLOGY

consumer debt
marginal efficiency of capital
annual percent rate of interest
truth-in-lending law
financial intermediaries
prime rate
credit unions
revolving credit

SELECTED REFERENCES AND SOURCES OF DATA

Caplovitz, David. *The Poor Pay More.* (New York: The Free Press, 1967).

Chapman, John M. and Robert P. Shay. *Licenced Lending in New York.* (New York: Columbia University Press, 1970). (A discussion of how legal rate ceilings and other restrictions have resulted in a denial of loans to many people.)

C.V.N.A. International, Inc. *Credit Unions—What Are They? How They Operate. How to Start One.* (Madison, Wisconsin: Box 431, Public Relations Department).

Katona, George. *The Mass Consumption Society.* (New York: McGraw-Hill, 1964).

Katona, George, *et. al. 1968 Survey of Consumer Finances,* (Ann Arbor: Institute for Social Research, 1969).

Katona, George, L. Mandell, J. Schmeideskamp. *1970 Surveys of Consumers.* (Ann Arbor: Institute for Social Research, 1970).

Mandell, Lewis. "Consumer Perception of Incurred Interest Rates: An Empirical Test of the Efficacy of the Truth-in Lending Law," *Journal of Finance,* Vol. XXVI, No. 5, 1971.

Mandell, Lewis. "Consumer Knowledge and Understanding of Consumer Credit," Journal of Consumer Affairs (Summer 1973).

Mandell, Lewis, ed. *Surveys of Consumers 1971/72.* (Ann Arbor: Institute for Social Research, 1972).

Mandell, Lewis. *Credit Card Use in the United States.* (Ann Arbor: Institute for Social Research, 1972).

National Consumer Finance Association. *Finance Facts Year Book.* (Washington, D.C.) (A valuable source of statistics and a fact book about consumer financial behavior and the consumer finance business.)

11

INSURANCE

The purpose of insurance is to protect the consumer against the unexpected. Unfortunately, this point is not well understood by many consumers who end up paying for much more when protection is all they really want—or want to pay for.

What the consumer wants to protect himself against is serious, unforseeable, financial loss. Here are some examples.

Premature Death

The death of a family breadwinner will cause a serious financial loss to the family. *Life insurance* protects against this loss.

Incapacitating Illness or Accident

With the current cost of medicine, a hospital stay of only a few weeks can wipe out the accumulated savings of a family that does not have *medical insurance*.

Unemployment

The loss of a job and its income may come on unexpectedly and through no fault of the jobholder. To protect against this, states have *unemployment insurance* which protects most workers against total loss of income during unemployment.

Outliving the Ability to Generate Income

People who are too old to work do not know exactly how many years they have left to live. Thus it is difficult to save for your old age since you don't know how long it is going to last. Insurance plans to provide for latter years include the federal *social security* program as well as private annuity, and pension plans.

Property Loss and Liability

A consumer's property may be lost, stolen, burned, flooded, or otherwise damaged. To protect against these occurrences, one can purchase fire, theft, and other types of *property insurance.*

A consumer may also damage the property of others, for which he is responsible. He may demolish someone's car with his car, or his dog may lacerate the leg of the neighbor or the postman. If the consumer is uninsured, the victim's loss must be paid from his assets. *Liability insurance,* however, can protect him against such a loss.

THE PRINCIPLE OF INSURANCE

Any consumer has a small but positive chance of incurring an unexpected loss during the course of a year. Let's suppose that the chances that you will total your car (worth $2,000) in the next year are one in twenty. The odds that you will are small, but if you do, you could be out a lot of money and be without a car for some time.

Now suppose that you had nineteen friends like yourself who have cars worth $2,000 and who have a one in twenty chance of wrecking their cars in the coming year. Since all twenty of you have the same odds, it is likely that one of you will, but of course no one knows which it will be.[1] The one person who does meet with the accident is out a lot of money, but the other nineteen people get off scot-free.

Now suppose that no one in your group wants to take the risk of losing $2,000 in an accident. All of you might get together and put $100 each in the kitty (a total of $2,000), and the one who has the accident will use the $2,000 to replace his car. In this manner, you are spending $100 per year to guarantee that you will not lose $2,000.

This is the principle of insurance. *You trade a small, certain loss* (the premium—in this case $100 per year) *for a much larger, uncertain loss* (the $2,000 to replace the car).

---

[1] Technically, in a group this small it is not unlikely that, in any given year, two people or no people will wreck their cars. However, losses over a number of years will *average* one car per year.

Our example using only twenty people was not realistic, since the group was too small to predict accurately the number of accidents in one year. With a larger and larger group, the accuracy can be predicted better and better. This is based on a rather complicated statistical concept popularly known as the *law of large numbers*. By studying accident rates in past years, insurance company statisticians known as *actuaries* can predict with great accuracy the number of accidents that will occur to a large group of people in the future. They can also estimate the total losses to the insured and use that figure to calculate *premiums* or annual payments for all policy holders. Premiums include not only these losses but the operating expenses of the company as well.

The Need for Third Party Insurance

The decline of the extended family and the increasing monetization of the economy are two of the most important reasons for the growth of the insurance industry.

decline of the extended family   One of the most important benefits of an extended family is what we have called insurance function. If a member became seriously ill, he was cared for by other family members who would likely undertake to share his economic function until he recovered. If a breadwinner died, the spouse and children would be provided for, thereby obviating the need for large amounts of life insurance. Old people didn't need social security or other insurance since their children generally cared for them when they could no longer work.

Using industry terms, we can say that the extended family was large enough to *self insure*. Today, very large companies such as IBM and A.T.&T. are able to self-insure, since they are large enough to cover the costs of employee accidents and other misfortunes without having to pay the costs of outside insurance.

While the extended family could also do this, the isolated core family of today is no longer able to.

If Fred Brown loses his job, the family is in real trouble since no member can be counted on to come up with the money they need to get along. When the Browns' house burns down, they can not count on all the Browns in town getting together one Saturday morning to raise a new roof.

The core family is just too small to self-insure. All their eggs are in one basket, and when the heavy foot of fate stamps down on that basket, there are no more eggs. Therefore, insurance companies, which in a sense *create* an extended family, serve an important function. Now, however, the insured consumer does not pool his resources with other family members. Rather, the insurance company pools his resources with complete strangers, but the outcome is the same.

AN EXTENDED FAMILY

the monetization of the economy   In our modern industrialized, specialized economy, one must pay for just about everything he gets. This means that money, and lots of it, is about the only effective cure for misfortune.

In other words, in today's society, services that would have been exchanged 100 years ago must now be bought. As we have been forced to specialize our skills, we have lost the ability to provide other needed services and must buy them on the marketplace with cash. Today's physician must call a carpenter to fix his stairs, just as the carpenter calls the physician to treat an injury.

If you can not have an extended family to see you through emergencies, cash is the next best thing. Thus, we have the great growth and success of the insurance companies.

HOW INSURANCE COMPANIES WORK

Earlier in this chapter we gave a simple illustration of twenty friends getting together to insure each other against a $2,000 automobile loss by each contributing $100 per year. Let's return to this group and observe their behavior.

At an early meeting, they elected Barbara to be treasurer. She now has $2,000 in her possession for safekeeping. What will she do with it? She could rent and furnish offices for the new company or use it for an excursion to Puerto Rico for all members. However, she realizes that the $2,000 is not company income but the *reserve* that must be used to compensate a member for an accident. Consequently, she must have that money available at all times.

Should she stuff it in her mattress or put it in a safe deposit vault or checking account? Although the last two are safe, they are unprofitable since Barbara would earn nothing on the money. Instead, she could put it in a savings account and earn 5 percent interest on it. This is what she does.

During the first year of operating, the club is very lucky—no one has had an accident; so it ends the year with $2,100 in its bank account (since 5 percent interest on $2,000 is $100). At the year-end meeting, one member suggests that no premiums be paid for the second year since the club has more than $2,000 in reserves. Another goes even further and suggests dividing up the earned interest as a *dividend* for the members.

Barbara speaks up. "You know, we were very fortunate that no one had an accident this year. It would have wiped us out. If a second member also had had an accident, there would have been no funds to compensate him. We should have started this thing with enough reserves to keep going even if several of us had accidents. But since we lucked out this year, I propose that we pay the same premium next year, or even a little more to build up our reserves."

They agreed to increase annual premiums to $125 with the understanding that when reserves were at a safe level, premiums would revert to $100 or even less since their funds were earning. The following year there was an accident, but the reserves were in good shape to handle it.

Within five years, the insurance association had grown to 100 members, and reserves were at a level that Barbara considered high enough to meet even the worst conceivable rash of accidents. At the annual meeting, she arose to say the following: "I am proud to have been with this insurance association since its inception six years ago. During that time the membership has increased five-fold and the reserves have gone from zero to $25,000. However, the burdens of managing finances have become too great to do in my spare time. Not only must I look after the reserves, making sure that they earn the highest possible safe returns, but I have to send out premium notices to members and even investigate accidents to insure proper payment to our insured. Consequently, I must ask that someone else assume my position."

As might be expected, no qualified persons came forward to take over. So after some debate, the club voted unanimously to offer to pay Barbara for her services. This raised premiums somewhat, but everyone felt it was worth it. In ensuing years, the expansion of membership made it necessary for Barbara to work full time for the insurance company, and gradually other paid employees were added.

Types of Companies

Barbara's company was owned and controlled by the insurance holders or *beneficiaries* who shared in the interest earned on reserves through dividends or reduction in premiums. This type of company is known as a *mutual* insurance company, and many of the biggest companies today are mutual companies.

A second type of insurance company is known as a *stock* company since it is owned and controlled by stockholders who put up the initial capital. In Barbara's company, each initial member might have begun by putting up $1,000, thereby establishing sufficient reserves for a much larger company, and selling insurance to other people who would neither own nor control the company. Any profits made by the company would be shared by the twenty initial stockholders and not necessarily by the company beneficiaries.

In reality, it is difficult for a beneficiary to see much difference in terms of cost, service, or control between stock and mutual insurance companies. Both are very large and impersonal, controlled by a small

group of top company officials, and generally to some extent by the states in which they are located so that the reserves are protected against loss.

Life Insurance

The concept of life insurance differs somewhat from other types. When you take out fire insurance on your home, you are insuring that you will be able to purchase a similar home in the event that it burns down. You are essentially protecting your family's home from loss by fire.

But what does life insurance protect? Certainly not your life—no amount of insurance is sufficient to resurrect the dead. What you are protecting is your earnings—your value as an income producer to your family.

how much are you worth? How much of a loss would your death represent to your family? First, how much do you earn each year? Let's say $10,000, after taxes. Would that represent your economic value to your family? No. You have certain expenses that must be taken care of when you are alive. You eat—that costs money; you spend money to get to work, to relax, to clothe yourself. Let's assume that you cost $4,000 to keep going; if you die, the net loss to your family will be $10,000 less $4,000, or $6,000. (To simplify matters, we will assume that these amounts do not change over the person's lifetime, either by salary increases or inflation.)

Therefore, how much will your family lose altogether with your demise? In order to calculate this, we must convert from a *flow* term ($6,000 *per year*) to a *stock* of dollars (a lump sum). Obviously, your total value to your family also depends on the number of working years you have left. If you are 69 years old and plan to retire in one year, your early death would cost your family one year's net income of $6,000.

But how about if you are 30 years old and have another 40 working years ahead of you? Your family's loss would be $6,000 times 40 years, or $240,000. Right? Wrong. The present loss to your family would be less than that, much less. Why is this so?

In order to guarantee your family $6,000 per year for the next 40 years, you don't have to have $240,000 in insurance (and savings). You actually need less than $100,000.

In chapter 4 we introduced the concept of *present discounted value* which enables us to convert a stream of future payments to a lump sum of money today. Table 4-3 shows us that at an interest rate of 6 percent, the present discounted value of $1.00 per year for 40 years is $15.05. Consequently, the present discounted value of $6,000 per year for 40 years is $90,300. This means that if you died today and left $90,300 in life insurance to your family, and they invested it at 6 percent, it would yield $6,000 per year for 40 years before it ran out.

Yet even this sum may overstate the true loss to the family since social security may provide substantial payments to a widow and minor children.[2] So an even smaller amount of insurance may be sufficient to protect your family against the loss of your income.

how much insurance?   The cost to a person of insuring the full present discounted value of his stream of future income, even if it is net of his expenses and anticipated social security payments to his family, may be very high. A man at age 30 earning a net of $1,000 per month would have an income with a present discounted value in excess of $180,000. Yet the cost of insuring himself for that amount, at the very low price of $5 per $1,000 per year[3] would be $900 a year, or 7.5 percent of his take-home pay!

In this context, insurance can be viewed as another item competing for the consumer's dollar, just like a new home, a steak, or a snowmobile. The expenditure of one's income on insurance yields a certain amount of utility—in the feeling that one's family will be financially secure in the event of the breadwinner's demise. Yet other possible uses of the same funds on less morbid items also yield utility. The extent of insurance coverage is a difficult decision for consumers to make—one for which there are no pat formulas or easy answers.

It is worthwhile to note that since the purpose of life insurance is to insure the continuity of an income flow, the sex of the earner is irrelevant. Families headed by females have as much need for protection of income as do those headed by males. And families with two earners should logically insure each in some proportion to expected lifetime earnings.

Straight Life Versus Term Insurance

Although every life insurance company offers a whole grab bag of policies with varying conversion plans, annuities, and bells and whistles which are beyond the scope of this book, it is worthwhile to examine the most basic distinction between life insurance policies—straight life versus term insurance.

term insurance   Term insurance is pure insurance. It insures a person's life for a fixed number of years at a certain price. If the insured person dies during that period, his beneficiaries receive the full amount

---

[2] Social Security tends to be far more generous as a life or disability insurance than it is as an old-age insurance. A widowed mother with two children may be eligible (in 1974) for payments of $707.90 a month, which is nearly $8,000 a year.

[3] Consumers Union, "A Guide to Life Insurance: Part I. Five-Year Term Insurance," *Consumer Reports,* January 1974, pp. 43, 54.

of the policy. If he doesn't die, he doesn't get any of the money that he paid into the policy. The premium for a policy with a certain face value increases as the insured person gets older, since it is more likely that he will die within a given period of time.

It is important that term insurance be *renewable,* which means that at the end of a term of, say, five years, the insured person can renew his policy for additional terms (at a higher price, since he is older).

straight life insurance   Straight life insurance, which is often called *ordinary, whole,* or *cash value* life insurance, provides more than just life insurance. It adds a plan of forced savings.

While term insurance is written for a specified numer of years and increases in price with each renewal, straight life is generally written for the entire life of the insured person during which he usually pays the same premium until he dies or until the policy is paid up. It also guarantees payment of the full value of the policy at some point (provided that premiums are paid), while term insurance pays off only if the insured dies during the term of the insurance. Another important feature of straight life insurance is the (slow) buildup of a *cash value* which the insured person can borrow on at relatively low rates.

With all of these advantages of straight life, you might ask, "Why does anyone buy term insurance?" Well, for one thing, straight life insurance costs a great deal more for young people. This is because term insurance is pure insurance—your premium covers the risk that someone of your age will die in any year. If you are 25 years old, the probability that you will die within the year is low, so your premium should be low to cover this risk. When you become 55 years old, the probability of your death would be much higher, and consequently your premiums will also be higher for the same amount of coverage.

You pay more for straight life insurance because you are buying more than pure insurance. You are also building up a type of savings account which will eventually be paid out to your estate (or in some cases to you at a certain age). And, although your premiums are generally higher than term insurance in the beginning, they remain the same throughout your life, so that at some point, often when you are about 50 years old, they become less than what you would pay for term insurance.

In deciding between term and straight life insurance, you should remember two points that we covered earlier. First, as you grow older and closer to retirement, the present discounted value of your earnings (that you want to insure) gets progressively smaller. Consequently, the ideal policy is large in the beginning and gets progressively smaller. In addition, in studying the life cycle of families, we see that most breadwinners have the greatest need for insurance (in terms of dependent children) in their earlier years—their 20s, 30s and 40s. In later years, when term insurance becomes more expensive than straight life, the need is no longer so great.

In terms of meeting the actual, pure insurance needs of a family, term insurance is cheaper and more flexible. However, consumers who cannot save on their own may value the forced savings feature of straight life and may be willing to put a higher amount of their current income into it.

An additional problem of ordinary life insurance is that it can easily be clobbered by inflation. Twenty years ago a person may have struggled to pay the premiums on a $20,000 policy, and today $20,000 provides relatively little protection. As Consumers Union has put it: "Fixed and guaranteed interest on savings (in an ordinary life insurance policy) is a proposition that few families can afford when price inflation is the long-term prospect."[4]

Table 9–1 shows the distribution of ownership of *individual* life insurance by income and life cycle. This excludes *group insurance* obtained through one's employer, since such insurance is often a fringe benefit of employment and not an option for all consumers.

More families own straight-life term insurance, although a number own both. Ownership of life insurance is heavily influenced by family income and life cycle, as we might expect. While two-thirds of all families had some individually purchased life insurance in 1970, only 40 percent of families with incomes below $3,000 had such insurance as contrasted with 89 percent of families with incomes above $15,000.

Among life cycle groups, it can be seen that families with children, who need life insurance protection most, are most likely to have some.

Other Types of Insurance

There are many types of insurance other than life insurance. Nearly every driver has automobile insurance, homeowners have fire insurance, many people have theft and liability insurance.

While many of these apply to specific objects such as a car or a house, they can be broken down into two primary types: one designed to cover a loss of fixed amount or value, and the other to protect the consumer against a loss of indeterminable value.

When your house burns down, when you drive into a tree (and aren't hurt), or when someone steals your mink coat, you suffer a loss of a certain amount of money equal to replacement or restoration of the lost or damaged items. Consequently, when you insure these items against loss, you know how much protection (in dollars) you need.

On the other hand, if you run down a child in the street or if your dog bites the banker who lives across the street, you may be in serious difficulty. In these instances you may be *liable* to pay an indeterminant amount of money to the victim or his family, depending not only on the seriousness of the mishap but also on the often volatile judgment

---

[4] Consumers Union, *The Consumers Union Report on Life Insurance* (New York: Harper & Row, 1967) p. 80.

TABLE 11-1

Type of Insurance Owned by Income and Life Cycle

(Percentage distribution of families)

Category	Type of Insurance[b]		
	None[a]	Term	Cash Value
All families	33	40	49
Total family income			
Less than $3,000	60	22	22
$3,000–$4,999	50	31	27
$5,000–$7,499	41	37	39
$7,500–$9,999	28	43	49
$10,000–$14,999	22	46	61
$15,000 or more	11	53	76
Life cycle stage of family head			
Younger than age 45			
Unmarried, no children	59	21	28
Married, no children	33	34	52
Married, youngest child under age 6	28	42	56
Married, youngest child age 6 or older	19	56	63
Age 45 or older			
Married, has children	18	44	61
Married, no children, head in labor force	23	43	61
Married, no children, head retired	35	39	41
Unmarried, no children, head in labor force	37	39	38
Unmarried, no children, head retired	56	21	22
Any age			
	51	29	30

[a] Families who have bought life insurance only through their employer are included under "none."

[b] Rows add to more than 100 percent because some families own both term and cash value insurance.

Source: Katona, Mandell and Schmeideskamp, *1970 Survey of Consumer Finances* (Ann Arbor: Institute for Social Research, 1971) p. 120.

of the courts as well. For this reason, *liability insurance* exists to cover losses to another person for which you are responsible.

Yet it is the open-endedness of the possible loss that makes it so difficult to determine the proper amount of coverage. Many, if not most, drivers take out the minimum amount of liability insurance required by their states, often the "10 and 20" insurance which covers a loss to one person up to $10,000 and a loss to *all* injured parties (if one accident) to $20,000. Yet newspapers regularly report court judgments in the hundreds of thousands or millions of dollars. If a young family bread-winner is killed, we have already seen the magnitude of his loss to his family. Yet even more tragic (and costly) is a permanent, disabling injury to a child who will need costly medical care and attention for the rest of his life. Court judgments in these cases have almost always been very high.

The risk of carrying too little insurance is that your liability does not end with your insurance coverage. You may also lose your life's savings and other assets that can be taken to meet the judgment. And many people do not know that the additional cost of an extra $50,000 or $100,000 in liability insurance is often only a few dollars. Compared to the additional protection, it is very often a great bargain.

no-fault insurance   For some time, many consumer representatives and insurance experts have argued that automobile liability insurance costs the consumer too much relative to the damage payments that are made. The reason for this is that in accident cases, it first had to be established who was liable and then the extent of damages had to be determined. This was both a time consuming and costly process, since lawyers for both sides often spent months or even years arguing their cases. Legal and related fees have amounted to almost as much money as was eventually paid out to injured parties. And injured parties often had to wait for years for their settlement, paying their own accident-related expenses in the interim.

As a result of these injustices, several states have adopted *no-fault* insurance. While each state has its own rules regarding no-fault, the basic feature of all plans is that fault in an accident is no longer the determinant of who pays damages. Each person basically insures his own car and its occupants, and if he is involved in an accident his company pays damages to his car and its occupants *regardless of whose fault the accident was*. If the accident involved a second car, damages to that car and its occupants would be paid by the insurer of that car. This feature eliminates the legal hassling over whose fault the accident was, which greatly reduces the legal expense involved in the insurance. Furthermore, the no-fault policies provide immediate payments for damages and medical expenses to those who were injured.

1. Insurance is essentially a method of protection for the consumer against unexpected and serious financial loss—sickness, old-age, unemployment, theft, accidents, and natural disasters that destroy property.

2. With the decline of the extended family and growing urbanization and monetization of the economy, insurance has become big business. The principle behind it is as follows: a person takes an insurance policy and pays a small amount of money. This payment, or premium, represents a certain loss for him in exchange for a much larger and uncertain loss such as serious illness which prevents him from earning a living, or death which means the permanent loss of income for his family. Since the amount of money spent on a premium represents resources that have alternative uses, this is again an area where it is possible to calculate costs and benefits. Consumers must decide what kinds of insurance and how much of it they want—premium payments naturally go up as the amount of insurance increases.

3. Some insurance policies protect consumers against specific loss such as theft, fire, property damage, natural disasters. Life insurance protects a person's earnings for his family. The value of that income is computed by calculating the present discounted value of the income over a period of years.

4. Liability insurance is also a useful mode of protection for the consumer since it protects him from payments he would have to make as a result of losses, for which he is liable, to another person.

5. Automobile insurance is another important category of insurance. In this field the concept of *no-fault* is becoming more and more popular. It is more efficient because in case of an accident, payments for damages and medical expenses are made more promptly and expensive legal proceedings are avoided.

QUESTIONS

1. Several times in this book you have come across the various problems arising in a modern society due to the break-up of the extended family. Discuss the effects of this decline of the system specifically in regard to insurance.

2. A 35-year-old man with two very young children makes $15,000 as an engineer. How much life insurance do you feel he should carry? Explain any assumptions you have made. Would the same answer apply if he were unmarried with no dependents? Why?

actuaries
premiums
mutual and stock insurance companies
present discounted value
straight and term life insurance
liability insurance
no-fault insurance

Before buying life insurance be sure to read the following:

Consumer's Union. *The Consumer's Union Report on Life Insurance.* (New York: Harper and Row, 1967).

Consumer's Union. "A Guide to Life Insurance," Part I - Five-Year Term Insurance - *Consumer Reports,* January, 1974. Part II - One-Year Term Insurance, Special Policy Riders, When to Switch - *Consumer Reports,* February, 1974. Part III - Whole-Life Insurance - *Consumer Reports,* March 1974.

Data on life insurance can be obtained from:

Institute of Life Insurance. *Life Insurance Fact Book* (most recent year).

Katona, Mandell and Schmeideskamp. *1970 Survey of Consumer Finances.* (Ann Arbor: Institute for Social Research, 1971).

Information on all types of insurance is available from:

Martin Cromwall. *The Collier Quick and Easy Guide to Buying Insurance.* (New York: Collier Books, 1963).

The Principles of Insurance are covered in the following:

Denenberg, Herbert S., Robert D. Eilers, G. Wright Hoffman, Chester A. Kline, Joseph J. Melone, and Wayne H. Snider. *Risk and Insurance,* (Englewood Cliffs, New Jersey: Prentice-Hall, 1964).

Mehr, Robert I. and Emerson Cammack. *Principles of Insurance.* (Homewood, Illinois: Richard D. Irwin, Inc., 1966).

Important information on social security is available in booklets from the Social Security Administration, U.S. Department of Health, Education and Welfare.

No-fault insurance is covered in:

Rokes, Willis Park. *No-Fault Insurance.* (Santa Monica: Insurors Press, 1971).

12

SAVINGS
AND
INVESTMENTS

There was a very stupid character in a play by Molière
who was also very rich. In an attempt to impress a *jeune
fille* whom he greatly admired, he engaged the services
of a professor to teach him how to write beautiful love
letters. After much clumsy effort, he inquired of the professor whether he was now writing poetry. No, said the professor, quite honestly, he wouldn't consider the gentleman's
effort to be poetry. "Then what is it," asked the stupid
man. "Well," said the professor, "all writing is either poetry
or prose. And since you do not write poetry, this must
be prose." This made the foolish man very happy because
he was no longer an unsophisticated boor, he could now
write *prose*.

Just as all writing can be divided into poetry and prose,
the disposition of all income can be divided into *consumption* and *savings*. Any income that you don't consume,
you save and any that you don't save, you consume.

Saving Stock Versus Flow

The term *saving* is often confused with *savings* which has
a totally different meaning. Saving is a *flow* term. It is
the amount that you save (or don't consume out of income)
for a given period of time. You save $20 *per week* or $100
per month or $1,500 *per year*—it is always measured for
some period of time. Other flow terms are *income,* which

is measured by the week, month, or year; and *consumption,* which is measured in the same way. If someone told you that he had saved $50, the statement would not be too meaningful to you unless he also told you the relevant time period.

Savings (with an *s* on the end) is a *stock* term that tells you the total amount that the person has saved to the present moment. If someone told you that he had $500 in savings, the statement is meaningful in itself, it doesn't need a time period reference. What he is saying is that he has a *stock of savings* with $500 at the present time. How and when he accumulated this savings is not relevant.

Of course, you cannot have a stock of savings unless you have done some saving. A very good analogy is a water reservoir. In order for that reservoir to hold a stock of 50 million gallons of water, on July 1, that amount must have flowed into it over many months or even years. That stock of water is stored and can be turned back into a flow in the form of consumption in the future. Similarly, people save money (refrain from consumption) so that they can accumulate a stock of savings which can be used for consumption in the future.

Figure 12-1 illustrates the relation between income, present consumption, present saving, savings, and future consumption. The gate on the reservoir, which is closed in the diagram, controls the outflow from the stock of savings to future consumption.

dissaving When the outflow gate in the savings reservoir is opened, *dissaving* occurs. If a person begins the year with $1,000 in savings and ends it with only $500, he has dissaved $500. Dissavings is the means by which people can consume more than their income.

Of course, it is not necessary to have a stock of savings to begin with in order to dissave. You can dissave by *borrowing money* (using someone else's stock of savings), and this may result in your having a *negative* savings stock. Instead of having $500 in savings, you may have a $500 debt. This means that you must save $500 from your income in order to bring your savings stock to zero.

Figure 12-1
The flow of saving and the stock of savings

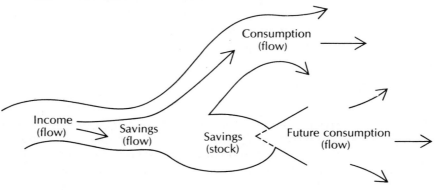

Wealth or Net Worth

Technically speaking, the value of a person's stock of savings is his *wealth* or *net worth*. The latter term is more often used by economists because of the somewhat ambiguous meaning of the term *wealth*. Net worth, practically defined, is the value of a person's assets less the total amount of his debts. In other words, your net worth is what you would have if you sold everything you owned and paid off all of your debts. Bright readers will, of course, recognize that net worth applies only to *nonhuman capital*. A thirty-year-old medical doctor, stripped of all his worldly possessions, is probably better off financially than a thirty-year-old uneducated laborer who has just inherited $100,000, since the return on the doctor's human capital may be $35,000 per year while the return on the laborer's inheritance may be only $6,000 or $7,000 in interest. However, at the time of measurement, the doctor's net worth (in conventional terms) is zero while the laborer's is $100,000.

measuring net worth It is often useful to measure net worth not only to satisfy one's curiosity but also to find out the size of one's estate for tax reasons or the protection of the family, or to gauge the financial health and resources of the family. In measuring net worth, it is generally best to consider assets and liabilities (debt) separately, and further, to break down each by relevant categories.

assets Everything owned by the family, from the 500 shares of IBM to the half-used tube of toothpaste is an asset. Yet assets differ greatly in terms of liquidity.

The term *liquidity* carries the analogy between savings and water one step further. Your stock of assets can be characterized by the ease with which they can be converted to a form which is ready to flow again. Most simply, if an asset can readily be converted to cash (with little risk of loss in value) it is said to be liquid. Therefore, liquid assets include such things as savings and checking accounts and U.S. Savings Bonds, while *non-liquid* or *illiquid* assets include a house and a car, which take time and effort to convert to cash and which may lose value if sold at the wrong time (the winter, for example). There are also *semi-liquid* assets which are somewhat riskier or more troublesome to convert to cash than the liquid assets. These include stocks and bonds, which fluctuate in value, and time certificates of deposit which can be converted to cash without loss of interest only at certain periods of time.

debt Debts that are classified as *long term* are generally for many years, mortgages being the most prevalent type; while *short term* debt might include revolving credit or credit-card debt. There is also *intermediate term* debt, which includes installment contracts of a few years.

TABLE 12-1

Net Worth of the Harry Houndtooth Family

Assets		Liabilities (Debt)	
A. Liquid Assets		A. Short-Term Debt	
Cash	$ 75	Charge Account—Ace Hard-	
Checking Accounts	$ 415	ware	$ 60
Savings Accounts	$2116	Bank Credit Card	$150
U.S. Savings Bonds	$ 150	Bank line of Credit	$225
Total Liquid Assets	$2756	Total Liquid Assets	$435
B. Semi-Liquid Assets		B. Intermediate-Term Debt	
100 shares Jones		Boat & Motor	$800
Shipping	$1500	Car	$750
2 year certificate		Color T.V.	$125
deposit	$2000	Total Intermediate-	
5 shares, U.S. Steel		Term Debt	$1675
Bonds	$4500		
Total Semi-			
Liquid Assets	$8000		
C. Illiquid Assets		C. Long-Term Debt	
House-market value	$35,000	Mortgage on Home	$23,500
2 year-old car-		Education Loan	$ 5,300
book value	$ 1,200	Total Long-Term Debt	$28,800
Boat & Motor	$ 1,300		
Antique Cabinet	$ 450		
Furniture, appliances			
etc.	$ 2,000		
Total Illiquid			
Assets	$39,950		
Total Assets	$50,706	Total Debt	$30,910

Net Worth = Total Assets − Total Debt = $19,796

Table 12–1 illustrates the calculation of net worth by examining the balance sheet of the Harry Houndtooth family. Many asset and debt items are fairly difficult to evaluate. The car bought two years ago for $3,500 isn't worth that today, and the house purchased for $30,000 seven years ago is worth a good deal more. Items such as these can only be evaluated by assigning a fair market value to them—what they would honestly bring if sold today.

This is relatively easy to estimate for automobiles since there are books that give the current value of all cars. Houses are somewhat harder to evaluate, and personal property hardest of all, since the value is determined by what you can get and varies greatly over time and by the personality of the seller.

It goes without saying that since debt is measured as a stock item, it must be evaluated as of the day of reckoning of net worth. A $3,000 automobile loan taken out two years ago is probably down to less than $1,000 today, while a $25,000, 30-year mortgage falls relatively little in seven years.

Other assets owned by many families but not the Houndtooths, include the cash value of any ordinary life insurance and the cash buildup of pension plans.

Methods of Saving

The most common conception of saving is an amount taken out of the paycheck and put in the bank each week or month. Yet this is not the only type, nor, for most Americans, the most prevalent.

According to our definition at the beginning of the chapter, saving is that part of income which is not used for consumption. A family may begin and end a year with $1,000 in the bank, but chances are that the family saved some money. Let's look at three possible ways.

1. *Regular voluntary saving.* This is what is most commonly thought of as saving: putting income aside, generally in liquid or semiliquid form such as bank accounts and securities.

2. *Consumption saving.* This occurs when income is used to buy a durable good which will yield consumption services for more than a year. A $3,000 automobile will yield service for more than one year. If it depreciates $850 that first year, we would say that consumption for the year is $850 and saving (held as savings in the form of a car) is $2,150.

3. *Forced saving.* Saving which is done as part of a formal agreement is *forced saving,* which is often related to repayment of debt but probably to other factors as well.

For most American families, the biggest forced saving is their house mortgage. In 1970, 58 percent of non-farm families were making house payments.[1] As we have seen in chapter 9, these are part interest (which is consumption) and part amortization (which is saving). The same breakdown applies for other types of debt repayment, where the interest may be viewed as a type of *rent,* which enables a consumer to use a good before he has fully paid for it.

Non-debt forced saving includes ordinary life insurance (discussed in chapter 11), which builds up a reserve, as well as pension plans and social security. Falling somewhere between forced and voluntary saving are

[1] Katona, Mandell and Schmeideskamp, *1970 Survey of Consumer Finances.* Ann Arbor: Institute for Social Research, 1971, p. 44.

Christmas Club accounts, savings bond payroll deduction plans, and stock and mutual fund plans that invest a regular amount for the consumer. These are not forced in the sense that the consumer can quit at any time without loss, yet people join them in order to force themselves to save money.

Why People Save

Everyone has reasons for saving—or wanting to save, which determine the manner in which savings are held. The goals may be arbitrarily divided into *short term* and *long term*.

short-term goals People may want to accumulate savings for possible use over the short run, say a few years, to be prepared for emergencies (reserves) or to make relatively large expenditures.

Emergencies may include accidents, illness, or periods of unemployment as well as property loss or car breakdown. Savings designed to meet emergencies should be in fairly liquid form so that they can be utilized quickly.

People also save in order to buy something too expensive to purchase out of current income—a new car, vacation, and so on—where the incurrence of debt is not desired or possible. People also save to make downpayments on houses and other items where debt will figure as well. Since there is often discretion over when such a purchase or expenditure is made (see chapter 5), the form of savings may be somewhat less liquid than for emergencies. For example, time certificates of deposit may be more suitable.

long-term goals Some savings goals are for things that will not occur for many years or involve sums of money that take a long time to accumulate. Sending a child to college, for example, may cost $20,000 or more, an amount that few people can spare from current income. Longer-run goals may be built up to a reserve to make retirement as comfortable as possible (which means reducing the drop in income when salaries cease and one is forced to live on pension and social security). And the longest-run saving goal is to leave a large estate to your heirs when you die. Some even want to accumulate great wealth (and power) that they can enjoy during their own active lifetimes.

Savings held for long-term goals need not be put into liquid assets. As we will see, liquid assets generally yield lower returns over time than less liquid assets and are also often more susceptible to the ravages of inflation.

HOW SAVINGS ARE HELD

The stock of savings, as we have seen, may be held in many forms which differ on the basis of risk, liquidity, and yield.

Money

The most liquid form of savings is *money,* which is generally defined as including *cash* and *checking accounts* (the latter can be used just like cash). However, each form of money has its own advantages and disadvantages.

Cash can be used everywhere, while checks may not always be accepted. Holding cash is risky because it can be lost or stolen; checks are a good deal safer.

These differences apart, both types of money share major advantages and disadvantages as a method of holding savings. The major advantages are in liquidity and (with safety precautions for cash) risk. Money is instantly usable, and since it constitutes the basis for the measurement of liquidity, it is the *most liquid* type of savings. Money is similarly protected against loss of value. Since *risk* is generally measured in terms of money, money is riskless—the value of a dollar bill (nominal value) can never go below a dollar. The *buying power* of the dollar can decrease with inflation, but that's another matter.

The *disadvantages* of holding money result from its *lack of yield* and *susceptibility of erosion by inflation.* Cash yields no monetary return to its holder, and banks are prohibited by law from paying interest on checking account balances. Therefore, there is a cost to holding savings in the form of money—the *implicit interest* which could have been earned if the money were held in, say, a savings account paying 5 percent interest. Savings held in checking accounts often have a *negative yield* since depositors are frequently forced to pay a service charge.

The fact that money has a fixed nominal value makes it susceptible to loss of buying power as the result of inflation. Throughout this country's history, and particularly within the past thirty years, inflation (rising prices) has been an almost constant fact of life, while *deflation* (falling prices) has rarely occurred. If prices rise by six percent within a year, the buying power of savings held in the form of money declines by 6 percent.

The twin disadvantages of money—no yield and likely erosion by inflation—make money very costly to hold. Then why hold it?

Lord Keynes, the great British economist, whom we cited earlier as the discoverer of the consumption function, listed three possible reasons for holding savings in the form of money rather than as an earning asset.

1. *Transaction* People keep ready money to use between income payments. In our economy (and in nearly all others as well), income is paid to earners in discrete intervals, like once a week or once a month. However, they must spend money all through that period—for groceries, gasoline, restaurant meals, and so on. The $500 that Tom gets on the last day of each month must last until the final day of the following month; it must be kept in a readily accessible form. Money is the most accessible means of storing funds needed for transactions. Therefore, for short

periods of time, the convenience and accessibility of money outweigh the cost of holding that relatively small quantity.

2. *Precaution* Keynes' *precautionary reasons* for holding money are similar to the emergency needs that we discussed earlier. You may need funds for immediate use; money is the handiest form.

3. *Speculation* A third reason, particularly important to Keynes in a personal way, was what he called the *speculative* value of holding money. Lord Keynes was not only a brilliant economist, art patron, and *bon vivant,* but proved the veracity of his economic advice by making several million dollars in the stock market himself.

He observed that when an investor or "speculator" feels that the price of a security or securities is about to rise, he will invest his money in them. However, if he feels that prices will fall, he will sell his securities and maintain a "cash position" so that he can purchase the securities at (what he hopes will be) their lowest level, and profit when they bounce back up again. Since securities prices may reverse their downward movement at any time, money is the best asset to hold in order to get back into the market quickly.

Savings Accounts

Savings accounts at banks and the so-called thrift institutions (savings and loan associations, mutual savings banks, credit unions) are generally as riskless as money (or even less so, in the case of cash) but have slightly less liquidity.

The decrease in liquidity is due to two factors:

1. They are often time deposit accounts (particularly at banks) which allow the financial institution to delay withdrawal up to 30 days. Although this is seldom if ever exercised by the institution, it is conceivable that one day when you want to withdraw $10,000 from your bank, they may tell you that you will have to wait several days.

2. They can only be withdrawn during banking hours. If you need $1,000 at 6 P.M., you will be out of luck and forced to wait until the bank opens the following day, which makes your funds even less liquid on weekends.

risk Assets in savings accounts are at least as risk-free as money. Since balances are payable to depositors in the form of money, there is no risk that the value of your account will decline relative to money. A $500 savings account balance cannot be lost or stolen. In fact, one of the basic functions of banks and other financial institutions is to safeguard the depositor's money. The assumption has been that steel bank vaults and alert bank guards offer your funds more security than your mattress.

However, until the creation of the Federal Deposit Insurance Corporation (F.D.I.C.) in the mid-1930s, bank failures and loss of depositor's money was a recurring phenomenon in this country. Banks, as we have seen, are relatively fragile institutions which do not have all the depositor's money sitting in the big vault behind the cashier. In order to make money for themselves and pay interest to their depositors, banks must lend most of their money to borrowers—for mortgages, business loans, consumer loans, and so on. At any point in time, they could put their hands on only a fraction of total deposits—certainly less than a quarter. The rest of the money is contractually tied up in loans for periods of days, weeks, months, years—even decades, in the case of mortgages.

To make matters worse, depositors know from experience just how vulnerable banks are. Since it takes the withdrawals of only a relatively small proportion of depositors to cause a bank to be illiquid (fail), depositors who sniff trouble will try to get their money out before the bank goes under. This, of course, becomes a self-fulfilling prophecy: if depositors suspect (rightly or wrongly) that a bank is about to fail, their withdrawal of deposits guarantees that it will fail.

Many banks, including some of the largest, failed during the early years of the great depression, costing many depositors their life savings. In order to prevent this situation from happening again, the F.D.I.C. was set up to insure depositors' accounts in commercial banks. Today, all but a handful of commercial banks are members of the F.D.I.C., and many of the "thrift institutions" have their own Federal insurance programs.

The coverage on depositor's insurance has gradually increased over the years. Currently bank accounts insured by the F.D.I.C. have had a limit of $40,000 per individual account (and $80,000 for a joint account). Insurance limits on thrift institution accounts are generally similar. It must be remembered that banks still fail (although not as frequently as before) as the result of mismanagement, embezzlement, or terrible luck. Consequently, one should always inquire as to the insurance coverage because it might just be necessary to protect your savings. Insured banks don't often fail because there is little incentive for depositors to "run" on them, and because their operations are closely watched by officials of the insurance agencies. If they do fail, however, you are still protected for at least the insurance limit.

Differences Among Savings Accounts

Savings accounts that appear to offer identical rates of interest often differ significantly, particularly in *compounding, computing,* and *crediting* interest (the three Cs).

Let's begin with a savings account that pays 4 percent interest per year. This basic rate is known as the *nominal* rate of interest.

compounding If you deposited $100 in the bank and held it there for a year, 4 percent interest would give you $4. However, most banks (and other financial institutions) compound your interest several times per year, which is to your benefit.

Suppose the bank compounds quarterly (four times a year). Each quarter you would be paid one percent on your money (the 4 percent annual rate divided by 4 quarters). Thus, at the end of the first 3 months, you would have $101 in your account. In the next quarter, you would get one percent interest on $101 (not just $100), so your interest for the second quarter would be $1.01, which is a penny more than you would have received otherwise. At the end of the second quarter you would have $102.01 in your account and 1 percent of that for the *3rd* quarter would be $1.02. At the beginning of the fourth quarter you have $103.03. One percent of that is $1.03, so at the end of the fourth quarter you have $103.03 plus $1.03, or $104.06. This is 6 cents more than you would have had with no compounding.

Compounding increases the *effective* rate of interest over the *nominal* rate, and the more times it is compounded per year, the greater the rate. However, the actual effect of compounding is relatively small. As we saw above, compounding quarterly at 4 percent increased the interest by 6 cents per year or .06 percent on the $100 which we invested. And although the yield increases as compounding is made more frequent, the difference is never very great (see table 12-2). Rather than worry about compounding, you need merely ask the *effective rate of interest* (which includes compounding) and compare institutions.

computing The computing method, often more important than compounding, determines when and for how long your money must be on deposit in order to earn interest. Many banks compute interest quarterly only on money left in the bank for the whole quarter. In other words,

TABLE 12-2

Interest on $100.00 at 4 Percent for One Year, Compounded Variously

Compounding Period	Interest (rounded to nearest cent)
Annually	$4.00
Semi-Annually	$4.04
Quarterly	$4.06
Monthly	$4.07
Weekly	$4.08
Daily	$4.08
Continuously	$4.08

if the quarter begins January 1, they pay interest only on money in the bank on January 1 and left there until March 31; they do not pay a cent in interest for money withdrawn before March 31 or deposited after January 1.

In recent years, as the result of greater demand for bank loans as well as more savings available from consumers, banks have begun competing for consumer savings by making savings accounts more attractive. One way they have done this is by compounding and computing interest on a shorter and shorter time period.

Accounts that cannot be touched for three months without loss of interest are less appealing (and less useful) than those that are computed much more frequently and can be withdrawn at any time with little if any loss of interest. Many banks now even compound and compute on a daily basis. With daily interest, you earn from day of deposit to day of withdrawal and cannot be penalized for deposits or withdrawals made at the "wrong time," since there is no wrong time.

crediting A third influence on savings accounts is when the interest is *credited*—when you can get your hot little hands on it. Crediting (or *paying* as it is sometimes called) often has nothing to do with the compounding or computing period. Many credit unions, for example, compute interest quarterly or monthly, but credit it only at the end of the year. So you may have earned interest after six months, but you can't get it yet. If you are counting on the interest to help you buy something, the crediting system might make a difference.

Certificates of Deposit (Time Certificates)

Another type of bank deposit has become popular in the past ten years: the *certificate of deposit* or the *time certificate,* which in some banks involves no actual certificate at all. Money is left with the bank for a period of time—generally three months to four years—and earns a higher rate of interest than a regular savings account. To insure that the funds remain for the specified period of time, most certificates of deposit call for the loss of some or all of the interest if they are withdrawn before maturity.

Banks are willing to pay more interest on certificates of deposit because they can make loans with guaranteed funds that otherwise would be impossible.

The Relation Between Yield and Liquidity

Banks pay more interest on long-term deposits to attract funds from depositors that can be loaned out for longer periods and, generally, bring a higher yield.

The inverse relation between yield and liquidity has long been recognized. Generally speaking, the greater the liquidity (or shorter term of commitment), the lower the yield in interest. This is so for these reasons:

1. *Liquidity Has Utility for Consumers.* All other things (such as interest rate) being equal, more liquid assets are nicer to have than less liquid assets because they are easier to spend or invest. In order to get people to give up the utility of a nice liquid savings account that they can tap any time they want, banks bribe them with higher rates of interest to tie up their funds for a longer period of time.

2. *Liquidity Is Less Risky for Banks.* Although risk is seldom a factor for the consumer depositing money in a bank, it is an important factor for the lender using that money. The longer the period of the loan, the greater the chance the borrower cannot repay. A bank who has carefully examined the client can be pretty sure of getting its money back on a one-month loan; but over five years, who knows what may happen?

3. *Liquidity Is Bad for Borrowers.* Borrowers, particularly commercial firms, greatly value longer-term loans (and are generally willing to pay more for them) because they provide more room to carry out plans. If firms had to borrow on a daily basis, never knowing if the loan would be renewed the next day, they would not be able to invest in equipment that takes several years to pay off. Also, consumers would hardly consider using a day-to-day or week-to-week loan for buying a car.

CONSUMER INVESTMENT

Thus far we have spoken of ways the consumer may employ his savings with virtually no risk of losing either principal (the amount he began with) or interest (amount earned on the principal). Since there is no risk of loss (assuming that deposit insurance exists and limits are not exceeded), the consumer trades off between liquidity and interest. The most liquid form of savings—money—earns no interest.[2] The least liquid form—certificates of deposit—ties up funds for several years but pays the highest.[3]

---

[2] Recently, however, banks and other financial intermediaries in some states have experimented with a type of interest-bearing checking account which has generally been called a Negotiated Order of Withdrawal (N.O.W.) account (since such interest payments as such are illegal).

[3] There are also risk-free bonds offered by the United States government. *Savings bonds* tie up funds for a long time (7 to 10 years) and generally pay rates of interest that are lower than long-term certificates of deposit. When a consumer buys savings bonds, patriotism must be one of his motives.

Short-term *government bills* are also available at competitive rates, but these 3- to 6-month obligations can only be purchased in $10,000 denominations and are out of the range of most consumers.

Consumer savings may also be placed in risky forms, where neither the principal nor the interest is guaranteed, referred to as *consumer investment.*

Returns to Consumer Investment

Savings accounts yield only one return: fixed interest; $1,000 at 5 percent (effective rate) earns $50 in interest per year—no more and no less.

Most consumer investment can produce two kinds of returns—an *annual yield* and a *capital gain.* The annual yield may be in the form of interest (on bonds), dividends (on stocks), or even rent (on real property such as land or buildings). The capital gain results from an increase in the value of the investment (the *capital* or *principal*).

If a consumer buys $1,000 worth of stock in the ABC company, his annual yield might be $60 in dividends during the year. If at the end of a year he sells his shares for $1,100 (not counting broker commissions), he has realized a capital gain of $100. Adding this to his dividends, he has made $160 for the year, or a total return of 16 percent on his principal.

Of course if that 16 percent return could be guaranteed, everyone would buy stock. However, investment is by nature risky, and the return could have been only 6 percent or 0 percent or even *minus* 6 percent (if the value of the stock went down).

The Relation Between Risk and Yield

Why, then, do consumers invest their money rather than put it in a nice secure savings account? The answer is that *added risk is compensated for by added yield.* We have already seen the inverse (backwards) relation between liquidity and yield where less liquid forms of savings pay more interest. There is a direct relation between risk and yield—the riskier the investment, the greater the return *on the average.* We must add "on the average" since return on investment is never guaranteed. In any one year the consumer may do better by putting his money in a savings account where the return is guaranteed than in the stock market where it isn't. However, averaged over many years, yields in the stock market have, on the average, been higher than yields on savings accounts.

There are other reasons why consumers might prefer riskier investments to savings. An important one relates to the *tax structure* of the United States while the other relates to *inflation.*

capital gains tax   According to the tax laws of the United States, capital gains (increase in value) of investments held for at least six months are taxed at a much lower rate than other types of income.[4]

The rationale behind this policy is not entirely clear. Initially, it was thought to be the government's way of compensating investors for the added risk necessary to build up the nation's productive capabilities. When you use your money to help XYZ manufacturer get started (by buying stock in the company), you are also helping the economy by providing more jobs and building the nation's capacity to produce goods.

Nowadays, however, most of the stock market transactions involve the purchase of existing shares, and a relatively small proportion goes to support new physical investment in plants and equipment. For this reason, and others which are too lengthy to cover here, the justification for the reduced tax on capital gains has been called into question. But suffice it to say that it is a fact of life and helps make investments that offer possibilities of capital gains relatively more attractive.

protection against inflation Many types of investments have their value and yield linked in some way to the price level. When you buy shares of stock in the XYZ corporation, you are buying *equity* or ownership in that company. Therefore, as a part owner, you share in the earnings of the company as well as its increase in value.

Let's suppose that the XYZ corporation makes furniture. When inflation hits and prices rise, chances are that furniture will also go up, and the company will make more in *dollars* even if the amount of furniture sold does not change. It can therefore declare more in dividends, and your annual return on your investment in dollars will also increase.

In this way, the *buying power* of the returns on your investment may not decrease. If prices in general rise by 6 percent, your dividends may also increase by 6 percent to leave you no worse off than before. If, however, your money were in a checking account, the buying power of your fixed returns would have *decreased* with inflation.

But even more important than buying power is the value of your investment. If your $1,000 were in a checking account, a 6 percent rate of inflation would have reduced the value by that much. However, if your money were invested in shares of the XYZ corporation, you would likely have done better. Since the price that XYZ gets for its furniture increases with inflation, the company becomes worth more in dollar terms (since the dollar value of a producing investment is measured in terms of the dollar value of the goods it produces). Also, a general increase in prices probably means an increase in the value of the company's capital (physical plant and equipment) and inventory.

As a result, the price of the shares of the XYZ corporation will probably increase with increases in the price level, protecting the buying power

---

[4] Half the investor's regular tax rate, or 25 percent (for the first $50,000)—whichever is lower.

of your investment. Since inflation is a common occurrence in an economy, many people invest in things like stocks that will serve as a *hedge* against inflation.[5]

Types of Investments

We have discussed many characteristics of investments that are traded off against each other: liquidity, risk, yield, tax benefits, and hedge against inflation. In our brief discussion of possible consumer investments, we will refer to these to see what tradeoffs are made for each.

investment in human capital One type of investment made by all consumers is their own human capital. We have discussed this investment at length in chapter 4 and realize that there are costs and returns associated with education and training.

Investment in human capital is the least liquid investment that can be made. Your Ph.D. from M.I.T. cannot be converted directly to cash. In certain circumstances, great skill (such as a star football player's or an opera singer's) may be committed to a long-term contract for a lump sum, but this is rare. Money poured into training or education can seldom be recovered in a short period of time.

Human capital investment carries some risk. Teacher training may be a bad investment if, upon graduation, it is found that there are no teaching jobs, but college graduates are seldom unemployed for very long. The overall risk is not very great.

The yield on human capital has been variously estimated by many economists. Schultz estimated it to be 10 to 15 percent, which seems surprisingly low.[6] But this is only the monetary yield in terms of increased salary and does not include the nonmonetary benefits such as status and job satisfaction that we mentioned earlier.

Investment in human capital has no tax benefits (although several have been proposed), but it is well hedged against inflation, since wages and salaries tend to keep pace with price increases.

investment in housing This also is relatively illiquid, since it cannot be turned into cash in a short time with no loss in value. It has some risk associated with it since house values may decline. The yield on hous-

---

[5] Stock prices are not related entirely to current earnings. They also reflect *anticipated future earnings,* and if investors feel that a business recession is coming, stock prices may fall to reflect that. This accounts for the recent (1972–74) decline in stock prices which accompanied high rates of inflation. On the average and over the long run, stock prices and yields generally keep up with inflation.

[6] Theodore Schultz, "Optimal Investment in College Instruction: Equity and Efficiency," *Journal of Political Economy,* Vol. 80, Number 3, Part II, May/June 1972, p. 523.

ing cannot be easily measured in dollar terms (since it is largely in terms of satisfaction).

There are two types of tax benefits associated with investment in housing—the deductibility of interest, and the reduced capital-gains tax associated with profits from the sale of a house. An added tax benefit is that even the reduced tax on capital gains may be put off if the seller buys a new house at a higher price by a certain time. This allows consumers to delay payment of capital gains taxes until retirement when lower income reduces the tax liability.

Houses are often regarded as good hedges against inflation since values as well as the cost of building goes up with inflation. This may not happen in the future, however, if population growth levels off thereby decreasing the demand for new construction.

vacant land   Investment in vacant land is said to be highly *speculative* since there is no annual yield by which value can be gauged but only capital gain.

Investment in land is illiquid and risky. The yield may be very high if you are lucky or smart, or may be zero or negative if you are not. Tax benefits are the same as for any capital gain, and land is considered a pretty good hedge against inflation.

The important fact to remember before investing in land is that you must realize a relatively large capital gain to do well. Your lot or field just sits there producing no income and costing you explicit or implicit interest. If the annual interest rate is 7 percent and the real estate taxes are 3 percent, the value of your vacant lot must increase by 10 percent per year just to enable you to break even, if you bought the land with your own money (bank loans for vacant land are very difficult to get since the investment is so highly speculative). Under these conditions, a gain of 33 percent in three years would just about let you break even *before taxes*. Don't forget that you must pay capital gains tax on your profit, which sets you back even further.

vacation homes   Vacation homes are similar to land as an investment, except that you gain additional returns in terms of the utility or pleasure from their use. In economic downturns, vacation homes often tend to lose value faster than year-round homes that people need no matter what the economic conditions.

equities   Stocks (and mutual funds, which are generally bundles of stocks managed by someone else) are a popular type of investment for consumers. They are relatively liquid since they can be converted to cash in a few days by calling a broker.

All equities have risk, some more than others, with the direct relation between risk and yield that we have discussed. An example of a low-risk equity is a utility such as American Telephone and Telegraph and the electric companies. Consumer use of utilities does not fluctuate very much from year to year, and a certain rate of return is generally pretty much guaranteed. These low-risk equities (sometimes called "widow and orphan stocks" because of their dependability) also have relatively small yields, often only slightly above those paid by the banks.

The price of stock of companies whose earnings fluctuate widely, such as airlines and aircraft manufacturers, tends to fluctuate in a similar manner. Within a year's time, the value of these holdings may double or halve.

Between the utilities and the airplane stocks are hundreds of companies with different degrees of risk and yield. All equities offer capital gains tax benefits and an additional (small) tax break in that the first $100 in dividends ($200 for a married couple) is tax free. As stated earlier, under most circumstances equities tend to be good protection against erosion of savings by inflation.

other investments Some consumers purchase *industrial bonds* and *preferred stock,* where the annual yield in interest or dividends is pretty well guaranteed but the principal fluctuates. Others buy *rental property,* which has additional tax benefits as well as additional headaches. Still other consumers invest in *commodities, coins, art, antiques*—almost anything you can name. Each type of investment has its own set of characteristics—liquidity, risk, yield, tax benefits, and inflation protection—which should be consistent with the consumer's overall savings and investment plans.

1. The distinction between flow and stock is important in economics. The former is meaningful only in the context of a specific period of time while the latter refers to an aggregate without any reference to the time factor. Saving is a flow, while savings is a stock.

2. The net worth of an individual is the difference between his assets and his liabilities. Even though the available evidence indicates that investment in human capital increases a person's productivity and therefore his earning power, it is not included as an asset when calculating net worth.

3. Liquidity is significant when considering assets. An asset that can quickly be converted into cash without loss of value is considered highly liquid. Assets can yield income in the form of interest or increased value when held in forms other than cash and checking accounts. Generally speaking, the higher the liquidity of an asset, the lower the risk and also the lower the yield from it.

SUMMARY

4. Money or cash, which is the most liquid asset, is demanded for transactions and for precautionary and speculative uses.

5. There is a trade-off between the liquidity and the income-earning capacity of an asset. Consumer investment (distinct from consumer saving) is more risky but also produces more income. On the average, the riskier the investment, the more yield it will bring.

6. Consumer investments that increase in value over time are taxed at a lower rate. This tax is called the capital-gains tax and acts as an incentive to businessmen to invest to increase in asset value.

7. Different kinds of investments have different characteristics and purposes; they vary as to liquidity, risk, yield, tax benefits, and as hedges against inflation.

QUESTIONS

1. What is the difference between *saving* and *savings?* Can you have savings without first saving? Explain. Which of the two is the *stock* term and which the *flow* term? Tell whether the following are stocks or flows: consumption, investment, savings account balances, debt.

2. Melvin has $250 in his checking account, $1,110 in a savings account, and 100 shares of Acme Widget worth $8 per share. He has a $16,000 mortgage on his house whose market value is $25,000. He still owes $900 on his car which is now worth $1,300. Ignoring anything we haven't mentioned, what is Melvin's *net worth?* What is his *house equity?*

3. What are the advantages and disadvantages of *forced* (contractual) *saving?* List and explain several types.

4. Name some short-term savings goals. What types of consumer savings or investments are well suited to these goals? Do the same for long-term goals.

5. Why do savings held in a checking account often have a *negative yield?* Why are checking account balances considered to be money?

6. Is yield *directly* or *inversely* related to liquidity? Explain. How about the relation between *yield* and *risk*—is it direct or inverse? Explain.

7. Even though the holding of money yields a zero or even negative return, there are good reasons for holding some. What are these reasons?

8. Why are banks both willing and able to pay a higher rate of interest on time certificates of deposit than on regular savings accounts?

9. What types of investments would have the greatest appeal to gamblers? Why?

10. If you expected a great deal of inflation over the next few years, what would you put your savings into? Why?

TERMINOLOGY

stock vs flow
net worth
assets and liabilities
liquidity
certificates of deposit
transactions precautionary and speculative uses of money
compounding, computing, and crediting interest
capital gains tax
preferred stock

ADVICE TO
THE CONSUMER

Dear Consumer Advisor:

I have $5,000 in a savings account at the bank and want to buy a $3,500 car. I can't decide whether to take the money from my account or borrow it from the finance company. What do you think?

Steve

Dear Consumer Advisor:

My husband recently passed away and left me $20,000 in a checking account, along with the house and some stocks. Friends tell me that the $20,000 in the checking account is protected by Federal insurance so I shouldn't move it and risk losing it. Do you agree?

New Widow

Dear Consumer Advisor:

Congratulate us! My wife just gave birth to a beautiful daughter. I have decided to begin putting away money for her college education since it is expensive now and will probably be much more expensive (with inflation and all) by the time she is ready to go.

What would you suggest as a good place to put my savings for this purpose?

Proud Papa

Dear Consumer Advisor:

My husband is hot to buy a vacation house in Colorado. He says that although we will only be able to use it for a month a year, vacation homes are terrific investments—better than the bank or the stock market. Is he right?

Reluctant

Dear Consumer Advisor:

Last week I came upon 50 acres of land that would be perfect for a shopping center. When I went to the bank for a loan, they said no, but that same week they loaned my friend money to buy a new house. Isn't this discriminatory?

Ralph

SELECTED REFERENCES AND SOURCES OF DATA

How to Invest in Stocks and Bonds. New York: Merrill Lynch, Pierce, Fenner and Smith. (Free copies are available.)

How to Read a Financial Report. New York: Merrill Lynch, Pierce, Fenner and Smith.

Katona, George, Lewis Mandell and Jay Schmeideskamp. *1970 Survey of Consumer Finances* (Ann Arbor: Institute for Social Research, 1970).

Keynes, J. M. *The General Theory of Employment, Interest and Money*. (New York: Harcourt, Brace and World, 1964).

Lawrence, Michael. *Playboy's Investment Guide*. (Chicago: Playboy Press, 1971). (An investment guide discussing all major investment media for use particularly for people in their 20's and early 30's with money and who are willing to take risks.)

Smith, Carlton and Richard P. Pratt. *The Time-Life Book of Family Finance*. (New York: Time-Life Books, 1969). (Chapter 11 explores the problems of saving money and gives numerical examples of the way banks compute interest.)

Unger, Maurice A. and Harold A. Wolf. *Personal Finance,* 3rd edition. (Boston: Allyn and Bacon, 1973). (Part III contains an exhaustive survey of different kinds of investments.)

13

BUSINESS ORGANIZATION

Earlier we observed that while the family wishes to maximize its utility, businessmen wish to maximize something else—namely, profit. This, of course, has the same ultimate purpose, since businessmen are also consumers; the more profit they make, the more they have to spend.[1]

An important question that must be asked is whether the businessman, in his quest for maximum profits, serves the best interests of consumers. This is a complex question that, like all other complex questions, must be answered both yes and no. In the first instance, a businessman attempting to maximize profits may resort to illegal or merely misleading methods which are not in the consumer's interest. Such methods involve false advertising, failure to live up to warranties and other such acts which are generally recognized as being against the law. These illegal or unethical practices will be dealt with more fully in the next chapter.

Competition

Businessmen may operate in a completely legal manner that is still not in the best interest of the consumer. If

---

[1] In many of today's large corporations where management owns only a tiny portion of their companies, actions may be influenced by non-profit-related considerations such as maximizing sales and size to boost executive salaries. There are limits to this type of activity, however, and companies that are not profitable soon hire new managers. Therefore the objective of profit maximization closely approximates the behavior of most businesses.

there is no governmental regulation, one important ingredient necessary to insure that businessmen work in the best interest of the consumer is *competition*.

What exactly do we mean by competition? Although economists define competition more technically than we need to here, we can say that it requires at least two conditions: that there are several firms in the market selling the same product; and that there are no barriers to entry in the market—that is, new firms are free to enter the market for a product, and old firms are free to leave.

In the statements above we have intentionally used two vague terms: *several* and *market*. How many firms is several? It is certainly more than one, for one has no incentive to be competitive. But do two firms cause a competitive situation? This really depends upon their behavior and the degree to which they compete, as opposed to *collaborating* with each other.

The term *market* is equally hard to define, but the concept will become clear with an example. A butcher with a shop in East Podunk may view his market as consisting of the town of East Podunk. However, if his prices were low, people from West Podunk and South Podunk might choose to come and buy their meat from him. In fact, it is not inconceivable that people from as far away as Miami and Los Angeles might hear about his terrific prices and order from East Podunk. Now how large is the market of this butcher? This is largely a matter of judgment on the part of the butcher, and may only be judged relative to the actions that he takes. If he confines his advertising to East Podunk, then he pretty much feels that that town is his market. If he also advertises in West Podunk and offers to deliver within a 25 mile radius, then he would define his market as being larger. So price changes (within a reasonable range) can determine "market," regardless of population or town size.

In order to explain the value of competition to the consumer, let's look at our butcher in East Podunk—the Meely Meat Market. Three years ago it was the only meat market in town. If people didn't buy their meat from Meely, they had to drive 125 miles to Stix over terrible roads with ugly billboards. For a long time the market had been run by old man Meely, who didn't believe in germs because they weren't mentioned in the Bible. Meely's meats were aptly named, and it was a tough decision for many townspeople whether to buy from him or turn vegetarian. But yet, Meely sold his meat. Why? Because there was no competition. There may not be strong incentive for a businessman to be responsive to consumer needs—when you have the only game in town, you can pretty well play it as you please.

Now, it is conceivable that Mr. Meely, with his slovenly, unsanitary ways, was not maximizing his profits. Perhaps he could have sold more meat and made more profits by cleaning up his shop. However, it was neither within his ability nor his knowledge to do so. So given his resources, knowledge, and energy level, he may very well have been maximizing profits for the Meely Meat Market, and unless competition opened up and forced him to change his ways, he may have been able to go on making a living like that forever.

About four years ago, however, old man Meely's son Adam graduated from college with a business degree and came back home to East Podunk to take over his father's business. The first task for young Adam, who had taken many marketing courses, was to clean up the butcher shop. Gleaming white porcelain counters were installed, an electronic cash register was put in, and customers were asked to take a number to stand in line for their meat orders. This was a welcome change for the citizens of East Podunk, but they did not realize what was in store for them.

Before we proceed with this fascinating tale, we must refresh our minds about something that we learned in chapter 6, the demand curve. You will remember that the market demand curve for any product, such as meat, slopes downward and to the right. In figure 13–1 below, you will see the market demand curve for meat in East Podunk, made up of the individual demands of all those living within the market (town). The Meely Meat Market was a *monopoly* in the town, meaning that there was only one seller of meat and that was Meely. Therefore, the market demand curve became the demand curve for Meely meat.

Since a monopolist faces a downward sloping demand curve for his product he has control over its price. He can charge a dollar for his steaks or three dollars, and the only thing the consumers can do is buy less when the price is high, more when the price is low and grin and it. A monopolist, therefore, is often called a *price maker*.

Now sharp young Adam Meely notices right off that his father had been charging low prices for his meat. Meat prices had been averaging a dollar a pound, and his father sold 500 pounds a week. After some calculations of his costs as well as his revenues, Adam found that by

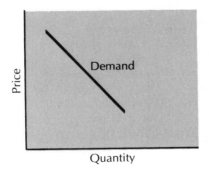

Figure 13-1

charging two dollars a pound, his total sales would fall but so would his expenses of running the business, and his total profits would go up. So Adam doubled the price of meat, and the consumers of Podunk responded by buying only half as much.

The exact reasons why Adam chose the specific price of two dollars concerns more than just his revenues. It also concerns a consideration of his cost which is beyond the scope of this chapter but is considered in great detail in more advanced courses in economics. Suffice it to say that Adam found he could make better profits by charging a higher price and selling less meat. The reader should also remember that the consumer is not indifferent about buying 250 pounds at two dollars a pound or 500 pounds at a dollar a pound; he would much prefer the latter.

Profit

We have already noted that not only is Adam charging more money for less, but he is also making very large profits. Before we proceed further, we should consider what we mean by *profit*. A business, like a household, has both income and expenditures. *Gross income* is the total income generated from all sales of the business. Let's look at the income and expenditures of the Meely Meat Market in order to calculate its profits.

After Adam takes over, the weekly sales are 250 pounds at two dollars per pound or $500 per week. The first item of expense that must be considered is the cost of goods sold. Adam pays $.75 a pound for the meat that he sells, so that 250 pounds a week costs him $187.50.

Let's assume that Adam runs the shop without any helpers. Does this mean that his profit is the $500 in revenues less the $187.50 for cost of goods sold? The answer is No; there are other explicit expenses that Adam must incur. The first of these is the rent on the building, which costs $100 a month or $25 per week. Then there are utilities and telephone, which come to $10 a week. There are other miscellaneous expenses, such as paper and twine to wrap the meats, gasoline for the delivery truck—these amount to $25 per week. His total explicit or *out-of-pocket* costs are $247.50, leaving him $252.50 per week. Is this all profits? The answer again is No. There are certain *implicit* costs borne by every business that must also be considered.

The first is Adam's own salary. While it is true that he draws no salary as such from the business right now, it does not mean that the value of his wages is zero. He has other opportunities. When he graduated from college a local bank offered him a job in its training program at $150 per week. So his salary cost in the meat market would be at least this much.

Second, there is some capital tied up in the business. When Adam took over from his father, he paid $10,000 for the equipment, machinery, and "good will." Adam could have put the $10,000 in the bank to earn 5 percent. In fact, since any business is riskier than money in the bank, he could have invested in an equally risky venture for more than 5 percent—let's say 7. So, 7 percent of $10,000, or $700 a year, is what Adam foregoes in interest to keep his business open. This amounts to approximately $13.50 per week.

Total implicit costs are, therefore, $163.50, and adding them to the $247.50, we come up with total costs of $411. Is the $89 left over from the $500 in revenues profit? The answer is finally, Yes. But the $89 is broken down by economists into two types of profit: *normal* and *excess*.

Normal profit is what is needed to stay in business. For example, if Adam Meely made no profit at all, would he keep the meat market? He is, after all, covering his income of $150 per week and all of the other expenses, but with no profits there would be no incentive for him to continue. Aside from the number of hours he works, there are other troubles of running a business for which the businessman must be compensated. Adam worries about getting supplies, he must bear the insults of old customers, he must remember to save doggie bones for the St. Bernard dog living down the street. If he worked for someone else, many of the worries of *entrepreneurship* would be on someone else's shoulder, and he could presumably go home at the end of the day and not have to worry. So normal profits, which cannot be exactly determined, are necessary just in order to keep the business in operation.

Let's suppose that this minimum amount is $25 per week. If Adam could not make a profit over and above that, he would just as soon close down the meat market, sell the equipment, and take his job at the bank at $150 a week.

But he still has $64 of the gross revenues as excess profits, which is more than needed to keep his business going.

These excess profits serve a function to society which is more important than merely keeping Adam happy: they are an incentive to other businessmen to enter the market and to compete.

The Economic Function of Excess Profits

When a potential competitor sees that a business is making what appears to be excess profits, he may well be tempted to compete in order to capture some of the excess profits for himself. In chapter 2 we said that there are scarce resources in every society—land, labor, capital, and entrepreneurial ability. What causes these resources to go to the production of automobiles or snowmobiles rather than buggy whips and whalebone corsets? The answer, of course, is profit.

Profits, or excess profits as we have been calling them, are the incentive used to attract the scarce resources of production to an area where they

are needed. The existence of excess profits in any market or industry indicates that consumer demand is not being satisfied as well there as in other industries where there is no excess demand. If a new fad catches on, like funky clothes and waterbeds have in the past, the excess profits that accrued to the first entrepreneurs attracted additional businessmen and additional resources. As soon as there is enough supply so that more businessmen cannot expect to make excess profits, the process stops and no new resources are brought into the industry. If the latest waterbed manufacturer found he was not making any excess profits but that manufacturers in a new fad like cross-country skiing were really raking it in, he may well be attracted to move his resources to the new industry.

Figure 13–2 shows how this works. Take the cross-country ski industry. Before the recent increase of interest, the demand curve looked like D, the supply curve looked like S, and the price of cross-country skis was P. That price was sufficient to let all manufacturers earn just the normal profit; there was no excess. All of a sudden demand for cross-country skis shot up, and the demand curve shifted up to D'. At this point the price was P', which was greater than that needed to make a normal profit (P_o), so excess profits were being made, and producers suddenly found that their relatively quiet business had become very profitable. Before long, other entrepreneurs noticed this enticing development, so they diverted their resources to the production of cross-country skis, shifting the supply curve downward to the right to S' until the price was back to the old level, P_0, which was just sufficient to produce normal profits for everyone.[2]

In East Podunk the inevitable happened one day. While visiting the town to view the famed statue of Chester Allen Arthur in the main square, Sidney W. Neet was nearly hit by a big long Cadillac while he was crossing the street. Grasping the arm of a passerby, he asked "Who owns that big long Cadillac?" and the passerby responded, "It can only be one man in town, Adam Meely, who owns the meat market." "You mean," asked Neet, who himself had spent many years working in his father's butcher shop in Brooklyn "that the owner of the meat market in this small town makes enough money to drive a big long *Cadillac?*" "Well," said the townsman, "his prices are high, his service is low, and he is the only meat dealer in town, so people have to buy from him."

To Sidney Neet, this was a sign of excess profits being generated, so, after checking things out and getting a loan from his father, he opened a competing meat store, known as Neet's Meats, right across the street from Meely Meats, and began by setting his prices well below Meely's.

---

[2] Actually, since firms are not equally efficient in their production, the dollar amount of profits would differ among firms. However, while more efficient firms make more dollar profits, they would also be more efficient in other industries, so the implicit value of the resources is higher and no excess profits may be made.

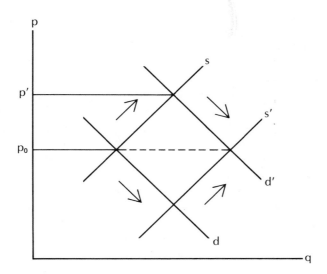

Figure 13-2

While Meely had been selling meat for two dollars a pound, Neet began selling for $1.50 a pound. Of course, everyone went to buy from Neet, since his prices were lower. Not to be outdone, Meely lowered his prices to $1.25, and Neet retaliated by lowering *his* to $1.00. At $1.00 a pound Neet could no longer earn any excess profits, but Meely came down to $1.00 a pound also, and the happy result for the town of East Podunk was that they were getting their meats cheaper, there were no excess profits being generated, and faced with the competition across the street, Meely began offering better service to his customers.

Imperfect Competition

The scenerio on meat need not have worked out exactly this way, for when you have only two competitors, there is often a chance of *conspiracy* whereby they would agree not to compete with one another in order to both earn excess profits. The case of two sellers is known as a *duopoly*. In fact, when there are only a small number of sellers, there is also the possibility of conspiracy. A small number of sellers is known as an *oligopoly*. The consumer is, in most cases, best served by competition or *perfect competition,* as it is sometimes called, which is characterized by a large number of sellers, none of whom sells enough of a share of the market to affect the price.

Some producers in America are actually perfect competitors. Farmers are a traditional example of this. A wheat farmer in Kansas, for example, is a *price taker*. He goes to the granary and he takes for his wheat whatever price is given. No matter how much he produces, whether one bushel or a hundred thousand bushels, he's going to get the same amount per bushel as all of the other wheat producers in his area. He just has too small a part of the market to be able to have any control over the price.

But we are far more familiar with so-called imperfect competitors—monopolies and oligopolies—which constitute most of big business in America. There are really only three major automobile producers and one small one, only a couple dozen major steel producers, a relatively small handful of tire producers, aluminum producers, beer producers, and cigarette producers, just to name a few. In some industries and markets there is only one producer, such as American Telephone and Telegraph, which is the only national telephone company, and the local utility company, often the only supplier of electric power to an area. Ask yourself when the last time was that a competitor came in to offer you lower rates on electric power.

MONOPOLY

RING THE CONSUMER

WIN A HOUSE IN CONNECTICUT

We can sum up the bad points of monopolies or other types of imperfect competition in two ways. First, prices are likely to be higher than they would be with competition; and second, the business may not be as responsive to consumer needs—that is, it may offer lower product quality and poor service and fail to anticipate changing consumer needs. These are the primary economic drawbacks to monopolies and other types of imperfect competition.

There are also political drawbacks in that power is concentrated in the hands of a relatively small number of people who have ultimate control over the means of production. In this manner they can exert pressure on the political system far in excess of their numbers. Also, monopoly profits make the distribution of income even more unequal.

anti-trust The dangers of monopolies have long been known. During the last half of the nineteenth century, increasing manufacturing and productive power led to the establishment of monopolies and oligopolies in several industries. Often, in industries where there were a few competitors, the magnates got together and said "Why should we compete against each other? It's like beating our heads against the wall. Let us agree to the same policies and, therefore, we can keep prices higher than they would be and keep excess profits flowing in." One method was to turn their companies into a trust. This would guarantee that pricing and other policies would be consistent with the maximization of excess profits. As the power and effect of these trusts became stronger and stronger, public resistance against them also became stronger, and political pressures finally resulted in the passage of the first anti-trust legislation, the Sherman Anti-Trust Act, in 1890.

This act essentially made it illegal to conspire in restraint of trade or to agree to keep competition at a minimum in order to keep prices high. This legislation was followed by others including the Clayton Anti-Trust Act in 1903, and over the years, a fairly sophisticated body of anti-trust laws has come into being. An end result today is that representatives of oligopolistic companies in the automobile or steel industry, for example, are often very fearful of discussing anything with their competitors that could even be remotely construed as representing conspiracy or common action. A fairly recent case involved identical bids submitted by major companies for government contracts resulting in a court decision against the companies. This decision cost them millions of dollars in damages and even put company executives behind bars for a short time.

some justification for imperfect competition   If we look around we see that many of the familiar businesses are certainly not competitive. Monopolies predominate in the utility field and oligopolies exist in many of our major industries. If these are harmful to the consumer, why doesn't the government take efforts to break them into smaller competitive units? The answer is that there are instances where monopolies are beneficial to society, particularly if they are regulated. First, they may save the duplication of scarce resources of society; and second, they may make production of certain goods economically feasible and often at lower cost than in a more competitive situation.

duplication of resources   In every town there is but one electric company. If you, the customer, feel that the rates are too high, you can have your power cut off, but you cannot buy electrical power from another company in the next town. Utilities are, in many cases, a regulated monopoly made possible by law.

Why have regulated monopolies? In the case of utilities, a good deal of effort is needed to supply each house. Lines must be strung on poles or laid underneath the city streets. While it is true that competitors could enter the market, this would be highly wasteful, not only in terms of additional copper wire necessary, but also of the streets which must be ripped up or new overhead poles installed, which would look even more miserable than the ones we have.

Since society, in an effort to best use its resources, grants a monopoly to only one utility company for an area, it also has an obligation to keep its citizens from being exploited by that monopoly. As one may easily realize, unregulated electric utility companies could easily double or triple rates without losing a good deal of business since people today are highly dependent on electricity. However, the companies that are given monopoly powers are generally not given the right to set their own rates. Public service commissions are put in control of rates, and prices are set in such a manner that the utility companies make no excess profits. In other words, the philosophy is that they should be constrained to making no more profit than they would if they were in a competitive industry, so the prices of competition are simulated. This generally means that after all expenses are met, a certain rate of return, which we here-tofore called a normal profit, generally 6 or 7 percent, is guaranteed.

reducing cost   Industrial operations differ in terms of the skills or processes needed to produce goods at the lowest possible cost. Often this is related to the *capital intensity* of the industry. If a huge investment is needed in capital equipment in order to manufacture a certain item, relatively large numbers must be produced in order to sell at a reasonable price. Let's assume that a certain process requires new machinery that costs $1,000,000 a year. If there were no other costs, such as labor, and if only one unit were produced in that year, it would cost a million dollars. Ten units would cost $100,000 apiece; to get the cost down to one dollar per unit, a million units must be produced.

But industries use both capital and labor. Generally speaking, the more capital intensive an industry, that is, the higher the proportion of production costs that must go for the payment of capital relative to labor, the greater the number of units that must be produced in order to reach lowest cost. To illustrate this let's take examples of two industries: waterbeds, which are characterized by relatively low capital to output ratio, and automobiles which are just the opposite.

Figures 13–3 and 13–4 show how the average cost of production behaves for each of the two industries. In a waterbed factory, there are some fixed costs, including rent, sewing equipment, and so on. So the production of 100 units per year may be relatively inefficient with an average cost of $100 per unit, while producing two or three times that volume spreads fixed costs over a greater output, and the average cost falls. At some point, however, say 300 units, when the average price is down to $50 per waterbed, we may start running into difficulties. The production of more units is going to result in overcrowding the facilities, people will get in each other's way, and overall efficiency will go down. So, past some point, say 300 waterbeds, the average cost of producing additional waterbeds tends to rise.

The same thing happens in an automobile company. However, because of the huge amount of capital investment that is necessary, and because of the hundreds of complex steps that must be taken to assemble the automobile, lowest cost is not reached until, perhaps, hundreds of thousands of one model of car are made in any one year.

What does this mean for anti-monopoly laws? It means that automobile factories may be too big to be completely competitive. Certainly, we see that when the price of one automobile goes up in a year, the other automobile makers generally follow. However, would society be well served by breaking the three or four existing automobile manufacturers down into 100 or 1,000? The answer is definitely No. In order to produce a relatively low-cost automobile, somewhere around 100,000 must be made of any one model. This means that if companies were

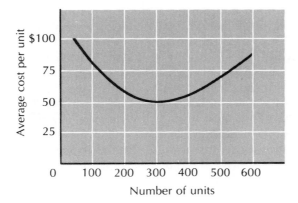

Figure 13-3
Cost curve for
waterbeds

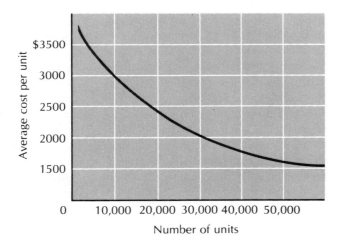

Figure 13-4
Cost curve for
automobiles

broken up so that each could produce only 10,000 cars, sufficient econo-mies of scale could not be realized, and the consumer would end up paying more money. For this reason, society is willing to tolerate the existence of imperfect competition in order to achieve a lower price, but it also demands that, wherever possible, collusion and practices that are guaranteed to work against the consumer are held to a minimum.

Differentiated Products and Advertising

The advantages of having a monopoly, in terms of generating excess profits, are so great that often producers of what may be considered competitive goods try to establish a monopoly position for themselves.

This is done through advertising. Take the manufacturer of ordinary aspirin and look at his returns. In discount drug stores we often see ABC aspirin selling for 23 cents a thousand tablets. If XYZ aspirin came into the store and started selling at 25 cents a thousand, few would buy it because they can get it from ABC at 23 cents.

If XYZ is clever, however, it may advertise and make special claims for its particular aspirin—that with it you never get flat feet or that it is good for your soul. And if enough people believe that XYZ aspirin is different from other aspirin, that it is sufficiently *differentiated,* they may be willing to pay more for it. Graphically, the demand curve for XYZ aspirin slopes downward and to the right like the demand curve of a monopolist.

This is the reason for high advertising expenditures on the part of producers of essentially similar goods, such as aspirin, soap, detergents, deodorants, cigarettes, and beer. Each wishes to differentiate his product in the mind of the consumer so that he can charge more for the product than he would get under competitive situations. When the consumer succumbs to such advertisement and pays more for the XYZ aspirin, he is paying for the advertising and also for the excess profits going to the producers as well as the 23 cents the aspirin really costs.

There are many other types of "non-price" competition in America. The main method for automobile makers has been to change the model every year or two and not compete on prices alone. These changes result in great additional expense to the consumer, since the industry must be retooled far more frequently than would otherwise be necessary. This may run to billions of dollars annually, much of which could be saved and the savings ultimately passed on to the consumer if model changes were not so frequent.

It is interesting to note that, as the result of foreign competition within recent years, American manufacturers are changing styles less frequently, particularly for small cars, and are beginning to engage in types of price competition beneficial to the consumer.

SUMMARY

1. Nearly all individuals, consumers as well as producers, try to maximize utility. Businessmen do this by trying to maximize profits which are the difference between their receipts and their expenditures.

2. The consumer's best interest is generally served by competition in the business sector. Conditions of perfect competition (the ideal situation) exist when there are (1) enough producers of a good so that no one individual has any control over prices, and (2) no restrictions on free movement in and out of the market. Competitive markets best suit the consumer's interest because prices are the lowest possible, allowing

for only normal profits for the producers. When profits rise because of increased demand (or any other reason) and there are no barriers to entry into the market, more producers will be attracted and supply will expand to meet the demand. Consequently prices and profits will fall to a point where no excess profits are made.

3. A monopoly is said to exist when a producer of any good or service controls its supply, and therefore is able to fix the price. Consumers are at a disadvantage in such cases because 1) they may not be able to get as much of the good as they want, and 2) they pay higher prices.

4. Monopoly, duopoly, and oligopoly are all forms of imperfect competition and characterize some industries in the U.S. today. Such producers control price and output either alone or in concert with like businesses.

5. Various anti-trust laws to restrict business collusion to control prices and output levels have been passed by the government in an effort to safeguard the consumer.

6. Sometimes only one producer, or a few, are both economical and more efficient than competition. Public utilities are regulated monopolies since society has deemed that duplication of services in any area is wasteful because of the high capital costs of machinery and transmission costs.

7. One wasteful aspect of imperfect competition is that producers, by spending a lot on advertising instead of improving the product, are able to convince consumers to pay them higher prices. Often the brands are basically indistinguishable except for the intensity of advertising campaigns. The automotive industry plays this game, as do detergent and drug companies.

QUESTIONS

1. Which is likely to be operated along more competitive lines, the tractor business or children's toys? Why?

2. We discussed two assumptions or conditions that must be satisfied before perfect competition can be said to exist. Can you think of any other conditions implied by these two?

3. Advertising is one way of differentiating between products for the consumer. Some people consider it wasteful; can you suggest good aspects?

4. One frequent statement by oil companies is that they need excess profits to continue production. Is this justifiable? Give reasons.

TERMINOLOGY

perfect competition
monopoly
imperfect competition
oligopoly
capital intensity
excess profits
normal profits
entrepreneurship
anti-trust legislation

SELECTED REFERENCES AND SOURCES OF DATA

For a discussion of the problem of separation of ownership and control of today's companies:

Berle, Adolph A. and Gardiner C. Means. *The Modern Corporation and Private Property*. Rev. ed. (New York: Harcourt, Brace & World, 1968).

Galbraith, John K. *The New Industrial State*. (Boston: Houghton Mifflin, 1969). (A discussion of the change in the nature of business organizations.)

For an excellent, but more technical discussion of imperfect competition, see:

Backman, Jules. *Advertising and Competition*. (New York: New York University Press, 1967).

Samuelson, Paul A. *Economics*. 8th ed. (New York: McGraw-Hill Book Company, 1970). Chapters 25, 26.

14

THE BUSINESS–CONSUMER RELATIONSHIP AND THE ROLE OF THE GOVERNMENT IN PROTECTION AND REGULATION

Within recent years, a great deal of attention has been focused upon the relation of business to the consumer, particularly on practices harmful to the consumer, and out of this has come a great deal of consumer-oriented legislation.

Largely as a result of publicity given to harmful or unscrupulous business practices, attitudes toward business in general, as measured by reputable survey research organizations, have greatly deteriorated. In this chapter we will attempt to present a balanced analysis of the business-consumer relationship, discussing first the benefits and then the possible harm to the consumer—and the role of government protection in these instances.

POSITIVE ASPECTS OF THE BUSINESS-CONSUMER RELATIONSHIP

In the last chapter we took a fleeting glimpse at the invisible hand, the mechanism pointed out by Adam Smith in the eighteenth century, that insures the fact that the capitalist system will meet the needs of its consumers. We see that profits serve as an incentive for business to be efficient and to anticipate consumer needs. When the fickle consumer shifts interest from one good to another, it is the profit system that insures the shift of resources, guaranteeing that the consumer makes his wishes felt on the production system.

Capitalist and Non-Capitalist Systems

The automatic functioning of the invisible hand diminishes the need for government intervention. If consumers want to wear Levis rather than gray flannel pants, the capitalist system insures that someone will recognize this, that there are profits to be made in Levis, and will slow down on grey flannels and step up the production of Levis. In countries where profits do not exist, where the invisible hand cannot operate, the government must anticipate consumer needs. In the Soviet Union, for example, there are often severe shortages of goods which are in demand, and very often there is great overproduction of goods which consumers no longer want. Who signals the manufacturer of gray flannels in the Soviet Union to switch over to Levis? Since the plant manager is not affected by profits, the only feedback that he gets is when other perceptive government officials notice that gray flannel slacks are going unsold while Russian citizens are buying more and more Levis (sometimes literally off the bottoms of visiting tourists). Only then is it possible that the switch will be made. But multiply this example by the millions of products, and you will see that if you don't have an invisible hand, you must have a visible and huge bureaucracy to make the same production decisions with much less hope of satisfying the customer.

The market system in the United States does more than just insure that shifting consumer demands will largely be met; it also insures that businesses that cannot deliver what consumers are willing to buy have a very short life. In smaller communities, word-of-mouth is a powerful influence. In larger cities, where the great number of people diminishes the power of oral communication, consumers often tend to be more cynical and wary of merchants and products whose reputation is not known to them.

The magnitude of this self-policing action may be seen in the hundreds of thousands of American businesses that fold every year. The fundamental cause of business failure is the inability to produce and sell enough to cover expenses (including normal profit). The number of businesses that are closed by action of the government as the result of fraudulent or otherwise illegal practices is miniscule when compared with the number that fail of their own accord and would continue to be so even if the government were far more active and diligent in protecting the rights of the consumer than it is.

This does not imply, however, that all businesses now act wholly in the interests of consumers; there are some serious flaws in the market system. In the first instance, as we discussed in the preceding chapter, a lack of competition can enable a producer to get a higher price for a lower quality good than he would otherwise get. So the government takes steps to protect and encourage competition.

A second imperfection in the market system is its often slow pace. While it might be argued that a merchant selling a fraudulently represented product cannot stay in business indefinitely, since people will soon learn about his unethical practices, it is first necessary for many consumers to suffer before the word gets around.

What business practices may be contrary to the interests of consumers, and what, if anything, is the government doing to remedy the situation? As we explore these questions, the reader must continually bear in mind that the cost-benefit tradeoff discussed in other chapters certainly is relevant here as well. The consumer benefits from government protection, yet it does not come for free.

increased tax burden   The effectiveness of consumer protection from unsafe or fraudulent business practices is strongly related to the number of people employed in searching out and preventing these practices. If there is one thing in common about attorneys general, biologists with the Food and Drug Administration, advertising specialists with the Federal Trade Commission, and others employed by local, state, and federal consumer protection agencies, it is that they all eat and must be paid. Consequently, increased government protection increases government expenses and, hence, taxes for the consumers. The decision that must be made is how much protection are consumers willing to pay for.

other increased costs   Business-consumer regulations often require increased business expenditures. Examples include child-proof aspirin bottles, automobile safety equipment, and unit-price labeling. Generally, these costs are passed on to the consumer in the form of higher prices.

lack of flexibility   As we saw earlier, a major benefit offered by our economic system to the consumer is its flexibility in meeting changing consumer needs and demands. Government regulations, even the best intentioned, involve red-tape and bureaucracy which can slow down or even discourage new products and businesses. It is one constant criticism of the Food and Drug Administration that the thoroughness of their testing before a new drug is allowed on the market may cost consumers who need that drug pain and suffering and perhaps even their lives.

GOVERNMENT REGULATION OF THE BUSINESS-CONSUMER RELATIONSHIP

In the last chapter, we learned that the first substantial piece of government legislation designed to protect the consumer was the Sherman Anti-Trust Act of 1890. Although the end result of this act was to protect consumers from higher prices resulting from conspiracy and restraint of trade, it is not often cited as a major piece of consumer legislation, which has mainly taken place in the twentieth century, much of it since 1960. Protection of the consumer is not situated exclusively in the branches of the federal government. Every state in the union and many cities have their own regulatory arms; yet for various reasons, federal legislation has had much greater impact. This is partly because of the greater power and policing ability of the federal government, but there are other reasons. If New York City passes a law banning the sale of a flammable piece of clothing and no one else in the country passes such a law, the manufacturer will almost certainly continue to manufacture and distribute his product. It is not at all unlikely that it will end up in the stores of New York City where it will be virtually indistinguishable from the hundreds of thousands of other products that are sold daily. In order to make sure that it is not sold in New York, a considerable effort, in terms of notifying shop-keepers and policing efforts, is necessary to insure compliance with the law. If, on the other hand, it is the federal government that passes a law banning flammable clothing, the manufacturers will probably quit making it, and if not, the government can sue them. This is a far more feasible solution to the problem.

Unsafe or Inadequate Products

There is often little incentive for business to design products that are safe for the consumer if they cost more to make. For many years automobile manufacturers resisted safety devices because safety was not a big thing, there was no great consumer pressure for safety features. In fact, it was not until Ralph Nader came along in the 1960s and documented the extremely unsafe condition of automobiles that the movement toward safety began to pick up momentum. The great tragedy in the production of unsafe automobiles is that the consumer who values safety really does not have a choice if cars are being made unsafe. As we saw in the last chapter, economies of scale necessitate the production of a very large number of automobiles in a small number of companies, so that the consumer has long been faced with the choice either to not drive at all or to buy a relatively unsafe product. It finally took government regulation to get safety features installed in automobiles.

Other examples have occurred in children's clothing. For many years much of it had been made from highly inflammable materials. However, the incidence of children badly burned was so low as to not really affect the consumer attitudes toward the product. Again, it was only through the action of the government that safety standards were adopted by the industry.

Consumer Product Safety Commission

On May 14, 1973, government actions to prevent unsafe products were greatly increased when the Consumer Product Safety Commission began operations. The new federal agency has been given the authority to set safety standards for a wide variety of products and has the power to ban something outright if it feels it is hazardous to consumers. The new commission is attempting to reduce the approximately 20 million injuries and 30,000 deaths caused annually by products commonly found in the home.

Food and Drug Regulations

Guarantees of the purity of food and drugs taken by consumers is of utmost importance. This appears to be a legitimate area for government protection, since few consumers can be expected to be able to ascertain the purity of foods that they eat, and particularly the quality of drugs that they must use. A hundred and fifty years ago when most Americans lived on farms and most food was sold as unpackaged, undifferentiated goods, a large proportion of people might have been able to evaluate the quality of food that they were buying. Nowadays, however, when only five percent of us lives on farms, and when most goods that we buy come packaged and processed, we can tell little about the quality or substance of food that we buy except by reading the label. In the case of drugs, the consumer is even more helpless. How many are capable of understanding the molecular composition of drugs, let alone educating themselves as to the possible side effects and reactions based upon years of test research done in laboratories?

For these reasons, increased pressure was put on the government during the nineteenth century for the passage of laws guaranteeing the purity of food and drugs. Throughout the nineteenth century many states passed laws to this effect, and between 1879 and 1906 over a hundred food and drug bills were brought up in Congress. It wasn't until 1906, however, that the first federal legislation was signed into law, the federal Pure Food and Drug Act. It was relatively weak, however, and was superceded by the present federal Food, Drug, and Cosmetic Act of 1938. This has been amended a number of times since then regarding such things as pesticide chemicals, food additives, and color additives. In 1966, in response to numerous complaints by consumers regarding unfair and deceptive packaging and labeling, the Fair Packaging and Labeling Act was passed.

Although the laws relating to foods have been well received by consumers, considerable controversy has resulted from enforcement of the drug laws. As was mentioned above, critics have alleged that the very cautious way in which new drugs are approved for consumer use has kept many from reaching consumers when they need them.

MISLEADING THE CONSUMER

A variety of techniques have been used by some businesses to have the consumer pay for goods that are inferior to those that he thinks he is paying for. Some techniques constitute outright fraud and deception. Other, more subtle techniques, rely on the consumer's own ignorance.

Fraud and Deceptive Advertising

The profit system often produces an incentive for a business to deliver less than it promises. Of course, well established businesses seldom resort to fraudulent or deceptive practices because their interest is long-run. They wish to establish a good name with the consumer and keep his patronage through the years. The fly-by-night firm has no such incentive. It is organized quickly and attempts to exploit the market as quickly as possible, and then dismantled to reassemble in another area. Examples of outright fraud have been numerous through American history. The consumer column in your local newspaper can illustrate the latest tricks used by fraudulent merchants, including door-to-door sales routines, mail-order products that are never delivered, and other such trumpery. With the increasing political activism of the consumer, governments have become more aware of fraudulent practices of this type and have begun to police them much more carefully.

The larger American companies often engage in deceptive or misleading advertising. Some years ago in a TV advertisement, a can of soup was poured into a bowl and all of the meat and vegetables were forced to the top by marbles placed at the bottom of the bowl in order to illustrate how rich and hearty the soup was. Another example involved bread advertised as low calorie because it was sliced thinner and each slice contained less bread and therefore fewer calories. Aspirin commercials have recently come under attack because tests show that there is relatively little difference between brands.

Legitimate advertising serves an information function. Your television set may show you what the new model car looks like, or how you can unclog your drains without calling a plumber. It also pays for all your programs. Misleading advertising may cost the consumer three ways: by not getting the product as advertised; by paying for the advertising (in the add-on price); and by paying "monopoly profits" or excess profits accruing from product differentiation due to advertising.

Federal Trade Commission

While much of the protection against fraud is on a state and local level, often centered in the Attorney General's office or with local prosecutors, large-scale offenders whose operations might encompass several states or the whole country may be handled by the Federal Trade Commission. When the Federal Trade Commission Act was passed in 1914, the FTC was largely designed to help maintain competition and prevent monopolies, but it was also given responsibilities of policing unfair or deceptive trade practices. What is seen as unfair or deceptive has changed over the years as types of products have changed and become more sophisticated, as devices used by sellers have also become more sophisticated, and as advertising has proliferated into one of the big businesses in our economy. Although the FTC does not have the authority to levy fines against violators of trade laws, it can institute court action through the Department of Justice. Within recent years much of the publicized activity of the Federal Trade Commission has been in the area of policing advertising. Initially, unfair advertisers were penalized in the traditional manners with injunctions to stop their advertising and sometimes even with fines. Recently, a new method has been used that demands that violators in effect be forced to counter-advertise or buy commercial time to explain to the public that their former ads were misleading. Although actual decisions of this type have not been numerous, the effect of the FTC has been felt by the advertising industry, and commercials are now far more sparing in the amount of puffery used to boost products.

Insufficient Consumer Information

Part of the consumer's bad luck in dealing with business must be laid squarely at the feet of the consumer, who as we said in chapter 1, is often poorly equipped to go into the marketplace. (Of course, it is not always entirely the consumer's ignorance that does him in. He has a little help from his friend, the avaricious businessman, on many occasions.)

Examples abound in today's society. In the supermarket, cans and boxes of goods are found using the most difficult possible system of sizes. Cans of tunafish, for example, may be sold in 1 7/8, 3 5/8, and other unusual sizes so that it is very difficult for the consumer to calculate exactly how much he is paying per ounce. Of course, if the consumer had the ability and wanted to take the time, he could make this calculation. But few have either the ability or the time, or, if so, lack the inclination. Where unit-pricing laws have been instituted to guide the consumer by telling him the price per ounce or per pound, it has been found that relatively few use the system, and those who do tend to be the richer and better educated. Again, as we have seen in chapter 1, the welfare

of the rich and the welfare of the poor are separated a little bit further.

Enlarging Consumer Knowledge and Information

Since it is both impossible and undesirable to regulate every transaction between consumers and businessmen, the efficient functioning of our economy depends to a large extent on the assumption that consumers are knowledgeable in most transactions that they make. In fact, if cases of outright fraud and deliberate deception are excluded from the market-place, consumers probably do well for themselves most of the time. But in many of the more complex areas their knowledge and information must be expanded, and recently the government decided that it should play a role in this expansion. For quite a long time it has provided information to the consumer who knew how to ask for it. Government agencies, particularly the Department of Agriculture, have prepared thousands of booklets on everything from cooking to plumbing to raising hogs. More recently it has been getting into areas such as credit and the Truth-in-Lending Law, and passing legislation requiring labeling of foodstuffs. A number of bills are under consideration right now that would, among other things, indicate the nutritional value of foods, and tell the consumer how many miles he could expect to get per gallon of gasoline for new cars. Other more radical legislation would force the government to disclose the results of its own tests of the thousands of products it buys each year. Under this plan the government would, in essence, become a public Consumer's Union and would pass on information to the consumer, for example, on the durability of automobile tires. Of course, the largest and most important job that the government can do in increasing consumer knowledge must take place in the schools. Consumer courses are a part of many regular curriculums, but it will take some time before we learn their general effectiveness.

THE CREATION OF WANTS

There is another completely legal, if not completely ethical, way in which business practices may not correspond to the best interest of consumers: the creation of virtually unlimited wants through advertising and product promotion. While it can have a positive information value for the consumer by telling him something about a product that he did not know, we also saw in the previous chapter that it could effectively persuade the consumer to pay a higher price for a product which is not much different from other brands. Another effect upon the consumer, however, may be neither misleading nor fraudulent. By continually assailing him with his need to consume, and by portraying on the very persuasive mass media norms of families who are very consumption

oriented, many people buy more than they would have without these advertisements.

While businessmen will almost invariably argue that high rates of consumption are necessary in order to keep the economy going, a matter which we will study in chapter 16, encouraging exceptionally high rates of consumption may have two detrimental effects. First, some segments of the population may be encouraged to consume to the extent that their financial health is endangered. Since, as we saw in previous chapters, much consumption is possible only through borrowing, many consumers end up in deep difficulty, and these financial difficulties often have an impact upon their families, their marriages, and their mental health. The second possible disadvantage of abnormally high rates of consumption has been recognized only recently. Nearly all consumption involves depletion of scarce resources. As some ecologists claim, consumption is pollution. Every new car that is sold is some day going to be an old car that must be disposed of, every package of frozen cake has a bulky wrapper that must be put somewhere, and every good that burns gasoline puts its own pollutants into the atmosphere as well as depleting the world's source of usable energy.

For these reasons, we have seen a strange turnabout in recent years. For quite a long time electric companies, natural gas companies, and gasoline companies were shouting "Consume, consume, consume!" to all Americans. Almost at once, however, commodities became scarce, and the advertising was turned completely about: turn off the switch to save a watt, go easy on the accelerator to save gasoline. In the last analysis businessmen and consumers are constrained by the same limited resources, and so the era of pushing unlimited consumption may be coming to a close.

PRODUCTS THAT FAIL TO PERFORM

In our discussion of durable goods in chapter 7, we recognized that a highly desirable attribute of a durable good is its durability. What we really are paying for is the services of a car or television or washing machine for a certain period of time. A spiffy new car may not lose any of its beauty if its engine breaks down after two months, but the owner is likely to feel that somehow he hasn't gotten his money's worth. Consequently, many goods that the consumer expects to last for a while are covered by *warranties*. As we pointed out earlier, an understanding of many products implies such a high level of technical expertise that it is nearly impossible to acquire the information necessary to buy intelligently. The advice of such excellent publications as *Consumer Reports* is certainly useful, but beyond that we often have to rely on warranties issued on consumer durables.

Warranties

A warranty is an agreement given to a buyer at the time of purchase by the seller that a good will perform satisfactorily for some period of time or it will be repaired or replaced under set conditions. Most sellers put this in written form called *expressed warranty*. Common law, however, maintains that a seller guarantee that a good be in usable condition and perform to certain expected criteria even if there is no written warranty. This is known as *implied warranty*. While we do not intend to give full coverage to warranty laws here, there are certain economic considerations that come into play that make it more or less likely that the seller will live up to the terms of his agreement.

It is possible to enforce the terms of the warranty by taking the seller to court, but this is not often a workable or practical solution. Small claims courts exist in many states and enable the consumer to seek satisfaction for a nominal fee without a lawyer. However, if he accounts for the implicit value of his time, it is often not worth suing for an item costing $15, $30, or even $100. While written warranties are often useful on relatively expensive items where a substantial amount of money is tied up and where it might be worth the time to pursue the matter legally, warranties on less expensive items are often as valuable as the integrity of the seller. For that reason, it is useful to look at economic considerations behind warranties. First, there is economic incentive for certain types of firms to stand behind merchandise, particularly if these firms sell many different types of items or items which are needed frequently by customers. A firm that depends for its business on repeated patronage must strive to keep a good reputation with its customers, and they often take back merchandise almost without question for replacement or refund. In addition, those who market in a relatively small area where everyone knows everyone else, can face a substantial loss of business from consumer dissatisfaction as word of mouth passes the message. There are other firms that have no incentive to honor warranties or give very good service, that sell items a customer is likely to buy only once or twice—new or used cars, automobile parts such as mufflers, and home remodeling. Other slippery sellers deal in large market areas where chances are that someone who is dissatisfied, even if he told all of his friends, would have no significant impact on the seller's business. For these reasons, it is often in the consumer's interest to forgo a price savings of a small magnitude in order to deal with a merchant who is known to have a good record of service, particularly when buying goods that are likely to require a lot of service such as automobiles and appliances.

externalities and protection of the environment　An increasingly important area of conflict between the businessmen and the consumer concerns the environment. The problem simply stated, is that the producer maximizes profit by keeping his costs as low as possible, and if he can save money by discharging pollutants into the environment, he may be tempted to do so unless he is prohibited by law. The costs of production passed off on to society by effluents into the water or pollution into the atmosphere are not borne by the company, and therefore are known as external costs or *externalities*. Since they are borne by society as a whole, they are also known as *social costs*.

The problem of externalities is one that cannot be effectively dealt with by the internal operation of the profit system. There are few cases where a businessman can maximize profits by voluntarily installing expensive devices to restrict the output of polluting materials in his production process. The only solution to this problem is government intervention and regulation of the production process.

The failure of the profit system to cope with the externalities of business production has been explored by the conservative economist Milton Friedman. In an article a few years back, Friedman argued persuasively that not only do businesses *not* have an obligation to voluntarily restrict production for the sake of the environment, but that to voluntarily do so would be a distortion of the optimal allocation of resources. Friedman argued that society must make the laws and that businessmen faced with the laws should respond in a manner designed to maximize profits. In that way, the profit system will tend to allocate resources in a manner consistent with the desires of the consuming public, and also consistent with laws designed to protect the environment.[1]

You will recall that we explored this problem for the consumer with regard to his use of the automobile. Few consumers might be expected to voluntarily restrict the outputs of their polluting automobile engines at a cost to themselves since others might not comply with the voluntary system, and the level of air pollution would not improve materially. Neither the utility of the consumer nor that of the businessman, in terms of profits, is maximized by their paying to control their external diseconomies.

Government Actions on Behalf of the Environment

In recent years the government has created new standards for air and water quality and has begun to enforce existing laws on the books but hitherto ignored.

Government activity of this sort is often costly to the consumer. Devices to restrict the flow of pollutants from private automobiles have their original equipment cost passed on to the consumer in the form of higher prices. To the extent that these devices reduce mileage, the

[1] Milton Friedman, "Social Responsibility of Business is to Increase Profits," New York Times Magazine Section, September 13, 1970, pp. 32–33.

consumer is also hit by higher operating expenses. And, of course, when factories are required to install expensive devices to restrict their flow of pollutants, that cost is largely or entirely passed on to the consumer. So although laws insuring the cleanliness of our environment do help the consumer, they also end up costing him quite a lot of money. Here, as everywhere else, there are only tradeoffs, no absolutes.

SUMMARY

1. Government intervention and regulation is useful in protecting the consumer, but it costs the consumer in three ways: higher prices of goods that most probably would have been cheaper in the absence of government regulation, more delay in getting some new products to market, and increased taxes resulting from increased government expenditures. Therefore, the extent and degree of government regulation is also an area where the cost-benefit principle could be applied before decisions are made.

2. Major legislation to safeguard consumers is of relatively recent origin. State and local governments play a part, but federal legislation has been found to be the most effective, especially in preventing production and sale of unsafe products, in insuring the quality of foodstuffs, and in protecting consumers from misleading and deceptive advertising.

3. It is true that the consumer, in whose interest all these measures have been taken, has not made full use of the facilities and services available to him. Consumer ignorance, aided by certain business practices, has made the problem worse. Government intervention to expand consumer expertise in areas of correct decision-making is of recent origin. The school systems are beginning to provide a valuable service by offering courses in consumer education.

4. The question of who should pay for the undesirable side effects of pollution resulting from large scale industrial production is an area of conflict between consumers and businessmen, increasingly subject to government intervention and regulation.

QUESTIONS

1. The extent of government intervention in the market system is an area where cost benefit analysis is useful. Do you agree? Why?

2. Which would you prefer, a system of perfect competition or a certain degree of government intervention? Why?

3. Economics assumes that man is a rational being who tries to maximize his utility or returns. Is this realistic? What problems does this cause for consumers and businesses?

4. Do you think businessmen have an obligation to voluntarily restrict production for the sake of protecting the environment? Do you agree with Milton Friedman that this will result in a distortion in the optimal allocation of resources? Why?

TERMINOLOGY

truth-in-lending law
warranty
externality
optimal allocation of resources

SELECTED REFERENCES AND SOURCES OF DATA

Environment Reporter. Washington, D.C., Bureau of National Affairs (1970-). Contains discussion of federal laws, federal regulations, state air laws, state water laws, current developments and cases.

Federal Trade Commission. List of Publications. Listing of a number of publications of interest to the general public is available free from the Division of Legal and Public Records, F.T.C., Washington D.C.

Gordon, Leland J. and Steward M. Lee. *Economics for Consumers,* 6th ed. (New York: Van Nostrand Reinhold, 1972). A Discussion of the influence and power of the consumer and the factors affecting consumer demand.

Mather, Lays L. *Economics of Consumer Protection.* (Danville, Illinois: The Interstate Printers and Publishers, 1971). Results of a seminar by a group of agricultrual economists on the various aspects of consumer protection.

Peterson, Mary B. *The Regulated Consumer.* (Los Angeles: Nash Publishing, 1971). A discussion of the effects on the consumer from the increasing government regulation by examining various agencies, like F.D.A., F.T.C., N.L.R.B., I.C.C., F.C.C., etc.

U.S. Consumer Products Safety Commission. First Annual Report, 1971. (Washington, D.C.). A comprehensive survey of actions taken in the fiscal year ending June 1973 under the Consumer Product Safety Act.

15

TAXATION
AND
GOVERNMENT
SERVICES

The economy of the United States is often called a "mixed" economy: it is run by a combination of business and government. Although the basic orientation of our economy is to allow businesses to supply as much of the goods and services as can be done efficiently, the economic role of the government has been steadily increasing over the past fifty years. Figure 15-1 shows the tremendous growth in government expenditures at state, local and federal levels since 1930. This increase has been financed by a growing tax burden which in 1971 amounted to $1337 dollars for every man, woman, and child in the United States—up $611 dollars from 1960 alone. The American consumer is heard groaning more and more about the increase in taxes, but the demand for more and better government services which causes it continues to grow. Just what types of services does government provide, and what accounts for this growth?

1. Services Providing Social Rather than Individual Benefits

In order for business to function properly, services and goods must be sold at a price that in some way reflects benefits to the consumer. There are some services, however,

Figure 15-1
Government
expenditures –
1939–1973

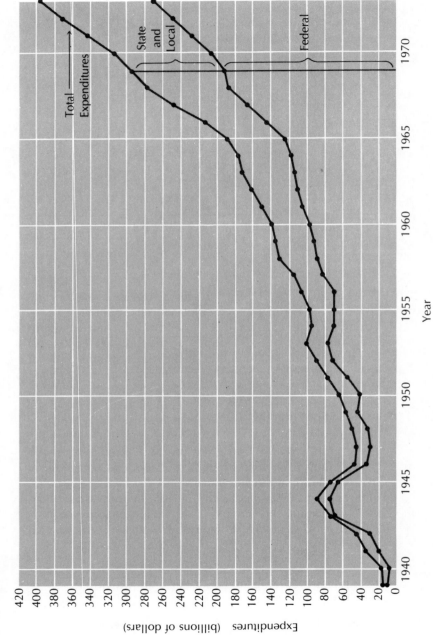

Source: *Economic Report of the President, 1974*, p. 328.

that cannot be sold in this manner; the government must provide them.

a. National defense. Presumably everyone in the country benefits from the armed services that protect us from foreign invasion. However, if a private business were running the army, navy, air force and marines, and citizens were asked whether they wanted to buy protection from foreign enemies, many would undoubtedly reason that as long as their neighbors pay for the service, they would also be protected. This is certainly true. It is relatively impractical to protect the Jones family at 118 Elm Street from invasion because they paid their national defense fee, and yet exclude the Smiths next door from the same protection because they did not.

b. Police protection. While it is somewhat more feasible to buy private police protection, as in fact many people do, public safety cannot be that narrowly based. A society must have protection on a wide scale. For example, it is in the best interest of all drivers and pedestrians to keep drunken drivers off the road. If the police protected only those who paid the fee, there would be less incentive to remove the drunken drivers because the probability of hitting one of the "protected" citizens is relatively slim.

c. Fire protection. Again, it is not feasible to offer fire protection only to those who pay. The classic example is the Schwartz home which is burning and uninsured right next to the Reilly house which is not burning but is insured. The fire department would have to put out the fire in Schwartz's home in order to save Reilly's. Consequently, Schwartz would not see the necessity for contributing if Reilly did.

d. Urban sewer systems. It is cheaper for a householder to discharge his sewage into the street or a nearby stream or put it into the ground; yet if everyone did this, the pollution problems could easily be imagined. Since it is undesirable for some people in an urban area to subscribe to the sewer system and not others, the government has had to get into the disposal business.

Consider our system of roads. In the early years, toll roads were actually constructed by private parties, and those who wished to travel on a relatively smooth surface had to pay for the privilege. Tolls are still charged on some highways, but it doesn't take much imagination to see the frustrations that would result from private ownership of all roads with tolls required every block or two.

Services that *regulate* relations between businesses (such as courts) and between business and the consumer cannot realistically be run by private business. Here again, government services are needed for effectiveness.

2. Services Whose Benefits Are Realized in the Future

An emerging government function which is solely oriented toward the future is its planning function. The unplanned development of our economy has led to many of our current problems such as urban blight, poor transportation and diminished environment. Today, most cities and states, as well as branches of the Federal Government have planning departments which attempt to anticipate problems of the future and suggest ways in which they may be avoided.

a. Education. Elsewhere in this book, we have viewed education as human capital. Its benefits partly accrue to the individual and partly to society as a whole. If each child were forced to pay for his education starting at grade one, it is probable that illiteracy would be far greater, and illiterate people are very inefficient in a modern society—as workers, soldiers, or just plain consumers. As a result, the United States and most other technically advanced societies provide free public education up to a certain level.

b. Social-overhead capital. A good deal of physical investment, which benefits many companies and most of the people, is necessary for the functioning of a modern economy—highways, bridges, airports, the dredging of harbors. Such services would clearly not be undertaken by a private company since the benefits are so diffuse.

There is also non-physical investment, such as the government's efforts to advance science through the National Science Foundation and other agencies.

3. Services That Do Not Pay for Themselves

The government has become increasingly involved in providing services that are not profitable for private businesses. An example is the part public, part private hospital. In wealthier areas, it is possible for a hospital to break even or even make a profit. In poorer areas, patients cannot pay for the services, so the government is faced with the choice of letting these people go without medical care or subsidizing some hospital services. It has increasingly opted for the latter course.

Commuter railroads provide necessary services but generally cannot support themselves. Their continued existence is justified by reasoning that the social costs of eliminating them, in terms of increased traffic congestion, air pollution, and lost time from work, are greater than the amount of the government subsidy.

4. Income Redistribution

Poverty is no longer solely the permanent problem of a small subgroup of our population. Many families dip below the so-called "poverty level" for short periods of time. Offsetting this are short-run government programs of transfer payments, many of which, like unemployment compensation, are automatic. Longer-run problems of poverty are approached by programs such as job training and education. The *negative income tax* has been suggested to eliminate both short- and long-term poverty by automatically transferring money to families at or below the poverty level. Experiments with this plan have generally proved its feasibility, but its actual implementation is a matter of conjecture.

PAYING FOR THE GOVERNMENT SERVICES

The theme of this book is that the individual family unit decides which goods and services it will purchase, a function ultimately constrained by its income. It can examine various costs and benefits to decide how it wishes to allocate that income.

However, with government services the costs are not so clearly related to benefits and so cannot be charged to the individual family on that basis. How then are these costs apportioned among families?

Figures 15-2 and 15-3 show what these government services are and how people pay for them. Many readers will be surprised to learn that the income taxes they pay account for less than half of total federal government revenues. This has remained fairly constant since 1960. More than a quarter of federal income (29 percent) comes from social security taxes (from individuals and employers), up from 16 percent in 1960. These funds, of course, are earmarked for payment to the contributors and their families. In the same period, corporate taxes have fallen from 23 to 14 percent of the total.

In terms of outlay, national defense and income security were almost equal in 1973, each taking about 30 percent of the pie. Since 1960, the share going to national defense has decreased from nearly 50 percent.

Another relatively stable but important item has been interest that must be paid to the owners of more than $400 billion of government debt. This came to 9.1 percent of the federal budget in 1973. We will go into this in greater detail in chapter 16.

Property taxes are the largest source of state and local revenues, with sales tax close behind (figure 15-3). The major expenditure is education which eats up over a third of state and local budgets.

a piece of the TAX PIE

PROGRESSIVE, PROPORTIONAL AND REGRESSIVE TAXES

A relatively simple solution to the problem of who should pay taxes

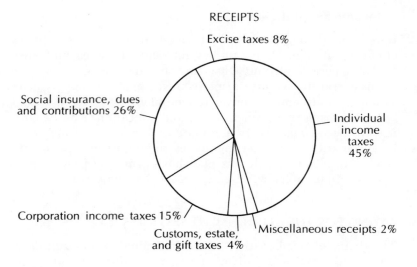

RECEIPTS

Excise taxes 8%

Social insurance, dues
and contributions 26%

Individual
income
taxes
45%

Corporation income taxes 15%

Customs, estate,
and gift taxes 4%

Miscellaneous receipts 2%

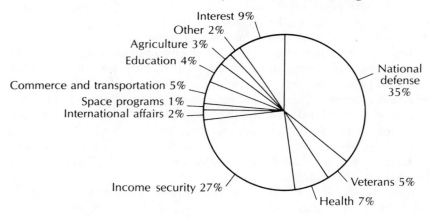

OUTLAYS
(Expenditures and net lending)

Interest 9%
Other 2%
Agriculture 3%
Education 4%
Commerce and transportation 5%
Space programs 1%
International affairs 2%

National
defense
35%

Income security 27%

Veterans 5%

Health 7%

Figure 15-2
The annual federal
budget: 1970 to 1973
(average annual
percent distribution,
by function. For fiscal
years ending June 30.

Source: *Statistical Abstracts of the United States,* 1973, p. 388.

is to assume that each family benefits more or less equally from government services and divide the taxes equally. The trouble is, the tax burden does not have an equal effect upon each family.

In chapter 1 we saw the great disparity in incomes among families of the United States. With an average tax bill per family of close to $4,000 it is easy to see that a family with only $4,000 in income would

Where it comes from . . .

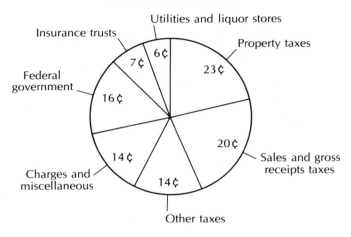

Where it goes . . .

Source: *Statistical Abstracts of the United States,* 1973, p. 411.

Figure 15-3
State and local
taxes and expenditures

be very hard hit indeed, whereas a family with an income of $30,000 would find the tax burden relatively light. Consequently, the notion of equal distribution of taxes is one that is not widely accepted. In other words, most people feel that, in some sense, a family's tax contribution should reflect its ability to pay.

But how can this best be done? The simplest formulation would be proportional taxation—an even percent of each family's income. If this were ten percent, families earning $5,000 a year would pay $500 and those earning $50,000 would pay $5,000.

Again, however, many economists have argued that the burden of a proportional tax still falls disproportionately heavy among poor families. A family earning $5,000, for example, may need all of its money to eke out a living, while $50,000 can supply a good life and quite a few luxuries. The outcome of this line of reasoning is that the tax rate should be higher on larger incomes—it should be *progressive*. The result is that a family near the poverty line pays very little, if any, of its income in taxes whereas a wealthy family would pay a very high proportion.

The proportional income tax in the United States dates back to the Civil War. From 1862 to 1872 such a tax was used as a measure to finance the war. In 1894, the Wilson-Gorman Tariff Act provided for an income tax of two percent on personal incomes above $4,000, but this was declared unconstitutional by the Supreme Court. This was reversed in 1913 with the ratification of the 16th Amendment and the Underwood-Simmons Tariff Act was passed in the same year. It provided for a one percent tax on all income in excess of an exemption of $3,000 for each taxpayer and of an additional $1,000 to a married person living with a spouse. In addition, a progressive tax was levied as a surtax on incomes over $20,000. The maximum rate of 7 percent—the 1 percent across-the-board tax and the 6 percent surtax—was applied to incomes of $500,000 or over. Since that time the progressive income tax has become accepted, although not without critics even today.

Many taxes do, in fact, appear to be *regressive,* that is, to place a proportionately greater burden on lower income families. The most cited example is the *sales tax* imposed by states and local governments. It is considered regressive since everyone, rich and poor alike, pays the same amount. Families with low incomes spend a high proportion of them on goods such as food and clothing, which are subject to sales tax. Higher income families, on the other hand, do not spend such a large proportion of their incomes on goods for two reasons: 1) higher income families save a higher proportion of their incomes, and savings are certainly not subject to sales tax; and 2) they use a larger proportion of their incomes to purchase services, such as household help, which are not subject to sales tax.

To illustrate the regressivity of the sales tax, let us assume that a family making $5,000 a year spends $4,000 of it on goods that are taxed at the rate of five percent. That's $200 per year, or 4 percent of the total income of $5,000. At the other extreme, a family earning $30,000 a year might spend only $15,000 on sales-taxable goods. At five percent that would be $450, which is only 1½ percent of their total income. Consequently, the poorer family pays more than twice the percent of its income in sales tax as does the rich family.

Let us examine the basic forms of taxation in the United States and see their impact upon the consumer.

1. Personal Income Tax

Individual income tax in the United States accounts for about a third of all taxes a person pays. According to their authoritative book entitled *Who Bears the Tax Burden,* Joseph Pechman and Benjamin Okner state that "the individual income tax is progressive over virtually the entire income scale, but it becomes regressive at the very top. This pattern reflects the fact that in the highest income classes a rising portion of total income as defined in this study is not subject to income tax at either the federal or the state level."[1] Working against the progressivity of income taxes are certain special provisions which tend to give preferred treatment to certain people or activities.

a. Tax exempt securities.

Interest from state and local government bonds is not subject to federal tax (although the income from federal issues such as savings bonds is). This benefits local governments since they can issue bonds for the purposes of constructing schools, highways, and other community projects at lower rates of interests than private companies would have to pay. This of course creates a demand for tax-exempt bonds, at least on the part of those in relatively high tax brackets, since someone in a low bracket would realize very little tax savings while at the same time getting rate of return on the bonds lower than what he could get elsewhere.

For example, consider Hilda and Janice, who are contemplating taking their money out of bank certificates of deposit that yield 7½ percent and buying $10,000 municipal bonds that yield 6 percent. Hilda is in the 60 percent tax bracket, so that her after-tax return from the bank certificate was 40 percent of $750, or $300, which compares with the $600 per year return from the tax-free municipal. Janice, on the other hand, is in the 15 percent bracket, and so her after-tax return from the bank certificate would be 85 percent of $750, or $637.50, as compared to only $600 from the tax-free municipal.

The growing demand for local and state government services has increased the supply of tax-free bonds in recent decades. Since demand for the bonds, however, has not increased proportionately, the rates paid have had to increase in order to attract enough buyers. As a result, this tax "loophole" has become increasingly more important to those who can afford to take advantage of it.

---

[1] Joseph Pechman and Benjamin Okner, *Who Bears the Tax Burden.* (Washington: The Brookings Institution, 1974), p. 57.

b. Capital gains.   Strangely enough, income earned by working is taxed at a higher rate than income earned by increase in the value of property. According to the tax law, property (land, stocks, and so forth) held for six months or longer which has appreciated in value when sold is taxed at only half the rate of other kinds of income, and to a maximum of only 25 percent of the total gain (up to $50,000). As a result, those in upper-income brackets have tended to concentrate on investments that yield a capital gain rather than ordinary income.

c. Homeowners.   As we have discussed in the chapter on housing, home ownership has been called the "tax loophole of the middle class," since mortgage interest payments and real estate taxes are deductible, and capital gains on the sale of a home may often be passed on to the purchase of a new house.

d. The aged.   Older people are given special tax benefits including additional exemptions, that is, amounts that may be deducted from gross income when filing their income tax. They are also allowed to deduct social security payments from income, and complex laws exist to cover pensions and annuities.

2. Corporate Income Tax

Corporations in America are subject to a tax on profits. Although this was initially seen as a device to divert revenues from wealthy stockholders, there is some question whether the corporation and the stockholders bear the brunt of the taxation or whether the taxes are, in fact, passed on to the consumer through higher prices. Although the argument is too complex to go into here, current feeling is that highly monopolistic corporations have the ability to do this, so that the tax burden is shared by the stockholders and the consumers.

3. Sales and Excise Taxes

As we have discussed earlier, sales taxes tend to be highly regressive. Excise taxes are like sales taxes except that they fall on a more limited set of goods, such as cigarettes, alcohol, gasoline, long distance calls, and other such "luxury" items.

Although the primary motivation behind the imposition of excise taxes has been to raise revenues for the government, it has also been used in some cases to attempt to moderate the consumption of socially "undesirable" goods. This is why the consumer pays $9 for a bottle of scotch that costs less than a dollar to manufacture and 50 cents for a package of cigarettes whose production may cost a nickel.

The effect of excise taxes, in general, is also regressive since the proportion of poorer people who smoke and drink is probably no smaller than that of their wealthier counterparts, and they pay the same tax on every bottle, pack, or gallon.

4. Property Taxes

According to the most recent study by Pechman and Okner, personal property taxes and motor vehicle licenses tend to be regressive for families at the lower end of the income scale and are proportional or even slightly progressive among higher-income groups.[2] Even poor people have to live in houses, and housing is a very large part of expenditures for low-income families. Since spending on housing tends to rise proportionately or even more than proportionately with income, higher-income families tend to have higher house values and consequently higher property taxes.

5. Payroll Taxes

The two basic payroll taxes imposed by the federal government support the unemployment insurance program and the social security system.

a. Unemployment. The payroll tax for the unemployment compensation program is levied only on employers and effects the employee or consumer only indirectly.

b. Social security. From the consumer's viewpoint, the most important payroll tax is for social security. It is paid jointly by the worker and the employer and for each amounted to 5.85 percent of the employee's wages in 1973. Self-employed persons are also eligible for social security but at a rate of 8 percent. These rates include one percent for hospital insurance under Medicare.

Social security tax is considered to be progressive up to the maximum income level—$12,600 per year in 1974, since many lower-income families derive a large proportion of their income from transfer payments such as welfare which are not subject to social security tax. Many low-income jobs are also exempt.

For incomes above $12,600 in 1974, the social security tax is clearly regressive, since those earning more than that pay no additional tax; consequently, the *percent* going to social security continuously declines as income goes up. Consumers can well anticipate continually increasing social security rates as well as limits. According to the current schedule the percentage will rise to 6.05 in 1978, 6.15 in 1981, and 6.25 in 1986. The hospital insurance part of the rate goes from 1 to 1.25 percent in 1978, 1.35 in 1981, and 1.45 in 1986.[3]

---

[2] Pechman and Okner, *op cit.,* p. 60.

[3] Social Security Administration. *Social Security Information for Young Families* (Washington: U.S. Department of Health, Education & Welfare, May, 1973), pp. 7–8.

Many critics of the social security system, however, feel that with continually expanding benefits and coverage and with the recent decline in the birth rate, the system may be in great financial difficulty within a few decades. In the future the tax may have to go far higher.

6. Estate and Gift Taxes

Aside from their value as a revenue producer, estate and gift taxes also imply a philosophical objection against the unhindered transmission of wealth from one generation to the next. To some extent, the ability of a person to become wealthy and powerful as the result of having the right parent is contrary to the ideals justifying the distribution of resources in a capitalist society such as ours. In chapter 2 we said that the justification for unequal shares of income in our system is that people who contribute more are given larger rewards. On the other hand, people who inherit wealth need not have made any contribution on their own and are therefore consuming scarce resources well out of proportion to their contribution.

In practice, however, estate and gift taxes are not very effective. According to Robert Haveman, "While this form of taxation has substantial potential as a major revenue earner, existing United States tax legislation has incorporated so many special provisions that it is only a minor source of federal tax revenue."[4]

THE NET EFFECT OF TAXES

When all of the various taxes paid by families are added together, what is the net effect? As a result of their study, Pechman and Okner conclude[5] that the tax system is virtually proportional for the vast majority of families in the United States, which as we mentioned earlier tends to hit lower income families harder. All told, taxes reduce income and equality by less than five percent. Those who gain from the tax system tend to be homeowners, rural farm residents, families with transfers as the major source of their incomes, and those with large numbers of children. Other population subgroups which tend to pay somewhat more taxes than average rates include renters, urban residents, families who draw their major source of income from property or business, and single persons.[6]

---

[4] Robert Haveman, *The Economics of the Public Sector.* (New York: John Wiley and Sons, Inc., 1970), p. 137.

[5] Joseph Pechman and Benjamin Okner, *op cit.,* p. 64.

[6] *Ibid.,* p. 82.

WHAT CAN THE CONSUMER DO ABOUT TAXES?

For most consumers, about the only thing they can do about taxes is pay them and complain. Those with low and moderate incomes tend to have little discretion to vary the amount of taxes they pay; about the only alternatives are 1) in the choice of a house and the attendant real estate taxes, which differ not only by the value of the house but also by the location and government services provided; and 2) the decision of whether or not to itemize income taxes or to take the standard deduction. While the former decision is a matter of taste, the latter is an empirical question that can best be decided by working the tax out both ways.

In many communities, consumers have an opportunity to help determine local expenditures and taxation. This is done at election time through voting on bonds to raise money for capital expenditures or on real estate tax rates. Beginning in the late 1960s, voters in many areas began to reject additional services and taxation. This may well be an indication that a growing number of consumers are satisfied with the mix of public and private services they are receiving.

It is only when the family achieves a somewhat higher income that it becomes worthwhile for its members to worry a great deal about taxes. Higher-income families have higher taxes to worry about, but also the wherewithall to greatly reduce that burden as the result of the special provisions or loopholes in the tax laws. It often becomes worthwhile for the consumer at this income level to invest his time in a study of the tax laws or to invest his money in hiring an expert who will be helpful to him.

SUMMARY

1. The U.S. economy is mixed; it is run by a combination of business and government. The increasing role of government calls for increased taxes to provide the desired services.

2. The government provides five essential services: those that provide collective social benefits, future benefits, and income redistribution; and those that business cannot provide or that do not pay for themselves.

3. The family cannot apply traditional cost-benefit analysis to tax expenditures. The cost of government services is apportioned among families by various kinds of taxes paid.

4. Proportional taxes take the same percent of everyone's income, and though at first glance appear fair, are actually unfair to poorer families who must spend more of their income on necessities. A regressive tax

places the heaviest burden on lower-income families. A progressive tax is the fairest: as income goes up, the proportion of income paid in taxes also goes up.

5. The basic forms of U.S. taxation are personal income, corporate income, sales and excise, property, payroll, and estate and gift taxes.

6. Studies show that when all is said and done, the U.S. tax system is virtually proportional.

7. The consumer can affect his own tax payments by the purchase of a home for its accompanying tax benefits, by deciding to itemize tax returns or take standard deductions, and by voting on local bond and tax issues.

8. The higher a family's income, the higher its expected taxes should be. At some point it becomes very worthwhile for the consumer to study tax laws or seek professional help in order to benefit from tax-law benefits.

QUESTIONS

1. Which government services are growing most rapidly, federal or state and local? What is the reason?

2. Under what circumstances can government provision of parks and playgrounds be justified?

3. Would you consider that a state lottery is a form of regressive, proportional, or progressive taxation? Why?

4. How can a consumer's choice of housing affect the amount of taxes he pays?

5. Cite arguments for and against the following tax "loopholes":
   a. capital gains tax
   b. tax-free bonds
   c. extra tax exemptions for the blind and the elderly
   d. tax deferment of profit made on sale of a house

The American Economic Association. *Readings in the Economics of Taxation.* Vol. IX. (Homewood, Ill.: Richard D. Irwin, 1959).

Buchanan, James M. *The Public Finances.* An Introductory Textbook. Rev. ed. (Homewood, Ill.: Richard D. Irwin, 1968).

Haveman, Robert H. *The Economics of the Public Sector.* (New York: John Wiley, 1970).

Horber, Bernard P. *Modern Public Finance.* (Homewood, Ill: Richard D. Irwin, 1967).

Pechman, Joseph A. *Federal Tax Policy,* Rev. ed. (Washington, D.C.: Brookings Institution, 1971).

Pechman, Joseph A. and Benjamin A. Okner. *Who Bears the Tax Burden?* (Washington, D.C.: Brookings Institution, 1974).

SELECTED REFERENCES AND SOURCES OF DATA

16

FISCAL POLICY

Through much of this book, we have discussed actions that the consumer might take to better his economic welfare. We have discussed how the consumer through proper planning may increase his income, make wise decisions regarding investments, purchase the best insurance, and get the best terms on credit.

We have also seen the role of the government as rulemaker or mediator between the consumer and the businessman, thereby insuring that the consumer is in a fair position to bargain in the economic system.

There are, in addition, certain major economic events that affect the consumer in which he is almost powerless to act—events that affect the entire economy. Although the consumer may not be able to change these events, by being able to recognize and understand them, he can perhaps minimize their detrimental impact.

Two of the most important economic effects that can adversely affect the consumer are inflation and unemployment. While these were at one time viewed as almost inevitable in the context of so-called business cycles, economists have learned much more in the past thirty-five or forty years about their causes and about methods of preventing them. As we will see, a relatively new and important role for the government is to control the economy for the benefit of its citizens.

National Product

Just as there are certain indicators, such as income, net worth, and debt, that show how well a consumer is doing, there are also indicators that show the health of an entire economy. Perhaps the most important such indicator is the Gross National Product (GNP), which is equivalent to the total income earned by all elements of our economy. The Gross National Product is derived by tabulating the final value of all goods and services produced in our economy in a year's time and is the sum of all *final products* produced.

Intermediate products are not counted in the costs in summing up the GNP. The baker who buys 20 cents worth of flour and shortening to bake into a loaf of bread sells it for 45 cents. The value of his contribution to the GNP is not 45 cents, but only the 25 cents that he has added to the process himself. If we count the 45 cents that the consumer pays for the bread and add to it the 20 cents that the baker pays for the supplies, that comes to 65 cents which is more than the loaf of bread costs. So, in order to avoid double counting, we either must add up the final price or value of goods produced in a year, or, alternatively, add up the value added during each step of processing. In the case of the bread, the value added by the farmer who grew the wheat might be 10 cents, the value added by the miller who milled the flour might be another 10 cents; add 5 cents for shortening for a total of 20 cents when it all gets to the baker. The baker adds 25 cents for his service, thereby coming to the same price of 45 cents.

In 1973, the GNP was close to 1.3 trillion dollars. Not all of that, however, ends up as income for the nation's consumers. Why is this so?

First, a certain amount of capital, the machinery of production, is used up in the process of creating goods and services. This, we know, is called depreciation, and a certain amount of current income must be put aside to replace worn goods. If we subtract depreciation from GNP, we arrive at another often cited statistic called Net National Product (table 16–1). But even this doesn't all reach consumers as income. There are taxes levied on corporations and other businesses before the money reaches the consumer, and these must be taken out to arrive at a statistic called *National Income*. In addition, corporations do not distribute all of their profits to shareholders, so corporate profits are taken out while dividends are added back in. After we subtract all of these things, as well as social security contributions taken from our paychecks, and add in transfer payments, or non-earned income such as welfare payments, we reach the personal income of the consumer. Then, of course, the consumer must pay his own income taxes before he gets to spend what he has left, which is called *disposable income.*

In essence, national income, whether we measure it by GNP or Net National Product (NNP) or even personal income, is one measure of how well the economy is doing.

TABLE 16-1

National Income in the United States

1970 (billions of dollars)

	Gross National Product	$976.5
Less	Depreciation	- 84.3
Equals	Net National Product	= 892.2
Less	Indirect Business Taxes	- 92.1
	Social Security Contributions	- 57.1
	Corporate Income Taxes	- 37.5
	Undistributed Corporate Profits	- 13.8
Plus	Transfer Payments	Z109.3
Equals	Personal Income	= 801.0
Less	Personal Taxes	-116.2
Equals	Disposable Income	= $684.8

Of course, the GNP figure alone is somewhat meaningless, since it must be viewed relative to something else. If someone told you that the GNP of Foo Foo Island was three trillion gil-gils, you might be very impressed. Similarly, if I tell you that the GNP of the United States is 1.3 trillion dollars, that sounds like a tremendous amount of money. Yet we must know some other things in order to know just how well the economy is doing.

growth A GNP of 1.3 trillion dollars sounds pretty good unless you hear that last year it was 1.5 trillion. Generally speaking, economic growth is a sign of health in an economy. When more goods and services are produced, people have more and, generally, are better off.

Of course within recent years the concept that more is best has been challenged by environmentalists who say that more means more pollution; but still, very few would be willing to say that a declining GNP was a very desirable situation. So one sign of health in our economy is to see GNP growing year by year at a fairly stable rate. There are others.

stable prices If GNP, measured in current dollars, increased 5 percent over last year, but prices increased by 10 percent, it is a sign that our economy is not in the peak of health. For this reason, economists suggest adjusting for price increases to account for differences in the price level.

The consumer price index (CPI) is more popularly referred to as the cost of living index and is measured each month in various places throughout the United States by the Bureau of Labor Statistics. The Bureau has determined the items that families ordinarily buy and their importance in their budgets. Then, professional shoppers from the Bureau of Labor Statistics go around to various stores in their areas and actually price some of these items. When you read in the newspaper that prices

HEY! THIS IS A $10,000 SUIT-THAT PANT LEG ALONE IS WORTH $2,000!

(TAX DOG)

have gone up by two tenths of one percent, this means that the average, weighted for the importance in budget, of all of the goods purchased by consumers has increased by two-tenths of one percent over the preceding period. In table 16-2, the CPI for several years is given with 1967 as a base. Periodically, this base is brought up to date.

Table 16-3 shows wholesale prices, the prices of intermediate goods before they are eventually sold to the consumer. Wholesale prices are often reported in the media because they tend to be a leading indicator of increases in consumer prices. If wholesale prices are up sharply in a month, it is a fairly good indication that soon consumer prices will be up as well.

In order not to distort current income figures by including inflation, a method is used to put prices in "real" terms. There is no one real price. By real we mean prices measured with respect to a particular year which is known as a base year. Often, for example, you will see income for 1973 measured in 1968 prices, or changes from 1968 to 1973 may have been 30 percent in measured income and only 15 percent in *real* income. In order to deflate prices you merely set a price index equal to 1.0 in your base year, say 1968, and add to that the proportionate increase in prices in the intervening years—say 15 percent. Then the price index for 1973 would be 1.15. In order to deflate income in 1973, merely divide income measured in 1973 prices by the price index base 1968, or 1.15, to arrive at the income for 1973 at 1968 prices. Having done that, the comparison between 1968 and 1973 will be a measure of real change in income.

unemployment Another important measure of health in the economy that the GNP alone will not tell you is the amount of unemployment. Although human labor is just one resource input into the production process (like land, capital, and entrepreneurial ability), it has detrimental social effects if not enough of it is used.

When a person is unemployed, his income ceases. To some extent, he puts a burden on the state to provide him with a means of support, but far more important are the social effects that no income has upon his family and his children. Consequently, one of the goals of the government is to maintain full employment.

The Employment Act of 1946, which established the President's Council of Economic Advisors, gave three goals for the federal government: no unemployment; stable prices (no inflation), and continued economic growth.

One fact that continually amazes noneconomists is that full employment involves a certain amount of unemployment—3–4 percent is considered normal. The reason is that in our economy, there is always a certain amount of "frictional" unemployment caused by people shifting between jobs. Labor is a resource that responds to different job conditions; in

TABLE 16-2

Consumer Prices, 1929–1973 (1967 = 100)

(For urban wage earners and clerical workers.)

Period	All Items	Food	Housing	Apparel and Upkeep	Transportation
1929	51.3	48.3	—	48.5	—
1945	53.9	50.7	59.1	61.5	47.8
1960	88.7	88.0	90.2	89.6	89.6
1965	94.5	94.4	94.9	93.7	95.9
1970	116.2	114.9	118.9	116.1	112.7
1971	121.3	118.4	124.3	119.8	118.6
1972	125.3	123.5	129.2	122.3	119.9
1973	133.1	141.4	135.0	126.8	123.8

Source: *Economic Report of the President, 1974*, p. 300.

order for our economy to be efficient, it must be free to shift from declining industries, like horse carriages, to growing industries, like automobiles. There are always going to be some unemployed.

Of course, we find that in many years there is unemployment beyond the expected 3 or 4 percent.

Table 16-4 shows some important facts about unemployment in the United States. First, for all workers, the rate since 1960 has mainly fluctuated between 4 and 6 percent. In wartime, with the great need for the labor of every able-bodied person, rates may decline substantially (it was 1.2 percent in 1944). On the other hand, in the depth of the Great Depression in 1933, the figure was 24.9 percent.

A second important point to remember is that everyone is not treated equally in the labor market. Whatever the overall rate of unemployment, it will be much higher for teenagers, and higher for women and nonwhites than for white men. In 1973, for example, while total unemployment

TABLE 16-3

Wholesale Prices: Summary

(1967 = 100)

Period	All Commodities	Farm Products	Processed Foods and Feeds	Industrial Commodities
1960	94.9	97.2	89.5	95.3
1965	96.6	98.7	95.5	96.4
1970	110.4	111.0	112.0	110.0

Source: *Federal Reserve Bulletin*, September 1972, p. A 68.

TABLE 16-4

Unemployment Rates by Selected Groups

1960–1973

Year	All Workers	Teenage Workers (Aged 16–19)	Men (Aged 20 and Over)	Women (Aged 20 and Over)	White	Non-White
1960	5.5	14.7	4.7	5.1	4.9	10.2
1961	6.7	16.8	5.7	6.3	6.0	12.4
1962	5.5	14.7	4.6	5.4	4.9	10.9
1963	5.7	17.2	4.5	5.4	5.0	10.8
1964	5.2	16.2	3.9	5.2	4.6	9.6
1965	4.5	14.8	3.2	4.5	4.1	8.1
1966	3.8	12.8	2.5	3.8	3.4	7.3
1967	3.8	12.8	2.3	4.2	3.4	7.4
1968	3.6	12.7	2.2	3.8	3.2	6.7
1969	3.5	12.2	2.1	3.7	3.1	6.4
1970	4.9	15.2	3.5	4.8	4.5	8.2
1971	5.9	16.9	4.4	5.7	5.4	9.9
1972	5.6	16.2	4.0	5.4	5.0	10.0
1973	4.9	14.5	3.2	4.8	4.3	8.9

Source: *Economic Report of the President, 1974,* p. 279.

was 4.9 percent, it was three times as high for teenagers and twice as high for nonwhites. In spite of laws against discrimination in hiring, relative unemployment rates among subgroups appear largely unchanged.

Relationship of National Income and Employment

The income of our economy, measured as either the Gross or Net National Product, is related directly to the number of people in the labor force: more people can produce more goods. A country like Sweden with about eight million people has a much smaller GNP than the United States, even though the per capita product, the amount that each person produces, is about the same.

Since national income is directly related to the number of people employed, two things become clear. First, and most obviously, the more people you have employed the higher the national income. But another point not quite as obvious is: the lower the national income, the fewer jobs available. In other words, at some level of national income, say a GNP of 1.5 trillion dollars, we have full employment (less than 3 or 4 percent frictionally unemployed). At a GNP below that, say 1.3 trillion dollars, not everyone who wants to work can, so we have unemployment. Now the question is, what determines the level of national income and, consequently, the level of employment? And the answer to that question is *aggregate demand.*

In our economy, producers will hire people to help them produce only if there is a market for their products. If a snowmobile manufacturer has no sales for his snowmobiles, he will have to lay off his employees.

Demand for the goods and services in our economy is made up not only of the consumer but of business, which wants goods for the purpose of investment, and government, which buys goods and services for the benefit of the citizens.

In addition, there is a demand for American goods and services in foreign countries. To some extent this is offset by the reduction in domestic demand because of goods that we import, but as we will see in chapter 18, we generally export slightly more, so the margin contributes to aggregate demand.

In 1970, when our GNP was 976.5 billion dollars (see table 16-1), this was accounted for by consumer demand of 616.7 billion, investment of 135.7 billion, government purchases of 220.5 billion, and net exports (exports minus imports) of 3.6 billion.

To restate it very briefly, unemployment occurs when aggregate demand is not sufficiently large to sustain the employment of everyone willing to work.

Inflation

If aggregate demand is above the full employment level, it will cause *inflation.*

Let us suppose again that full employment GNP is 1.5 trillion dollars, and let's assume that total demand—consumers, business investment, and government—is 1.7 trillion dollars. There is just no way, given the number of people in the United States who are available to produce goods, that we are going to be able to produce 1.7 trillion dollars worth of goods. Consequently, the total demand of 1.7 trillion is higher than full-employment supply and constitutes what is known as *excess demand.* It means that more goods are wanted than are available at current prices. Thinking back to our analysis of supply and demand, we recall that whenever people want more goods than are available at a certain price, the price has a tendency to rise. This is, in fact, what happens in the aggregate: the price of goods and services combined will go up, and we have inflation.

This occurred during the last years of the Johnson administration when consumer spending was high, business investment was high, and the government was spending a great deal of money to fight an expensive war in Viet Nam. The demand for goods and services was greater than an

economy going at full capacity could produce, and prices went up.

This very simple relation between aggregate supply and aggregate demand was not very clear to economists for a long time. It was pointed out in 1935 by John Maynard Keynes in his famous book *The General Theory of Employment, Interest and Money*. What this meant was that if there were unemployment, say during a depression, which was caused by the fact that aggregate demand was less than full employment national income, the unemployment could be diminished by increasing aggregate demand.

How does one increase aggregate demand? Well, of the three major components, consumption is most difficult to increase since the government has very little control over consumption. Investment can be increased through monetary policy, which will be explained later. However, the easiest thing for the government to do is increase its expenditures. It can do this at will in a number of ways because it is not bound by tax revenues. Most of us—consumers, businesses, and state and local governments—cannot spend more than we take in except for short periods of time when we borrow money that must be repaid. The federal government, on the other hand, is not that constrained. It has vast borrowing powers, and since the currency of a country is only as good as its government, a debt obligation of the government in the form of a bond, a bill, or a note is as good as cash in terms of its safety. Consequently, the government is able to borrow large sums of money almost indefinitely and use that money to increase aggregate demand.

The Multiplier Effect

Now let us assume that current national income is 50 billion dollars below full employment national income. If the government wanted full employment, wouldn't it have to increase its own expenditures by 50 billion dollars? The answer is no. The government could conceivably increase its expenditures by only 10 billion dollars and cause an increase in aggregate demand of 50 billion dollars. Why is this so?

This is due to the so-called *multiplier effect,* whereby an increase in expenditures in one sector will result in a manyfold increase in aggregate demand. The cause of this phenomenon is what John Maynard Keynes called the "marginal propensity to consume."

Back in chapter 5, we talked about Keynes's idea that when a consumer's income increases, his consumption also increases, but not by as much. Let's say that, on the average, the marginal propensity to consume in this country is .8—that is, if a family gets an increase of $1,000, it will tend to spend $800 of it and save $200. Now let's take a look at an increase in government expenditures and see what happens.

To illustrate how this works let us assume that the government wishes to increase aggregate demand, and that it goes out in the community and hires unemployed people to dig ditches and fill them back in. Suppose that it went out and hired John Jones who had a reputation as a skilled ditch filler. Jones, who theoretically had an income of zero (although he may have been getting a little assistance from welfare) suddenly jumps up to an income of $10,000 a year. Since his marginal propensity to consume is .8, he will consume $8,000 of this and save $2,000 of it (assuming there are no taxes).

In the first instance, aggregate demand went up by $10,000 since the government increased its purchases of goods and services, namely the services of John Jones for $10,000. But then Jones turned right around and increased demand by another $8,000 with his consumption, so aggregate demand is now up by $18,000.

Now what did Jones do with this money? He bought groceries, paid the rent, bought clothing for the children, and so on—in other words, he spent the $8,000 on goods and services largely within his community. As a result, the merchants and landlords around town find that their incomes have suddenly gone up by the $8,000 that John Jones spent, and since these people too have a marginal propensity to consume of .8, they spend $8,000 times .8, or $6,400 of the $8,000 that they got from John Jones. So now we are up to $24,400, and the process still has more room to continue. When everything is added together, it comes out to very close to $50,000 (table 16-5).

What is the multiplier? For the $10,000 that the government spent, aggregate demand was increased by $50,000, or a ratio of five to one. The multiplier in this case is five. The formula for calculating the multiplier is very simply one divided by one minus the marginal propensity to consume, in this case:

$$\frac{1}{1-.8} = \frac{1}{.2} = 5$$

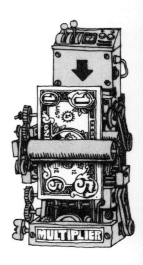

In terms of increasing aggregate demand, the government gets a lot of bang for the buck. Yet the government is not the only source of increased aggregate demand. If, for example, businesses decided to invest an extra ten thousand dollars, the same process would occur. They would order $10,000 more in capital goods which would make the capital goods manufacturer $10,000 richer, and he would spend $8,000 of it and so on. If businesses decided to invest extra money, that money would also go through the multiplier effect to increase aggregate demand.

Now what about the consumer sector? The same thing is true here. If consumers had previously been spending 900 billion dollars a year and suddenly decided to increase their expenditures to 910 billion dollars a year, an increase of 10 billion dollars, the same multiplier effect would

TABLE 16-5

The Income Multiplier

Process	Increase in Aggregate Demand
Government hires Jones for $10,000 per year	$10,000.00
Jones consumes	8,000.00
Recipients of Jones' money consume	6,400.00
Recipients of that money consume	5,120.00
Recipients of that money consume	4,096.00
Recipients of that money consume	3,276.80
Recipients of that money consume	2,621.44
Recipients of that money consume	2,097.15
Recipients of that money consume	1,677.72
Recipients of that money consume	1,342.18
Recipients of that money consume	1,073.74
Recipients of that money consume	858.99
Recipients of that money consume	687.19
Recipients of that money consume	594.76
Recipients of that money consume	439.80
Recipients of that money consume	351.84
Recipients of that money consume	281.47
Recipients of that money consume	225.18
Recipients of that money consume	180.14
Recipients of that money consume	144.12
Recipients of that money consume	115.29
Recipients of that money consume	92.23
Total	$49,676.04

work; and if the marginal propensity to consume were .8, income would increase by 50 billion dollars.

What causes consumers to want to increase or decrease their expenditures? One factor is consumer sentiment, which we discussed in chapter 5. Consumer spending may depend on a feeling of optimism or pessimism regarding the future of the economy. For that reason, George Katona of the University of Michigan's Survey Research Center and others who have studied the consumer suggest that the power of the consumer is very great.

It must be noted, of course, that the multiplier effect works just as well in the opposite direction. If government, business, or consumer expenditures fall by 10 billion dollars, aggregate demand decreases by 50 billion. When aggregate demand equals or is less than full employment output, a decrease in national income results in greater unemployment. However, if the economy is in an inflationary period where aggregate demand is greater than full employment output and prices are rising, any of these methods can be used to decrease demand to the point where we reach a non-inflationary full-employment economy, which is the goal of every government.

To fight inflation, the government can reduce the level of demand in two ways: it can lower its expenditures, or it can increase taxes. The combination of federal expenditure and taxation policies is known as *fiscal policy* of the government. (This may be contrasted with *monetary policy* which we will discuss later.)

Expenditures

There may be good reasons why the government does not want to cut its spending. For one thing, many funds are committed years in advance. For another, the government may not wish to cut its major expenditure, national defense, for fear that the defense stature of the United States may be weakened. Therefore, it may be forced to take the other alternative of increasing taxes.

Tax Policies

Strangely enough, an increase in taxes does not have the same dollar for dollar impact through the multiplier as a decrease in expenditures. Let us examine why this is true.

Take John Jones who is now making $10,000 a year as a ditch filler for the federal government. The government decides to increase taxes, so it charges Jones $2,000 in federal taxes. If the multiplier is five, as it was before, would not the increase in his taxes result in a decrease in aggregate demand of $2,000 times five, or $10,000? The answer is no.

If Jones's taxes are increased by $2,000, he does not decrease his consumption by $2,000. The marginal propensity to consume of .8 says that if he were given an increase of $2,000, he would spend 80 percent or $1,600. Similarly, if $2,000 of his money is taken away by taxes, he will decrease his consumption by eight-tenths of that, or $1,600. Where will the other $400 come from? From his savings. An increase in taxes of $2,000 means that John Jones will consume $1,600 a year less than before, but he will also save $400 less than before. So, if John Jones decreases his consumption by $1,600, with a multiplier of five, this results in a decrease in demand of $8,000. Consequently, a change in taxes always has a smaller multiplier effect than a change in government expenditures. For this reason, if the government both increased expenditures and paid for it by increased taxes of the same amount, the net effect would be an increase in aggregate demand. This is known as the *balanced budget multiplier effect*. This means that a government that is attempting to reduce inflation cannot raise expenditures and taxes *by the same amount* without also further increasing aggregate demand—which would encourage more inflation.

The Incompleteness of Government Fiscal Policy

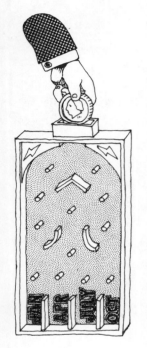

In the earlier sections of this chapter we tried to lay out fiscal policies available to the government as well as the reason and probable impact of their effect. The precise numbers we used, however, should not influence the reader to believe that the government has complete control over the economy—far from it. If it did, it would stand to reason that there would never be any unemployment other than frictional and that the rate of inflation would always be zero or very close to it.

Unfortunately, this is not the case. While economists can predict the probable direction of government fiscal policies, they can in no way predict the exact magnitude of the effect of a tax cut or increased expenditures, nor can they predict the timing of the effect. The fact that there is a multiplier is quite well established, but it does not operate with the precision given in table 16-5. If the average marginal propensity to consume is .8, this does not mean that when John Jones gets an additional $10,000 in income he will spend $8,000 of it. He may spend all of it, he may spend none of it; he will probably spend some amount other than $8,000. Small fluctuations in the desires of consumers to save can cause big differences in the multiplier.

Timing is also a critical variable. If the government attempts to counteract unemployment by increasing expenditures by an extra 5 billion dollars and the true multiplier is five, aggregate demand will go up by 25 billion dollars. But the question is, when will this effect occur? Ideally, it would occur the next day so that demand would be stimulated and people would be hired again. Practically speaking, however, this is impossible since the people getting the funds must re-spend them over and over, down the line of the multiplier, which may take six months or a year. The full impact of the additional 25 billion dollars may occur a year later when, for other reasons, the economy is on an upswing and unemployment very low. Consequently, the government action, because of its delayed impact, may contribute to inflation rather than reduce unemployment. Several economists who are critical of government fiscal policy admit that it is subject to a "long and variable lag" which may have ultimate effects contrary to those intended.

supply inflation   Inflation is not due exclusively to excessive government spending. Other factors contribute to price increases: consider the *supply inflation* of 1973–74.

As we recall from chapter 6, whenever the supply of an item is reduced and demand remains the same, the price will be driven up since the consumers will bid higher and higher to get what there is of it.

Ordinarily, when the price of one good in an economy goes up, the effect on prices in general is not very great. However, when that good is an important input to many other commodities, or when it constitutes a sizeable part of total expenditures, an increase in its price can cause a substantial increase overall. This is largely what happened in 1973 when the oil-producing nations of the world decided to greatly increase the price of petroleum. The Arab countries for political reasons also decided to entirely restrict supplies of petroleum to the United States. As a result, the cost-of-living index shot up. Why?

First, everybody uses lots of direct petroleum products such as heating oil and gasoline, and when prices went up substantially, the overall cost of living increased by a fair amount. Second, producers of other goods that use petroleum in their production processes had to raise prices because of more expensive petroleum. The cost of such goods as plastics and other petrochemically based products was increased. Third, since much of the nation's transportation is fueled by petroleum, the cost of delivering all goods went up, thereby raising prices. And fourth, since many utilities are powered by oil products, the cost of electricity went up.

While petroleum was the most dramatic example of supply inflation, other products are also responsible. When steel companies increase the price of their product (which may or may not result from increased wages to steel workers), the effect on the economy is also widespread. The reason is obvious—so many of our goods are made of steel or steel products. It is for this reason that President Kennedy took what, at the time, amounted to extreme measures to hold the line when companies announced a price hike in 1962. There is a vast difference in the overall impact on the economy of a ten percent increase in the price of steel as opposed to, say, a ten percent increase in the price of bananas.

wage-price inflation Once inflation gets going, it becomes relatively difficult to control because it gathers its own momentum. The *wage-price* cycle, a form of supply inflation, is often cited as a cause. This may occur because workers in many of the large oligopolistic industries in the United States such as steel and automobiles belong to large and powerful unions. If, for some reason, inflation increases prices by, say, 7 percent, unions may justifiably demand and receive wage increases that will cover at least the increases in the cost of living. In fact, many unions have such *escalator clauses* incorporated into their contracts. Often, large industries will agree to such wage increases because they can pass on the increased costs in the form of higher prices, since there is little competition to hold prices down. Increased prices in fundamental and widespread industries such as these cause a supply-inflation effect which further increases the cost of living. In the following year, the unions may demand and get a further increase in wages to offset the further increased cost of living. And so on and on the spiral goes until the government can step in and effectively interrupt it with policies that may, by that time, appear to be drastic.

Who is Affected by Inflation?

It is extremely important to realize that in most inflations the greatest effect is *redistributive*. This means that, for the most part, for everyone who is hurt by inflation, there is someone else who benefits from it. This may not be true in cases of supply inflation where the supply problem is the result of natural causes, such as a drought that drives up the cost of food; but in most types of inflation that we know today there is as much gain as loss.

From the consumer's point of view, since he is not able to control inflation individually, it is important that he learn which of his actions may cause personal gains or losses during the almost perpetual inflation that we know.

To put it in simple perspective, people gain from inflation if their assets increase in value more rapidly than prices increase, and they lose if their assets increase less rapidly. Assets in this case include human capital, pension rights, and other income producers.

Since the majority of consumers in America have most of their assets in human capital, we shall consider this first. Workers who have jobs that give them some type of market control generally fare better in inflation than those who do not. Market control is most easily achieved by a powerful union, which can bargain on equal footing with large employers and which also has the power to exclude non-union labor from competing against its members. This need not be a trade union—it may be any society that restricts membership and provides necessary goods, such as the American Medical Association, which has been called by some economists the most powerful union in America.

Another group of people who often benefit from inflation are businessmen who see the price of their products steadily increasing; their profits tend to increase as well.

Those who suffer most from inflation in terms of their human capital or working income neither share in the increased profits of business nor have strong market positions to bargain for higher wages. Government workers such as teachers and civil service employees have traditionally been in this position. In the last decade, however, organized labor has become increasingly important among government workers, and this pattern is changing.

asset distribution While many consumers may not have the ability to change occupations in order to keep up with inflation, they may be able to mitigate some of its effects by wise distribution of their assets. As we mentioned earlier, home ownership has generally proven to be an excellent hedge against inflation; other types of real estate have, too. The worst asset to hold during an inflation is one of fixed nominal value such as cash or money in a checking account, which pays no interest.

In periods of high inflation such as that of 1973 and 1974, consumers who held money in savings accounts saw it lose value. On the other hand, many who had $5,000 or $10,000 were able to invest in government bonds which yielded a higher rate of interest than that offered by the banks. Those who had even larger sums of money could invest in special certificates of deposit offered by commercial banks which occasionally paid rates in excess of the rate of inflation.

During periods of rapidly increasing prices, the physical goods that a consumer owns also increase with the cost of living. Just as many corporations found that they made "inventory profits" just on the basis of holding goods in storage and seeing their prices increase, so consumers may realize inventory profits by buying large quantities of food and storing them or buying appliances and other goods they know they will need before the prices go up any higher.

As we mentioned in chapter 12, in times of moderate inflation investments in the stock market are often a good hedge; however, in periods of great inflation this does not seem to be a good bet since the market tends to go down as prices go up, largely because of uncertainty in the economy.

In the past, those who were often hurt worst by inflation were on a fixed income, such as the elderly who had to exist on pensions and social security. Two recent factors have helped to mitigate the situation of the elderly. First, social security is now tied to the cost of living, or "indexed", so that as prices go up, so do the benefits. Second, the variable annuity, a fairly recent development, is available as a part of many pension and life insurance plans. All or part of the payments are put into common stocks and other investments that generally gain in value with inflation. This helps to insure that in thirty years, when Edgar Smith retires, he won't have to live on a pension, which in terms of current buying power, is worth one tenth of the dollars he put in during his working years.

1. A knowledge of basic principles of economics can equip the consumer to get the best return from his limited resources. The government also plays an important role in safeguarding and furthering consumer interests. Inflation and unemployment are two economic conditions that affect everyone. Even though a consumer by himself is powerless against these conditions, he can still act to minimize the deleterious effects.

2. There are indicators that give a measure of the health of the economy; Gross National Product and Net National Product are two.

SUMMARY

3. GNP figures must be placed in the context of growth of the economy, stability of prices, and unemployment figures. The Employment Act of 1946 gave the federal government three goals—to minimize unemployment, to stabilize prices, and to maintain economic growth.

4. A certain amount of unemployment must exist, even when "full employment" is achieved. Whatever unemployment exists above frictional unemployment is never spread evenly throughout the labor force.

5. GNP and employment are intricately linked and are dependent upon aggregate demand. Aggregate demand above full employment output is one form of inflation.

6. A change in expenditures by any sector of the economy will result in a manyfold change in aggregate demand. This phenomenon is known as the multiplier effect.

7. Inflation can be caused by aggregate demand above aggregate supply, by supply shortages, and by wage-price spirals.

QUESTIONS

1. Trace the effects of a tax cut on national income and employment levels.

2. If there are only two choices open to a government, which is the better in your judgment, inflation or unemployment?

3. Since marginal propensity to consume has such a direct effect on national income, is saving a virtue?

4. What are some of the kinds of unemployment in addition to frictional unemployment? What would be the effect of fiscal policy on them?

5. Would starting a war with another country increase one country's GNP?

TERMINOLOGY

inflation
gross national product
net national product
disposable income
consumer price index
frictional unemployment

multiplier effect
marginal propensity to consume
aggregate demand
index number
fiscal policy
balanced budget multiplier

Katona, George and Eva Mueller. *Consumer Responses to Income Increases.* (Washington, D.C.: Brookings Institute, 1968). (Report of interviews to measure the reactions of consumers to the tax cut of 1964.)

Keynes, John Maynard. *The General Theory of Employment, Interest and Money.* (New York: Harcourt, Brace & World, 1965).

McConnell, Campbell R. *Economics: Principles, Problems and Policies.* 5th ed. (New York: McGraw-Hill, 1972). (See Chapter 14 for a discussion on fiscal policy.)

Samuelson, Paul A. *Economics.* 8th ed. (New York: McGraw-Hill, 1970). (See chapter on fiscal policy.)

Smith, Warren L. and Ronald L. Teigen, ed. *Readings in Money, National Income and Stabilization Policy.* Rev. ed. (Homewood, Ill.: Richard D. Irwin, 1970).

17

MONETARY POLICY

The government's fiscal policy is only one of the instruments it has to keep the economy on an even keel. Another major control is its monetary policy.

Consumers who have bought or sold houses in the past several years have probably noticed very strange things happening to mortgages. For a while, interest rates appeared to be relatively reasonable, say 7 percent or less, and someone wanting to buy a house would have a good chance of getting a mortgage with a downpayment of perhaps 10 percent of the purchase price. Then, almost without warning, interest rates shot up to 8½ or 9 or even 9½ percent, and sources of mortgage money began to dry up, meaning that it was nearly impossible to get a loan. The few loans that were available required very large downpayments.

Of course, what was happening to consumers in the mortgage market was also reflected, to some extent, in the consumer credit market where, when interest rates went up, consumers not only had to pay more for a loan, but it was also more difficult to find lenders. At the same time, businessmen found it both more difficult and more expensive to get loans.

These occurrences were not coincidental and did not result from sunspots or comets passing overhead. Both high interest rates and decreased loan availability are largely the result of government monetary policies designed to slow down the rate of inflation.

How does the supply of money relate to inflation? To

a great extent, it works through the interest rate which is the price of borrowed money. If the supply of money is increased, more is available for borrowing and the price—the interest rate—goes down. If the supply of money is decreased, then interest rates go up. Now, what effect do interest rates have on inflation?

In the previous section we spoke of three components of overall demand which control the level of economic activity: the consumer and business investment as well as government. If the government controls interest rates, what does this do to business investment and consumer spending?

Let us take business first. In chapter 7, we said that a businessman will borrow money in order to make a capital investment if the yield on that investment is greater than the cost (interest) of the loan. Therefore, it follows that when businessmen have to pay only 7 percent for a loan, a great many more investments are profitable than if they had to pay 10 percent for that same loan. So, at a loan rate of 7 percent, there will be much more business investment.

That takes care of businessmen. What about consumers? As we have seen in earlier chapters, a great many costly items such as cars and appliances are made possible only through consumer credit. When interest rates go up, lenders charge more because the money is worth more. Therefore, to the extent that consumers are sensitive to the rate of interest, they will postpone buying things on credit if they must pay more for the loans.

While there is some question whether consumers are sensitive to general credit rates, when the government raises mortgage rates, the effect is to cut demand from the consumer sector as well as the business sector.

Money Availability

Because of the peculiar nature of banking institutions, high interest rates are not the only conditions that reduce borrowing. The government also has the power to limit the amount of money available, which causes interest to rise. That lack of money means that, at least in the shortrun, borrowers who are willing and able to pay higher rates of interest will often find that there is no money available for them to borrow. This will also limit the amount of consumer borrowing and business investment and help slow down the booming economy.

Of course, the system works the other way, too. Monetary policy can be used to increase business investment and consumer expenditures as well. When the government increases the money supply, this tends to decrease the rate of interest and stimulate business investment. To some extent, lower rates on consumer loans also stimulate spending.

The Chicago Approach

Another school of thought arrives at similar conclusions but by different reasoning. The "monetarist" school, led by Professor Milton Friedman at the University of Chicago (whom we have observed earlier), says that the supply of money itself has a direct effect on consumer expenditures *without* the necessity of having to raise and lower interest rates to stimulate consumer borrowing.

According to Friedman, consumers feel comfortable holding a certain amount of money—whatever is consistent with their income and their portfolio of assets, which include not only stocks, bonds, and bank accounts, but "real" assets as well, such as houses, cars, and even clothes.

Friedman feels that when the government expands the money supply too rapidly, consumers are left holding more money than they feel is consistent with their incomes and portfolios, and they change part of it into other assets. To some extent, they buy more stocks and bonds (which raises their prices and lowers their percent yields), but in addition—and this is most important—Friedman feels that consumers use some of their excess money to buy real goods—that is, they go out and get rid of their excess dollars by spending more money on consumer products. Conversely, when the money supply is cut, spending also suffers since consumers try to increase their holdings of money by buying less.

However, Friedman feels that increasing or decreasing money supply is not a good instrument for controlling the economy. His reasoning is that changes in the money supply affect the future economy in a way that cannot be determined. If the government cuts the money supply to slow down inflation, by the time this decreases consumer demand the economy may have moved from a boom period to a down-turn, and the ultimate effect is to make it worse.

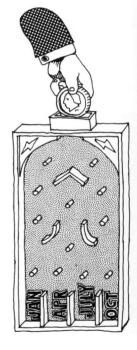

Controlling the Money Supply

Our government, like every other sovereign national government in the world, controls its own money supply. And, as we have seen, the supply of money is related to the level of economic activity in at least two ways: directly, an increase in the money supply causes consumers to spend their excess money; indirectly, it means that there is more money to lend out to businesses for investment, and just like the supply and demand for any commodity, the price goes down. In the case of money, the price is the interest rate.

But exactly how does the government increase the money supply? In the days of the feudal kingdoms of Europe, it was easy: they merely coined and printed more. However, this is not the way that it is done these days, largely because our currency—coins and paper money—constitutes only about 21 percent of our total money supply. The other four-fifths is in the form of demand deposits, more commonly known as *checking account balances*.

We recall from chapter 12 that holding money in cash or a checking

account is generally not a very profitable thing for a consumer to do. It could be generating revenue if invested in a savings account or elsewhere. Yet, people hold money for transaction purposes, for emergencies, or occasionally even for speculation, as we saw in chapter 12.

The 80 percent of our money supply which is in the form of checking account balances is held in the approximately 13,000 banks in the United States which accept checking deposits. These are known as *commercial banks,* the only kind that currently can give you a checking account. Other financial institutions such as savings and loan associations, mutual savings banks, and credit unions do not have this power. Recent legislation has been proposed that would give them power, and accounts resembling checking accounts are being tried on an experimental basis.

The instrument that the government uses for controlling the money supply is the Federal Reserve System, established in 1913. It is run by an independent seven-member board of governors in Washington, D.C., who are appointed for 14 year terms by the President. Although it is a creature of the government, the executive branch, or the President, cannot exert very direct control over its policies and has often come into conflict with the board of governors.

Fewer than half the commercial banks are members of the Federal Reserve System, but that includes virtually all of the very large banks, and they have about four-fifths of total checking deposits of all banks. In effect, therefore, the Federal Reserve System exerts control over about 80 percent of total checking account balances.

The Creation of Money

Before we learn how the Federal Reserve controls the money supply in the United States we should first learn how the banking system as a whole can create money. Suppose that Johnny Jones, while traveling through Las Vegas on business, plunks a dollar in the slot machine and hits the grand jackpot for a thousand dollars. Let us also suppose (which is not very likely) that he pockets the thousand and continues on his trip.

What is he going to do with all that cash? Why, put it in the bank for safe keeping. So, he deposits it in his checking account. He still has that $1,000 in money; however, it is no longer in cash.

Now his bank, the 19th National Bank of Sheboygan, has an extra $1,000 in cash. What is it going to do, put it in its vault? Of course not—at least not all of it. Banks do not stay in business by putting their depositors' money in the vault. In order to cover expenses and make profits, they have to lend it out to customers who will pay interest on it.

But can they lend all of the money out? The answer is no. By law, every commercial bank is required to keep a certain part of their deposits

TABLE 17-1

The Creation of Money by the Banking System

Deposit		Bank Reserves	Bank Loan
1st (Johnny Jones)	$1,000.00	$200.00	$800.00
2nd	800.00	160.00	640.00
3rd	640.00	128.00	640.00
4th	512.00	102.40	512.00
5th	409.60	81.92	409.60
6th	327.68	65.54	327.68
7th	262.14	52.43	262.14
8th	209.72	41.94	209.72
9th	167.77	33.55	167.77
10th	134.22	26.84	134.22
11th	107.37	21.47	107.37
12th	85.90	17.18	85.90
13th	68.72	13.74	68.72
14th	59.48	11.90	59.48
15th	43.98	8.80	43.98
16th	35.18	7.04	35.18
17th	28.15	5.63	28.15
18th	22.52	4.51	22.52
19th	18.01	3.60	18.01
20th	14.41	2.88	14.41
21st	11.53	2.31	11.53
22nd	9.22	1.85	9.22
	$4,967.60	$993.53	

held in reserves. Let us suppose that the reserve requirement of this bank is 20 percent. This means that, of the $1,000, the bank must keep $200 of Johnny Jones' money around but can loan out the other $800, which it does.

As it turns out, the money is loaned out to a businessman who needs some new office furniture. So, after drawing the $800 check from the bank, the businessman goes down to the office furniture showroom and pays $800 for new office furniture. At this point, the owner of the office furniture store has $800 more than he did in the morning. This is *new money* that has been created by the banking system, since Johnny Jones still has his $1,000, and now the furniture store owner has an additional $800.

Well, what does the furniture store owner do with his $800? At the end of the day he deposits it in his checking account at another bank. And that bank, also subject to a 20 percent reserve requirement, keeps 20 percent of the $800, or $160, and loans out the balance to another customer.

And so it goes, on down the line. As we can see in table 17-1, with

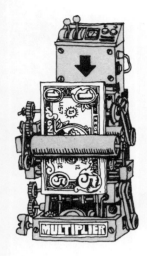

a 20 percent reserve requirement, the original $1,000 that Johnny Jones brought to the bank eventually becomes $5,000, meaning that $4,000 in new money has been created by the bank.

The fact that a small amount of new money put into the banking system results in a great increase in money supply is known as the *money multiplier effect*.[1] And like almost everything else in economics, it works just the same way in reverse. If Johnny Jones decided to go back to Las Vegas to parlay his $1,000 winnings into a $1,000,000 fortune and drew out the $1,000 in cash, the process would work exactly in reverse. The bank would be forced to call in some of its loans in order to have enough to keep up with the reserve requirement, and this would work the same way on down the system.[2] Of course, there are what are called *leakages* at every step, since each person who receives additional money might decide to keep some of it in his pocket as cash, but the main point is that a little bit of money put into the banking system goes a long way through the multiplier.

CONTROL OF THE MONEY SUPPLY

Now we may ask, how does the Federal Reserve System fit into the scheme of things? Basically, it can affect the supply of money in three ways.

changes in the reserve requirements The Federal Reserve System (the Fed) sets reserve requirements for each of the twelve Federal Reserve districts in the United States. Banks with larger deposits are subject to a higher requirement than smaller banks, and the Fed can raise and lower them for each bank. If, for example, it wanted to expand the money supply, one of the quickest ways would be to lower the reserve requirement. Why is this so?

Take the 19th National Bank of Sheboygan, which has a total of $1,000,000 in deposits. Since it has been subject to a 20 percent reserve requirement, $200,000 of its deposits have to be kept on hand. In actual fact, most of this money is probably on deposit with the Federal Reserve Bank in the district, and only a small proportion of it is actually on hand as cash in the vault. Now, if the Federal Reserve board lowers the requirement to 15 percent, this would mean that the bank would have to hold only $150,000, freeing $50,000 to loan out. This new money can run through the multiplier process and become much larger than the original amount. If this were done for every bank throughout the United States, the increase in the money supply would be enormous.

In the same way, if the Federal Reserve wanted to decrease the money

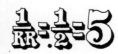

[1] The multiplier is equal to one dividend by the reserve requirement. In this case, $1/RR = 1/.2 = 5$.

[2] This assumes that the bank has loaned out all of its deposits not needed for legal reserves and must give Jones $1,000 from its reserves which it must then replace.

supply, all it would have to do would be to increase reserve requirements. In reality, changes in reserve requirements are not used very often because of the huge effect that even a small change of this type has on the money supply.

open market operations The most common method of controlling the money supply is through open market operations, which means the buying and selling of government securities by the Federal Reserve System.

To begin with, the Fed has billions of dollars worth of government bonds. If it wants to increase the money supply, it merely buys more bonds on the open market from individuals, corporations, or banks. Suppose it buys a $100,000 treasury bond from the 19th National Bank of Sheboygan. This means that the Sheboygan bank now has $100,000 in cash instead of a bond. Since this money is not necessary to meet the reserve requirement, it can lend it out and create a great deal more through the money multiplier.

In a similar but reverse manner, the government can tighten up on the money supply by selling some of its vast hoard of treasury bonds. If it sells one of its $100,000 bonds to an individual living in Sheboygan, he pays for the bond with a check drawn on his bank, the 19th National Bank of Sheboygan. As a result, the bank is now $80,000 short in its required reserves, since $20,000 has been held as legal reserve, and it must call in a similar amount of loans. This runs through the money multiplier to shrink the money supply by $100,000. Generally speaking, when we see money getting tight, it means that the Federal Reserve has been selling part of its supply of treasury bonds. It does not take very many billion dollars worth of treasury bond sales to tighten up the money supply considerably.

discount rates A third means of controlling the money supply by the Federal Reserve System is the regulation of the *discount rate.*

When consumer banks are short of reserves to meet the legal requirement, they can make up the difference by borrowing (discounting) from the Federal Reserve. If the discount rates are very low, it pays for banks to borrow from the Fed and lend out at higher rates to its customers. When the rate is increased, they are less likely to borrow and more likely to contract their own loans, thereby decreasing the money supply.

In recent times, however, changes in the discount rate have had a greater impact than the mere effect through this operation. This is generally the way that the Federal Reserve signals a change in monetary policy. If it announces an increase in the discount rate, it is saying to the banks, "Look, we think that money is too loose around here. We want things tightened up." Often banks will respond by decreasing their loans, even though they may not be very much affected by the discount rate as such.

other controls of the Fed The Federal Reserve System has other controls that do not relate to the supply of money, for example, regulation of the margin requirements for purchasing stocks.

Investors in the stock market do not have to put up the full price to buy stocks. If, for example, a person wants to purchase a hundred thousand dollars worth of American Telephone and Telegraph stock, and if his credit is good, he may be able to put up only $70,000 and the broker will in effect loan him the other $30,000. This may be advantageous from the investor's point of view if the stock goes up, since he profits from shares he didn't have the money to buy. If the price of the stock goes down, however, the investor can be wiped out much more quickly.

Prior to the Great Depression when margin requirements were not regulated by law, many brokerage houses were allowing people to buy with a 10 percent margin. That is, they could buy $100,000 worth of stock for only $10,000. This enabled many people to become quite rich in a short period of time, at least in terms of the current market value of the stock. But a small downturn in the market would have the power of wiping out the life savings of many investors.

Nowdays, the margin requirements are determined by the Federal Reserve System, and are generally around 50 percent. When the Fed wishes to tighten credit further and cut down on the volume of loans, it may increase this requirement to 70, 80, or even 90 percent.

The Federal Reserve also controls the ceiling on interest rates offered on time deposits at commercial banks.

monetary policy and the consumer An unfortunate aspect of monetary policy is that it often has unwanted effects. When the Fed tightens up on money, ostensibly to cut business investment, it almost invariably ends up by cutting off funds to the mortgage market so that consumers cannot get loans to buy houses. Consequently, someone moving from one city to another during a tight money situation may have great difficulty selling his house and buying a new one in the next community.

In order to overcome this situation, the government attempts to provide money for home mortgages by guaranteeing some mortgages, and by selling bonds in order to buy mortgages from banks and savings and loan associations. Although this provides partial relief, it is still difficult to get a mortgage when money is tight.

In chapter 16 we discussed actions that the consumer may take in anticipation of economic conditions caused by government fiscal policy. Similarly, he should be aware of monetary policies and the effect they may have on him.

If the Federal Reserve System takes actions to restrict the money supply (reported in the financial pages of the newspaper), it is likely that interest rates will go up and money will get tight. Consumers who

expect to buy a new house or add to an old one may save a considerable amount in interest by obtaining a mortgage before the rates increase.

If the tight money policy continues, the economy may well enter a downturn or even a recession (defined as a real decrease in national income over two successive quarters). Anticipating this, the consumer may wish to cut his spending and store funds against the possibility of a job layoff, which occurs more frequently during recessions.

On the other hand, a very loose monetary policy may eventually lead to an inflationary situation, some of whose effects can be avoided by the prudent consumer.

SUMMARY

1. Just as fiscal policy affects government expenditures, monetary policy also is a method by which the government affects aggregate demand and to some extent consumer expenditures. What monetary policy does is expand or contract the money supply in the economy to control the availability of loans for investment and consumption.

2. According to Milton Friedman, changes in the supply of money have a more direct effect on consumer expenditures than changes in interest rates. He is, however, skeptical of the results of such changes because of the time lags involved.

3. The Federal Reserve System, an independent agency, is the main instrument of the government's monetary policy. The three main weapons are changes in reserve requirements, open market operations, and changes in discount rates. The Fed also affects the monetary policy through its margin requirements for purchases of stocks, ceilings on interest rates in certain areas, and also by persuading its member banks to act in certain ways to support its policy objectives. Most of the bigger commercial banks in this country are members of the system. One disadvantage of monetary policy is that it limits home mortgages when it sets out to curtail business investment.

QUESTIONS

1. What are some of the possible leakages that will change the expected outcome of the money multiplier effect when a deposit is made and that deposit enters the money supply?

2. Which do you think is the most effective of the three main policy variables used to control the supply of money? Why?

3. Why do you think the housing market is susceptible to a contracting monetary policy?

TERMINOLOGY

portfolio of assets
Federal Reserve System
money multiplier effect
reserve requirement
open market operations
discount rate

SELECTED REFERENCES AND SOURCES OF DATA

Persons interested in the latest development in the area of monetary policy should look at copies of the *Federal Reserve Bulletin* which is published monthly by the Federal Reserve System.

Chandler, Lester V. *The Economics of Money and Banking.* 4th ed. (New York: Harper and Row, 1964).

The Federal Reserve System. Purposes and Functions. 5th ed. Dec. 1963. Board of Governors of the Federal Reserve System, Washington, D.C. 1963.

Friedman, Milton and Walter W. Heller. *Monetary vs. Fiscal Policy.* (New York: W. W. Norton, 1969).

Friedman, Milton and Anna J. Schwartz. *A Monetary History of the United States, 1867–1960.* (Princeton: Princeton University Press, 1962).

Marshall, Robert H. and Rodney B. Swanson. *The Monetary Process: Essentials of Money and Banking.* (Boston: Houghton Mifflin, 1974).

18

INTERNATIONAL TRADE

International trade is vitally important to the American consumer, yet there are few areas in economics where general understanding is so limited.

As the poet John Donne said, "No man is an island, entire of itself." No nation is really an island unto itself, either. No country on earth is so vast or so well endowed that it can continue its way of life without trading with other nations.

The United States ranks very low in terms of the proportion of national income accounted for by imports and exports. Table 18-1 shows that while in some countries export is as high as 33 percent of Gross National Product, in the United States it is only 4 percent. However, and this is important to note, because of the tremendous size of the United States economy, that 4 percent in dollar terms is greater than the value of exports by any other country. So, while trade constitutes a relatively small proportion of our total national income, it constitutes a large proportion of the world's international trade.

Advantages of International Trade

There are several advantages accruing to the consumer from international trade. Four of the most important are resource availability, economies of scale, absolute advantage of trade, and comparative advantage of trade.

TABLE 18-1

Exports as a Percentage of Gross National Product for Selected Countries
1968

Country	Percent
The Netherlands	33
Canada	19
West Germany	15
Great Britain	15
Italy	14
France	10
Japan	9
United States	4

resource availability Perhaps the most obvious advantage of international trade is that it supplies us with consumer items we cannot produce ourselves. These include mineral deposits that are either not found or found only in limited supplies, or alternatively, things that cannot be raised in a climate such as ours—bananas, coffee, chocolate.

There are other resources that, although available, cannot be supplied in an ideal form in our country. We grow grapes and process wine, but French wines are different, and some people prefer them. Also, and perhaps more important to the consumer, international trade also involves foreign travel. Americans go to Paris because there is no comparable city in the United States, just as Europeans come to marvel at the Grand Canyon. Although the citizens of the well-endowed United States could probably survive without international trade, our standard of living would be reduced.

economies of scale Earlier in the book we noted that there are goods that cannot be manufactured cheaply except in large quantities. An example we gave was the automobile, which is relatively uneconomical to produce in quantities of several thousand. For this reason, if every country produced all of its own manufactured goods, including automobiles, prices to their consumers would be very high. For example, the United States, with 200-plus million people, has a large enough market to support automobile manufacturing. However, a country like Israel, with only about three million people, would have difficulty producing a low-cost automobile. Similar arguments are valid for steel, aircraft, and electronics production. In these cases, it pays for one country to produce the item and utilize the larger market of other countries.

absolute advantage Due to combinations of resources and skills, different countries, just like different people, are better equipped to produce

TABLE 18-2

Types of Goods Imported to and Exported from the United States

1970 (millions of dollars)

Imports	Amount	Percent	Exports	Amount	Percent
Automobiles and Parts	$ 5,067	13	Machinery	$11,372	27
Petroleum and Products	2,770	7	Automobiles, Tractors, etc.	6,549	15
Electrical Machinery	2,272	6	Chemicals	3,826	9
Iron and Steel Products	2,032	5	Grains, Cereals, etc.	2,588	6
Nonferrous Ores and Metals	1,653	4	Iron and Steel Products	1,270	3
Coffee and Cocoa	1,360	3	Nonferrous Metals	893	2
Textiles	1,135	3	Other Exports	16,104	38
Other Imports	23,674	59			
Total	$39.963	100	Total	$42,602	100

Source: U.S. Dept. of Commerce, *Survey of Current Business,* March, 1971, pp. S-22,23.

certain items and can do so at lower cost. The United States, with its superior technology, can produce tractors much more cheaply than Korea, while Korea can make shirts less expensively because of its relatively cheap labor supply. Obviously it pays for them to trade their products with one another.

Consequently, whenever there are absolute advantages—and there are many in different industries—it pays for nations to trade with one another to capitalize on efficiencies in production.

comparative advantage Even when one nation is more efficient in the production of *all* goods than another nation, it still may pay to trade. This point, which is not well understood by non-economists, is known as *comparative advantage.*

Let's suppose, for example, that the United States could produce both tractors and shirts more cheaply than Korea. Would it pay, therefore, to trade with Korea? The answer is yes. For, although the U.S. has an absolute advantage in the production of both tractors and shirts relative to Korea, it can probably produce one good more efficiently than the other and would, therefore, be well advised to concentrate on its most efficient production, probably tractors. It would then trade tractors to the Koreans, who would concentrate on *their* most efficient good, shirts, and ship those back to the United States.

Although the benefits of comparative advantage can be proven mathematically, we can illustrate it with a simple example. Suppose that a highly skilled attorney is also a good typist and, in fact, can type much more rapidly and accurately than the secretary. Would it pay for that attorney to do his own typing? The answer is no. He is much more productive in the practice of law, although he has an absolute advantage in both law and typing over his secretary. He may only be half again as good a typist as the secretary, but he is probably a hundred times as good an attorney, so it would pay for him to devote all of his time to his law practice and let the secretary devote time to the typing.

Barriers to Trade

With all its advantages to the consumer, it would seem as if free trade should be encouraged among all nations. Yet, throughout history, we have seen nations attempting to restrict the quantity of goods imported.

These restrictions take two forms: *tariffs* (or taxes), which tend to make imports more expensive to domestic consumers; and *quotas,* which limit the amount that can be imported during any period of time. The question is, why do we have tariffs and quotas to restrict the movement of goods and services across international boundaries?

In many instances, imported goods compete with those manufactured at home. Producers of men's shirts in the United States certainly do not welcome competition of shirts from Korea manufactured at lower prices. In other words, tariffs and quotas are designed to protect American producers against competition, and those who favor the restriction of free trade are known as *protectionists*.

Of course, few manufacturers will give protection of profits against foreign competition as their reason for favoring tariffs in many foreign countries, and this should be preserved. What they generally say, with the support of labor in many instances, is that American workers enjoy a far greater standard of living and receive higher wages than the workers in many foreign countries.

Of course, this argument is correct, but we must examine whether it is best for our country to continue to protect the workers in the industry from foreign competition. Most economists feel that this is not the best possible policy. If free trade were allowed to operate, the principles of comparative advantage would result in resources within the United States—land, labor, capital, and entrepreneurial ability—being shifted to the production of those goods in which it has the greatest comparative advantage. If Korea has a comparative advantage of inexpensive labor in the production of shirts, then America would do well to move its resources out of the production of shirts and into the production of goods in which *it* has a comparative advantage. In that way, workers are not put out of a job, they are merely shifted from one industry to another, and consumers end up saving money.

arguments in favor of trade barriers Although most economists favor the removal of most barriers to trade, there are at least two arguments in favor of some restriction. The first is known as the *infant industries* argument.

Unless a new industry in a country can be protected against competition long enough to get established, the country will never know whether it has a comparative advantage in that good. Suppose, for example, that the Swiss were making all of the fine watches in the world. A Massachusetts firm might like to begin manufacturing fine watches. Until the management and workers acquire sufficient expertise—perhaps several years—they will not be able to compete with the Swiss watch makers who have been manufacturing fine watches for many, many years.

The infant industries argument would say, "Give the domestic manufacturer a chance to see whether he can make it. Perhaps America will prove to have a comparative advantage in the production of watches."

The trouble with this argument, as one might expect, is that it's very difficult to tell how many years an industry should be protected. The Massachusetts firm may not be as efficient as the Swiss companies for ten years, but if the government then proposed the removal of barriers, the domestic firm might yell that ten years is not long enough. So, once a tariff is set, it is very hard to get it removed. If nothing else, it might mean dislocating the workers in the Massachusetts watch factory, and this would be politically unpopular.

A second argument for the restriction of trade is based on national defense. During major wars, international trade is often severely disrupted. During the early years of the Second World War, for example, it was very difficult to conduct shipping because of German submarines. Consequently, the United States was forced to produce many of the goods that it formerly imported.

Suppose, for example, that some strategic goods could be manufactured less expensively in foreign countries, say airplanes or tanks. Under these conditions it would still be unwise for the United States to import its armaments since it may end up in a war against its supplier or otherwise be cut off from its sources of supplies.

This argument has been used not only to protect the manufacturer of arms but many other civilian goods, such as watches and shoes, which could conceivably be strategic necessities in the case of war. This is a valid argument; but unless severely checked, it tends to go too far.

The Movement Toward Freer Trade

In recent years, there has been a worldwide movement toward the reduction of barriers and the increase of international trade. Generally speaking, tariff reductions have been conducted on a bilateral, or two-nation, basis. Most recently, there have been multinational agreements, beginning with the General Agreement on Tariffs and Trade (GATT) which was signed in 1947 by 23 nations including the United States.

Of even greater significance, however, has been the creation of the European Economic Community, more commonly known as the Common Market. This is made up of several Western European nations who have banded together to abolish, over a period of years, tariffs and import quotas on all products among themselves and also to set up a unified tariff system for trading with nations outside of the Common Market.

Many economists feel that a good deal of the economic success of the United States is due to the fact that it constitutes in itself a large market which has not been subject to hindrance of trade. A manufacturer in California who produces a unique product may be able to count on a market in the 50 states without worrying about tariffs.

Until the Common Market was formed, this was not the case among the European countries. A French producer, for example, could count on a market of only the French, since the international market was subject to tariffs and negotiations. Now, they will have a tariff-free market comparable in size to that of the United States so that the development of all the countries involved may be speeded.

Foreign Exchange and the Balance of Payments

Consumers are undoubtedly familiar with hearing the terms such as *balance of payments deficit, devaluation,* and *revaluation.*

In order to understand the balance of payments, we must first realize that American dollars go abroad for reasons other than payment for our imports. Americans travel overseas and leave money behind—more and more, in recent years. In addition, they send money to relatives and charitable organizations in other countries.

The United States government gives billions of dollars each year in foreign aid. And most importantly, American business invests heavily in foreign countries and large corporations have subsidiaries in virtually all of the free-market countries in the world.

The other side of the picture shows foreign dollars coming into this country to buy our goods and services as well as to pay interest on the investments that we have made overseas. Furthermore, foreigners traveling in the United States leave a lot of their money behind. According to table 18-3, in 1970 the United States exported 53.3 billion dollars worth of goods and services and had returns of 9.8 billion on investments.

TABLE 18-3

The United States Balance of Payments

1970   (in billions)

(1)	United States exports		$+63.0
	(a) Goods	$+43.5	
	(b) Services	+9.8	
	(c) Income from United States investments abroad	+9.8	
(2)	United States imports		-59.3
	(a) Goods	$-44.7	
	(b) Services	-9.5	
	(c) Income from foreign investments in Unites States	-5.1	
(3)	Net balance due United States on exports and imports		$ +3.7
(4)	Net remittances		-1.4
(5)	Net government transactions: grants, loans, etc.		-3.2
(6)	Net capital movements		-4.7
	(a) United States capital outflow	$ -8.6	
	(b) Foreign capital inflow to United States	+3.9	
(7)	Balance due United States (+) or rest of world (-)		$ -5.6
(8)	Financing (balancing) transactions		
	(a) Decrease in United States holdings of gold and foreign currencies		+3.3
	(b) Increase in liquid dollar balances held by foreigners		+2.3
			$ 0.0

Source: *Federal Reserve Bulletin,* April 1971.

On the other hand, we paid only 44.7 billion dollars to import goods and services and 5.1 billion in interest on foreign investments in the United States. This left us a net inflow of 3.7 billion dollars.

However, this was more than compensated for by the grants, loans, private remittances, and net foreign investment that we made. So, when everything was added up, the United States sent or spent 5.6 billion dollars more overseas than all of the other countries sent or spent in the United States. This means that the United States had a deficit of 5.6 billion in its balance of payments.

What exactly happens when there is a balance of payments deficit? Foreign countries hold more dollars than we hold in foreign currency. Now, to the extent that foreigners wish to hold additional dollars, this is fine, and in fact for many years the dollar was regarded as the soundest

currency. Foreigners hoarded dollars as protection against their own disintegrating currency, economy, or, government.

What happens, however, if the foreign countries do not wish to hold the excess dollars created by a deficit in the United States balance of payments? Until several years ago the trading nations of the world were on a gold standard. This meant that the treasury of each nation would redeem foreign holders of its currency by giving them gold at some set rate.

This worked for a while, until a point was reached when there was more of the currency of many countries outstanding in foreign hands than they had gold to back it at the official rate. This meant, for example, that if all of the holders of British pounds suddenly got panicky and decided to convert their pounds into gold, the gold holdings (reserves) of Britain would be wiped out. So, what Britain did in several instances was to decrease the value of its currency (devalue her currency) relative to both gold and the other currencies of the world.

Devaluation has a great impact on both the domestic and the foreign consumer. When Britain devalued relative to the dollar, it meant that a dollar would now buy more British goods than before. Consequently, American consumers of British goods, including Americans traveling in Britain, found that their money would go further. At the same time, however, the British citizens who were paid in pounds found that the cost of imported goods went up, since the pound was worth less in foreign currency. So, one effect of devaluation was that it helped clear up a deficit in the British balance of payments.

The International Monetary Fund

While the Second World War was still raging, a number of the allied nations got together in Bretton Woods, New Hampshire, to plan for the orderly resumption of world trade after the war. Out of this meeting grew the International Monetary Fund (IMF). In order to insure stability of currencies, the IMF set the relationship between various currencies of the world, and member nations were obliged to abide by it. This meant, for example, that if the British pound started slipping in value relative to the dollar because people throughout the world thought the pound was overvalued, the British central bank would step in and begin buying up pounds on the world currency exchange with its reserve dollars. If it didn't have enough dollars, it could borrow from the IMF. This would increase the supply of dollars and decrease the supply of pounds on the world market and cause the price of the pound to keep its value relative to the dollar.

The success of that system did not endure. One reason was that the United States has been running deficits in its balance of payments almost continuously since the Second World War. For quite a long time this was not serious, since many foreigners, both citizens and central banks, wanted to hold the excess American dollars, and the dollar became more or less a substitute for gold in international transactions. However, the combination of continued overseas investment, the expensive war in Viet Nam, and American inflation, which made American goods more expensive to foreigners and foreign goods less expensive to Americans, resulted in such huge balance of payments deficits that the American dollar was no longer regarded as the ideal currency. People attempted to get rid of their dollars by changing them to gold and other currencies.

The United States, which by the IMF agreement was obligated to ship gold (or other foreign currency) for the dollars, did not have enough to pay for more than a fraction of those outstanding So, it suspended the payment in gold. Since that time, the world has been on a *freely fluctuating exchange* rate with laws of supply and demand determining the value of the dollar relative to other currencies. One result has been the devaluation of the dollar, particularly in comparison to currencies of countries with stronger economies such as Germany and Japan. To the American consumer this has meant that foreign goods are no longer as cheap as they used to be, and travel, in many places, is at least as expensive as it is in the United States.

Protection Against Changing Exchange Rates

Although international trade has great impact on the consumer in terms of the prices he pays for goods, there is little that he can do *as an individual* to alter the system. About his only action is to join others to exert influence on legislators to oppose new or increased tariffs that increase prices. As we will see, he can take some precautions to avoid the uncertainty of changing exchange rates—devaluation or revaluation. But this is done on a much more routine basis by businessmen, both at home and abroad, who must "hedge" to insure against large losses from exchange rate changes.

Take an American TV manufacturer who imports components from Japan. Scheduled delivery is in six months and is to be paid in Japanese yen since producers generally want to be paid in their own currency. The price is equivalent to one million dollars.

If, during that six month period, the dollar is devalued relative to the yen, the price of the components in dollars increases. If this increases 10 percent, the American producer will lose $100,000.

To protect himself against such a contingency, he may buy one million dollars' worth of yen *now*. That way he knows that the components will not cost more, no matter what happens to the dollar. The only problem is that he will probably lose interest for six months on the million dollars held in yen unless he lends it at interest in Japan. An alternative is to deal on the *forward exchange market* where a businessman can contract to buy a million dollars in yen six months from now at a slight premium without putting up the money in advance. This is possible because Japanese producers who have ordered American goods wish to protect *themselves* from possible devaluation of Japanese currency relative to the dollar. Many big banks act as intermediaries to protect both parties from losses due to shifting foreign exchange rates.

While few consumers have foreign exchange dealings large enough to warrant the services of the forward exchange market, there may be instances where hedging is warranted. If a traveler intends to spend the summer in Germany at a time when the newspapers are talking of a possible dollar devaluation, he would be wise to contact his bank and buy German marks in advance of the trip. He may lose a little in interest, but he gains the assurance that the vacation will cost him pretty well what he has put aside for it. On the other hand, if London is in his itinerary and there is serious talk of another devaluation of the British pound, the money should be kept in dollars and converted only for current expenses.

The best indication of pending changes in foreign exchange rates is a nation's balance of payments. If it experiences a continued and sizeable deficit, its currency may be expected to decline in value in contrast to those countries that have surpluses in their balance of payment accounts. Attention paid to these seemingly mundane figures may greatly aid the consumer in the timing and mode of foreign exchanges—be they purchases of imports or foreign travel.

SUMMARY

1. Even though it accounts for a very small percent of our Gross National Product, international trade is important to the United States economy. As with other countries, there are absolute and comparative advantages in the production of various goods and services. What is not available domestically because of climate and resources can still be enjoyed by importing. Foreign trade also provides a much wider market for domestic goods and therefore allows production on a large scale with the accompanying economies of scale.

2. Free trade is said to exist when all countries eliminate restrictions on the movements of goods and services. For various reasons, countries do create barriers to trade that eventually result in an increase in the prices of the imported goods. The U.S. is at an advantage in this respect because it is a large country—its products have a ready-made

large market. The European Common Market, by abolishing trade barriers between the different member countries, has sought to derive similar benefits for itself.

3. Foreign trade is complicated by the fact that it involves supply and demand of national currencies, creating fluctuations in the rate of exchange. A country's balance of trade and balance of payments are said to be in equilibrium when the value of the outflow of goods and services is equal to the value of the inflow.

4. The world has experimented with many monetary systems where the rate of exchange between different currencies was regulated artificially. At present, however, all the countries are on a freely floating exchange rate, which means the price of one currency in terms of another is determined by supply and demand factors.

QUESTIONS

1. In what situations would you consider barriers to trade between nations a legitimate action?

2. Describe what happens in a system of freely fluctuating exchange rates when one country has a high rate of inflation.

3. Is devaluation a good policy when a country has a balance of payments deficit? What could be a possible disadvantage of such an action?

TERMINOLOGY

absolute and comparative advantage
infant industries argument
free trade
protectionists
European Common Market
GATT
IMF
freely fluctuating exchange rates
devaluation and revaluation
balance of payments deficit

SELECTED REFERENCES AND SOURCES OF DATA

Economic Report of the President, 1971. (Washington). Chapter Five.

Ellsworth, Paul T. *The International Economy,* 4th ed., (New York: Macmillan Company, 1969).

Kindleberger, Charles P. *International Economics,* 4th ed. (Homewood, Ill.: Richard D. Irwin, 1968). (See Chapters One-Four)

Ohlin, Bertil. *Interregional and International Trade.* Rev. ed. (Cambridge: Harvard University Press, 1967).

INDEX